THE JUVENILE COURT
in a Changing Society

THE JUVENILE COURT IN A CHANGING SOCIETY

Young Offenders
in Israel

David Reifen

Chief Judge,
Juvenile Courts of Israel

Weidenfeld and Nicolson

Weidenfeld and Nicolson
11 St John's Hill
London SW 11

Weidenfeld and Nicolson Jerusalem
19 Herzog Street
Jerusalem

ISBN 0 297 76656 2

Printed by Keter Press, Ltd, Jerusalem, Israel, 1973

Contents

List of Tables

Foreword

Juvenile delinquency and judgments about the disposition of young offenders are of increasing concern to laymen as well as criminologists, lawyers, and child welfare workers. The functions and procedures of the juvenile court have become controversial issues, especially since the Gault decision in the United States. Despite the general consensus that the juvenile court should be a special court with its own philosophy and not "a replica of a court for adults," as Judge David Reifen says, there are important issues about the need for adequate presentation of evidence, proper representation by counsel, and protections against excessive sanctions sometimes given under the rubric of humanitarian motives and individualized treatment. Unfortunately, too often is juvenile justice administered by poorly trained, or untrained, court officers; and too often is "treatment" a form of punishment or institutional neglect.

Rarely do practitioners have the talent or time to articulate their concerns about their practice. Sometimes when they do write of their experiences, the field of knowledge or administration which they represent is little enhanced because anecdotes, while interesting, provide an insufficient basis for scientific statements or public policy implications. We are therefore especially indebted to Judge David Reifen for his insights and must applaud his capacity to relate his personal experiences in a way that enlightens us and provides general patterns for a broad analysis of juvenile justice. He offers us material from experiential and experimental activities. He gives data touched with the humanity of his help to others. Anyone who comes to know intimately 836 young people in a five-year period has done more than give a frequency count of their special problems. The experience yields a reflection of his special relationships with them that is at once perceptive, genuine, and meaningful to others who deal with these same problems.

In this volume is not only the story of a judge who knows his charges well. Here is also the analytic description and evaluation of a sociological process, the way in which a trained reactor to deviance responds to the young persons who have been identified and viewed as being in need of social control. Judge Reifen is a man of modesty whose message is based on his own vivid experiences as a street worker;

namely, that a juvenile judge should be well trained for his task, else
the clinical discretion suffered or enjoyed by that role will be denuded
of the eminence and rationality it deserves. He is right, of course.
Juvenile judgeships should not be held by persons merely trained in
the law or imbued only with sympathy for unfortunate lads who conflict
with the law. Not every juvenile court judge can duplicate Judge Reifen's
rich experience or his ability to analyze his contacts with youth. But
such judges should have special training for their tasks and learn the
kinds of lessons Judge Reifen has to offer.

I have noted that this volume gives especial attention to the influence
of economic conditions on the family, on the kinds of activities in which
youthful offenders engage, and on the disposition of delinquent cases
that have appeared before the court. I have also noted how alike are
the youth of Israel to the spirit of youthfulness expressed in Frederic
M. Thrasher's *Gang*. David Bordua pointed out several years ago that
the juvenile delinquents in Thrasher's analysis seemed less nasty than
those in the sixties in America and had more fun in their adventure-
someness during the days of the thirties in Chicago. Was the difference
due to the games juveniles played or to the social analysts in their
interpretations? Whatever the difference, Judge Reifen's accounts of
"idlers" and "loafers" sound more reminiscent of Thrasher than of
Lewis Yablonsky's *Violent Gang*.

Moreover, there is an emphasis in this volume on the factor of
boredom, which deserves more serious sociological treatment. Arthur
Miller, the famous playwright, wrote movingly about this factor some
years ago as a most important contributor to deviance and delinquency.
We have yet to have a systematic analysis of this variable as a contributor to the problems discussed in this volume. But Judge Reifen
is aware of the importance of the sociopsychological form of this factor
and how it functions in the genesis of criminological behavior.

There are special features about Israeli delinquency in this volume.
But, more importantly, the author lifts his readers beyond the territorial
parochialism of his own country when he describes the variables of
the human condition that generate delinquency and the imperatives of
society's response. Crosscultural in perspective, transferrable in wisdom,
this volume should prove its mettle before all who deal with young
lives in trouble.

Marvin Wolfgang, Director
Center for Studies in Criminology
and Criminal Law
University of Pennsylvania

June 1972

Preface

The ideas and impressions presented here are based on over thirty years of field work—the first ten years as a child welfare worker with wayward children and some twenty years with delinquent children as a judge in the juvenile court. A few remarks about the first group may be appropriate here, because my later understanding of juvenile delinquents and of their conditions has constantly been nurtured by my previous experience with wayward children and their parents. Through many years of close observation, I acquired first-hand knowledge of the behavior and personality of Oriental Jews, with whom this book is largely concerned.

Tel Aviv was, in the 'thirties and 'forties, the principal city of Palestine and drew a host of Jewish newcomers, attracted to it because it was the first all-Jewish city. It was an active, lively, commercial city whose very streets, marketplaces, cafes, and restaurants seemed bright and cheerful. It was also the country's main industrial center, insofar as the beginnings of an industry could be observed. Furthermore, as the commercial and spiritual center of Jewish life in Palestine, it was extremely susceptible to cultural and socioeconomic influences. Even then, every vogue, every fashion which appeared in Europe or in the United States was immediately imitated by those few who could afford to do so. It was hard to imagine that all the miseries of the slum areas— thousands of families enduring wretched living conditions, children playing in unpaved, muddy streets with no drainage or sewage system— were only a few yards from the center of the city. Thus, on the one hand, there were plenty of goods available and a great deal of luxury evident, and on the other, misery and want—all juxtaposed in the closest proximity.

When the children of the slums tired of playing in the muddy streets or of staying in their shabby rooms, they were drawn like magnets to the bright, attractive streets, where they saw people enjoying a way of life that was in sharp contrast to their own. Both children and parents felt instinctively that they could profit from the gay, busy life going on in the "real Tel Aviv." Children, sometimes as young as eight and nine years old, would go to the center to become street vendors or hawkers, to carry heavy packages, or to be shoeshine boys. The children viewed it as a wonderful opportunity to take part in the gay life of the city.

Their parents saw nothing wrong with this, for many of them accepted the necessity of their children's providing financial help from an early age. In fact, many of the young children I met were providing a livelihood for large families. It is of interest that this practice, which was often highly praised by the parents, frequently served as a motivation to delinquent behavior later, a reaction to and revenge for exploitation by their parents, as it were. These children could not continue to carry the burden expected of them, and when they tried to get a job or attend school, their parents objected, knowing that it would mean less time for them to provide for the family.

A host of vagrant children appeared in the streets of Tel Aviv in the years 1935–36, their ages ranging from eight to approximately sixteen. (It was often difficult to ascertain an exact age, because neither parents nor child knew it, nor were any official records available.) Most of the children were boys, but in marketplaces there were also girls, usually engaged in selling vegetables or fruit. Boys and girls alike sold their goods by relying on the pity and compassion of passersby rather than on the value of their wares. This sort of trading was in many instances a cover for begging. For a time, the number of vagrant children was constantly on the increase, and they became a general nuisance. Nothing was known about them—a fact which added to the feeling of unease caused by their presence.

The social services of the Jewish community in what was then called Palestine had only begun to develop on a small scale in 1932. Health, education, and social welfare were organized by a special department of the Jewish National Council. Social welfare services were especially limited because of lack of funds and professional personnel, but above all because of a deep-seated conviction that social services were not needed and should be discarded as a remnant of charitable attitudes of the past. Tel Aviv was the pioneer city in providing social services for its citizens. Clubs and schools for backward and problem children were opened in 1934, and two educational institutions for wayward and delinquent children were set up in 1935.

It was in 1935 that the Tel Aviv municipality appointed me as a street-corner worker. The responsibilities of my assignment were very vague; it was made clear only that I was to take care of children who were loitering in the streets and marketplaces, either selling a variety of goods or simply doing nothing. I was expected to get to know these children and then make appropriate placements in schools, at jobs, in clubs, and—if necessary—in one of the educational establishments for wayward and delinquent children that were already functioning. (There was then no legislation on compulsory education or apprenticeship for children and young persons.)

I started by going around the streets and marketplaces at odd hours, day and night, at times when the children generally appeared. I tried to contact them on the spot and endeavored to talk to them, individually or in groups. After this initial contact some would come to my office; others would be reluctant to do so, and for some time we would meet at places convenient to them, usually in the quarter in which they lived or at places where they spent their time. I remained reserved and abstained from asking questions or making any demands until they got to know me. Only when I was no longer a stranger to them did I tell them about my function on behalf of the Tel Aviv city government and of my interest in helping them to lead a more regulated life. It took quite a time before their suspicion was overcome—some even withheld their surnames and addresses—but once contact was established through repeated meetings in streets, marketplaces, hideouts, and their own neighborhoods, they gained confidence and became talkative. With the infallible intuition peculiar to children, they realized that they had nothing to fear and that I had no contacts with the police, of whom they had been apprehensive.

What had at first appeared to be an amorphous mass of children turned out to be something of quite a different nature. I often sat with them for hours at their meeting places, trying to become familiar with their way of thinking and listening to their stories and adventures, in order to gauge how best to handle them. Their eagerness to listen to stories was a great help, and I used to tell them about my own childhood in Germany in order to break down the barriers. It was then that I realized that each of them had distinct individual characteristics which became blurred when they appeared in groups.

The children's occupations fell into three major categories. Some were street vendors, trying to sell shoelaces, vegetables, fruit, chocolate, etc. Some children sold their goods only in the daytime, while others preferred to work during the evening and night hours. Some of them had fixed spots; others constantly roamed around, trying their luck in different places. It was my impression that those who roamed from place to place were the more aggressive. Both groups had specific techniques for imposing their goods on passersby.

Those who worked as carriers belonged to a different category. The younger ones, from eight to approximately twelve, were usually stationed in marketplaces, where they waited for housewives to hire them to carry their purchases home. They were young and inexperienced, but they knew all about the difficulties of earning a decent living. On their shoulders, these boys carried large baskets, which often covered most of their bodies. The older carriers, aged about fourteen to sixteen, had small carts at their disposal, and they sometimes bore heavy loads for grocery stores. Many of them had their fixed place at the markets, and store owners frequently hired the same boys. In a way, these boys were rather firmly established and a part of the market scene.

The loafers and idlers made up the third category. Most of them disliked the very idea of being tied to any kind of job, and the largest number of delinquents were to be found in this group. They were also rather difficult to handle. Occasionally, however, these masters of idleness were forced to do some odd jobs, just to keep body and soul together. The more mobile ones posted themselves near the bus terminals, trying to earn some money by carrying travellers' bags. Theirs was a more difficult job, based on competition and cleverness. Whenever a bus arrived at the terminal, some of the boys leaped to their feet, loudly offering their services to the passengers; even before it had stopped, a few of them had already jumped onto the roof of the bus, untying the luggage and thus gaining an advantage over the others. Their ingenuity gained them prestige and status, which they nonetheless had constantly to secure for themselves anew. Once the bus was gone, they fell back into lethargy, gambling or simply doing nothing. Innumerable times, day after day scenes of this kind recurred. Although they fought each other individually, the boys presented a united front when a newcomer tried to join their ranks. Entrance was usually very difficult indeed, and only those who had outstanding qualities of leadership succeeded.

In all the categories, the occupations sometimes changed, because the youngsters were easily bored by doing the same thing for any length of time. Parents did not take any real interest in such changes, provided their children brought home sufficient money. If the children did not comply with this demand, there was trouble at home, which often meant that a boy stopped working altogether and joined the group of loafers. It was obvious that the parents were almost exclusively concerned with the money their children earned, while the boys themselves gradually lost interest in supporting their families. The longer they were in the streets, the less they could be relied upon in this respect. Invariably, they became attached to street life for its own sake and became increasingly detached from affairs at home. This in turn led to a great deal of friction between the boys and their parents.

Over a period of five years I had intensive contact with 836 children and youths. Once they reached the age of about twelve, girls ceased to work on their own as street vendors because their parents feared possible negative repercussions and sexual delinquency. They were therefore sent by their parents to work as housemaids, sometimes performing heavy cleaning tasks. Some of them continued with their previous occupations, but working only with a parent and under close supervision.

Only 20 percent of the boys were caught committing an offense and eventually charged in court. Two reasons may account for this low figure. (1) Those who were engaged in one of the above-mentioned occupations had their minds set on earning money. Not much time was left to commit offenses. Most of those who were charged in court were the idlers and loafers. (2) Many of the boys had gained expert knowledge in street life and may have made use of this knowledge to avoid being caught while committing an offense.

Those who were charged in court usually told me the date of the trial beforehand, in an effort to enlist my help. All these children suffered from emotional and economic deprivations, and all had great difficulty in adjusting to permanent jobs later on. Moreover, many of them evinced symptoms and behavior patterns similar to or the same as those of their parents, and a certain repetition of the family pattern was evident. In fact, as a judge in the juvenile court, I came across children whose fathers I had dealt with as delinquents in earlier years.

During my work as a street-corner worker I made a point of becoming acquainted with parents in order to secure their cooperation. I came to know the cultural and socioeconomic background of the inhabitants of the slum districts and became acquainted with their way of life, their sorrows and pleasures, their habits and customs. I was sometimes present as a spectator when boys with whom I worked were brought to court, and it was on those occasions that I conceived the idea that a juvenile-court judge should be intimately acquainted with the social and educational problems of children and parents alike. This, together with legal training, seemed to me to be a basic requirement. Close observation of what goes on in and outside the juvenile court made it abundantly clear that the adjudication of children and young persons should not be just a replica of a court for adults, but rather a court in its own right, with its own philosophy. To implement this approach, training and knowledge in this special field would be indispensable.

In 1949, when the newly founded state of Israel was preparing and organizing its institutions, I submitted my ideas to the minister of justice, Mr. Pinhas Rosen, who accepted the basic concept and agreed to establish a juvenile court proper. In 1950 I was appointed the first judge for the whole of Israel, adjudicating juvenile offenders and children in need of care and protection. Since all such cases were brought before me, I had to travel throughout the country constantly. Dates for court sessions were fixed beforehand—once or twice a week in large cities, at least once a month in smaller places. My headquarters were in Tel Aviv, where the juvenile court was set up in a building separate from other courthouses. In other places I used the existing court buildings, but at hours different from the usual court hours in order to separate juveniles from adults. Since that time, the system whereby juvenile offenders and instances of care and protection are brought before judges especially appointed to adjudicate in the juvenile court has been continued.

This, then, is my personal experience in the field I am about to describe. My experience and my theoretical studies have convinced me of the following basic tenets:

1. The adjudication of juvenile offenders cannot be carried out according to the letter of the law or by common sense alone. Expert knowledge in the field of child psychology and child care is also essential.
2. The last fifty years have witnessed a growing awareness of the need for specialized knowledge for the understanding and evaluation of the dynamics of behavior problems among children and juveniles. Hence, the enormous development of child psychiatry, child psychology, child therapy, child-care workers—a development that has not taken place with the juvenile court.
3. The juvenile court, as a social institution, is in a most vulnerable position. In practice, however, the fact that there is a need for experts in child adjudication, who require specialized training in order to fulfill this function, has not been fully recognized. This applies to the different juvenile court systems, as well as to the child welfare boards which function in Scandinavian countries.
4. Whatever the official name of the institution concerned with the adjudication of children and juveniles, it belongs, by its very nature, to what may be called special social services within an authoritative setting. That it functions within the juridical field confers upon it an authority which may be an asset, provided it is manned by expert people. But to call such an institution by an impressive-sounding name does not enhance its real value.

I have tried to be objective in the pages which follow, but I have always been conscious of the fact that my personal experience has had a decisive impact on my feelings and thinking on the subject. What I have written in this book, and the way I have written it, is the result of a lengthy process, and is, therefore, inevitably tinged with subjectivity.

This attempt to convey impressions of my work in the juvenile court and of my contacts with juvenile delinquents is the outcome neither of preconceived ideas nor of a deliberate, conscious intention to collect material for a book. As events unfolded, I was impressed by the variegated nature of this human panorama, by its complexity and peculiarity. I found it helpful to make some notes, particularly when the impact of an experience was very strong. It soon became clear that these notes provided me with a tool with which to deepen my understanding of human behavior within the setting of my profession and that the varying facets of behavior are among the most important aspects of an extremely complex situation fraught with many potentialities, both negative and positive.

I am convinced that the juvenile court per se constitutes a dynamic situation which accords it potentialities for treatment of a special nature. The juridical setting increases these possibilities to a much larger extent and in a much wider sense than has hitherto been realized. It is to an exploration of these dynamics of behavior in a changing society that this book is devoted.

Acknowledgments

This book was inspired by Dr. Gerald Caplan, Professor of Psychiatry at Harvard Medical School and written upon his insistence and with his encouragement. I am glad of this opportunity to express my gratitude to him.

I am indebted to Prof. Israel Drapkin, Director of the Institute of Criminology of the Hebrew University of Jerusalem, for his valuable advice and assistance in connection with the publication of this book.

It gives me special pleasure to thank Prof. Marvin E. Wolfgang, Director of the Center for Studies in Criminology and Criminal Law, University of Pennsylvania, for the generous moral support extended to me while preparing the manuscript.

D. R.

I

Israeli Society

1

The Sociological Background

The sociological background of modern Israel is unique and requires a brief outline in order that the reader may better understand the problems raised here. A detailed discourse on sociology would be beyond the scope of this book; suffice it, therefore, to mention only a few aspects which bear on the complex problems of the juvenile court in Israel.[1]

There is first the remarkable fact that after two millennia the Jewish people have established an independent Jewish State. The tremendous upheavals which occurred in the world after 1933, and particularly after the outbreak of the Second World War, as well as the rapidly ensuing tide of nationalism, made the plight of the large Jewish masses most precarious. It may be regarded as a miracle of history that Israel came into being at that very time—the only place where large numbers of Jews were able to find refuge. Here they were accepted by their brethren and given a chance to build their own independent future as human beings and citizens, free of the threat of persecution.

Secondly, there has been the extraordinary phenomenon of ingathering of exiles from all corners of the world, which has been taking place on an unprecedented scale since. The former is a historic event of world significance; the latter is inevitably bound to play a decisive role in shaping the land and people of Israel. In Israel, we are witnessing a rapid process of acculturation. Not only has the Jewish population trebled in twenty years; the composition of that population is now a conglomerate of over seventy Jewish groups, who have for generations been influenced by differing cultures. These groups range from the sophisticated, scientifically trained to the primitive and illiterate. The process of acculturation is taking place not only within a brief period of time, but within a small territory that has hardly any natural resources and that is surround-

---

[1] The areas occupied by Israel during the Six Day War are not included in the scope of this book.

3

ed by enemies who are determined to annihilate the state. From the negative standpoint, this situation means a heavy drain on economic resources for sheer physical survival, while from the positive, the process of molding an integrated nation is accelerated.

At the beginning of 1948, when Israel was established as an independent state, the Jewish population numbered approximately 650,000. From 1948 to 1952 one of the peak periods of mass immigration, the number increased to over 1,450,000. Many of those who arrived during this period were survivors of the extermination camps in Europe. The influx of newcomers continued, and by 1961 the Jewish population rose to 1,981,000, and by 1967 to 2,384,000. The latest official figures for 1970 bring the number up to 2,561,000.[2] While more than two-thirds of the population increase among Jews was due to immigration during that period, among the non-Jewish population there was a growth of one-third, due entirely to natural increase. There is now a total of over three million inhabitants in Israel.

The major problem during the last twenty years has been—and will continue to be for some time to come—the absorption and integration of these masses of newcomers, of people who came from widely differing cultural and socioeconomic backgrounds, molding them into a free and democratic society. One feature which has seriously to be examined in this context may explain to a considerable degree many of the cultural and socioeconomic difficulties which we have witnessed during the past twenty years or so, and which continue to hamper the process of integration.

Before the establishment of the state of Israel, but especially until 1940 or so, those who came to what was then called Palestine were, in effect, selected immigrants; after the establishment of Israel, the characteristic feature was nonselective immigration. The declared policy of the government of Israel was that Israel, as a Jewish state, should admit every Jew who wished to immigrate there.[3] This has changed the ethnic distribution of Israel's inhabitants and its social structure as well.

There was no clear conception of the problems which might ensue from such a policy. Next to nothing was known about habits and customs of many of the Oriental Jewish communities. There was complete ignorance of the ways of life, and the low standard of general social conditions which constituted the plight of many Oriental Jews. And yet there was

[2] Central Bureau of Statistics, *Statistical Abstract of Israel*, 1971, No. 22, Table B/1, p. 21.
    [3] Law of the Return, 5710–1950, in *Laws of the State of Israel*, Vol. 4, 1950, p. 114.

some mystic conception that no specific problems would be involved in absorbing these newcomers, who differed so greatly from what had been experienced hitherto. It was accepted as a foregone conclusion that, as an independent state, with all resources at its disposal, Israel would reclaim these large masses of Oriental Jews within a brief period of time. Time, as a factor in the process of integration, was expected to lead only towards amalgamation.

It has not taken long, however, for field workers to realize that we are confronted with entirely new and manifold problems that will be very difficult to cope with. Doubts are now widespread as to whether successful integration for adults is possible at all. On the other hand, it was not considered a problem or even a matter of concern with the children and young persons. It was regarded a matter of fact that they would integrate into the existing pattern of the new environment without undue difficulties. Experience over many years has shown that this assumption cannot be taken for granted either. In part, this will emerge from the pages of this book.

Furthermore, there was practically no allowance made for the fact that the process of integrating large masses into a rather crystalized society entails in any case great difficulties for newcomers, the more so if the newcomers have come from entirely different cultural and socio-economic milieux. In Israel the absorbing society, although small in number, was very well-knit and purposeful, as well as very conscious of its abilities and leadership qualities. It was therefore regarded as natural that the absorbing society should impose its mores on those to be absorbed. The newcomers did not fail to be aware of these expectations. But it so happened that the rapid economic development which commenced about twenty years ago coincided with the large mass immigration which led to the numerical growth of the population. The onset of a new economic era and the needs of security have channeled almost all resources to strengthen further the economy; the special personal needs of many problem families who came under the aegis of nonselective immigration have as a consequence been almost entirely neglected. It has taken about twenty years to recognize that the magnitude of the problems among the latter has to be tackled in a well-planned and concerted effort.

As a result of the massive immigration of Jews into Israel, there are hardly any Jews left in many European countries, as well as in most countries of the Middle and Near East and in North Africa. Whole communities from Yemen, Iraq, Egypt and Syria migrated to Israel. From other Arab countries such as Morocco, Algeria, and Tunisia large numbers have come to Israel, while others emigrated mainly to France. Jewish survivors from Germany, Poland, Rumania, and other countries of Western Europe have come to Israel in large groups. Today, apart from Israel, there are large Jewish communities only in England, France, North and South America, and in Russia.

The Jewish communities originating from Moslem countries are of particular interest in this book. In Israel, immigrants from these countries face more difficulties than do those from Western countries. While both are exposed to increased stress, and both initially have difficulties in reorientation, this process is more painful for the Oriental Jew. He is often profoundly bewildered and feels more insecure than the newcomer from a Western country. There are a number of reasons for the greater difficulties faced by the Oriental Jew. For one thing, the very structure of Israeli society is foreign to him. For another, leadership in all walks of life in Israel is largely by Ashkenazim (i.e., by those who have come from Western countries). More important still, Oriental Jews encounter special problems which are, to one degree or another, common to them all. Those problems become more significant in Israel because of the confrontation with the Western world and the desire on the part of Oriental Jews to become part of it. It is a confrontation, as it were, between the knowledgeable and skilled on the one hand, and the illiterate and unskilled on the other.

Oriental Jewish communities on the whole constitute a less homogeneous group than their Western counterparts. There are great differences between those who come from Yemen, Egypt, Persia, Turkey, Tunisia, Morocco, and other countries. In fact, one often encounters considerable differences even among Jews who have been living in different regions of the same country. There are Oriental communities of whose existence American and European Jewry had no knowledge. Many of them had been in secluded ghettos for centuries, with hardly any contact with other centers of Jewish life. The members of these communities had had no idea whatsoever of the era of emancipation, or of the way of life among American and European Jewry. Time after time, one encounters resentment of and astonishment at the customs prevalent among Ashkenazim. In a way, it is the gap between the twentieth century in the Western world and the medieval age of the Oriental world, and the result is often a feeling of malaise in both groups.

From the end of the First World War until the establishment of Israel in 1948, approximately 90 percent of the immigrants to Palestine came from European countries. Most of them had a common ideology—political Zionism—which was to bring about a change and a renaissance in the social structure of the Jewish people, gave purpose to their interpersonal relations, and determined their way of life in Israel. The result was the development among the Jewish immigrants of a strong bond and a feeling of belonging, which became particularly important in the face of Arab hostility and British antagonism towards Zionist aspirations.

Among Oriental Jewry, however, motivations to immigration were basically emotional. Once Israel had come into being, they were driven by a messianic-mystical idea of the rebirth of Zion. It was this which inspired them to make their way to Israel. From 1948 to 1952, 70 percent of the newcomers originated from Moslem countries. During the last fifteen years or so, large groups have again arrived from time to time from Moslem countries, including a large influx of immigrants from Egypt after the Sinai campaign of 1956; and since 1948, the number of Jews originating from Moslem countries has increased to about half the Jewish population. Thus, a radical change in the distribution of the various ethnic groups has taken place.

All their differences notwithstanding, both Western and Oriental Jews felt united by the two important factors which played a vital role in their decision to come to their own land and live among their own people. There was their common adherence to the Jewish faith as laid down in the Old Testament. And because of this faith, both groups had experienced great hardship, discrimination, and persecution for generations.

Nevertheless, Oriental Jews, in contrast to their Western counterparts, faced an entirely new and unfamiliar situation in Israel. Their emotional insecurity and anxieties overshadowed their fears as to whether they would be able to make a living in the new environment. They sensed that old and established habits and customs were out of place and felt strong pressures to become a part of, or at least familiar with, a new mode of life. In fact, they themselves also looked upon this as a most desirable objective and as a requirement for being accepted in the new society. On the other hand, they encountered difficulties in adapting themselves to prevailing standards. The vacuum thus created enhanced insecurity and gave rise to bewilderment and resentment.

Economically and sociologically there was a considerable similarity between Jews and Moslems in most Oriental countries. There was the very small group of well-to-do, often erudite people, and on the other hand, large masses who suffered from economic deprivation and were largely illiterate. Among Jews and Moslems alike, the family was the only center for social contacts and each member of the family adhered strictly to obligations which the clan had decided to accept. Strong forces were at work to preserve that state of affairs and to counteract social movements with a different outlook. In Israel, however, family life and community organization are patterned on the conceptions and values of the Western world, a factor which is of no mean importance in the process of reorientation into a new society. Centuries of living in different countries under heterogeneous cultural, economic, and political systems made their impact on the Jewish inhabitants, even if they did live within ghetto walls, creating the great differences which distinguish the Oriental from the Western Jew.

To practically all of the Oriental Jews, immigration to Israel meant transplantation to a competitive society, urbanized and industrialized on the pattern of the Western European and American model. Few of these Jews had had previous experience in systematic manual work, however. Fewer still had any training in or knowledge of technical matters, and a systematic, formal education was foreign to the great majority. In Israel, all these are basic requirements, and they confer a specific social status upon the individual, as well as upon his ethnic group.

For these people, immigration has also meant a change from a society with strong taboos on social contacts and modes of behavior to a society in which no such taboos exist. It was of decisive importance that in this situation the values of the family were immediately affected, and the changes that took place within the family unit were often most painful. The characteristic family structure among Oriental Jewish communities bestowed unquestioned authority upon the father. In most instances he was the main provider, and it was natural for him, apparently, to have the main say in all family matters. But even when he was not the chief breadwinner, he was still highly esteemed as the head of the family. Immigration to Israel, however, has led to a change in his status. In most cases the father was unable to remain the provider for the family because of his inability to meet the requirements of Israel's competitive society. Moreover, his lack of general knowledge in a society where such knowledge is the most important yardstick for social status meant that his influence in all family matters diminished. In the new environment, the children often know better, and indeed, even become the interpreters of this environment for their parents. Thus, although the traditional status of the father should have been of particular importance in guiding the children in the new environment, he has been unable to provide this guidance, a fact which has, as a result, given rise to feelings of inadequacy, frustration, and anxiety.

Similar changes can be observed in the status of the mother, and of women in general. Equality of the sexes has become a matter of course in many Western countries and in Israel in particular. Those who come from Oriental countries, however, have never encountered this situation before. The mere fact that a woman may work outside the home, meeting men and women freely in factories, in workshops, and elsewhere, has tended to enhance her status and has brought about an enormous change in the pattern of many Oriental families.

The case of Moshe, aged twelve, illustrates the change that often takes place in the status of both parents. It was the boy's third trial for stealing. Previously he had come to court with his mother, but I felt that the matter should now be discussed with his father as well. When I asked the father how he explained the delinquent behavior of his boy, he became rather agitated, and among other things, said the following:

"When I was still in Morocco, I knew what was right and wrong, and my family obeyed me. Here I know nothing. My wife interferes in things, which she would not have done at home, and she thinks she knows better than I do." After some further conversation, he added: "When the police came home with the boy and asked me to certify that the the boy would appear in court when summoned to do so, the policeman immediately added, 'But don't beat him because of this!' Now you see, even the police are sheltering the boy, even though he committed an offense. Anyway, I have stopped beating him, because my neighbors said that this is not done in this country, and I was ashamed of behaving differently from others. I really don't know what to do with my boy."

The problem expressed by this father is quite common, although it is not always put as clearly. Two major and distinct reactions can be observed among fathers who sense the loss of their authority. There are those who give up and withdraw, who no longer interfere and subsequently become indifferent. There are others who try by all ways and means to maintain their authority, which is, in most instances, detrimental to family unity.

Many Oriental families face an additional problem caused by language difficulties. For two thousand years the Hebrew language was used only for prayers. Now, in a modernized form, it has become the official spoken language of Israel. The renaissance of the old Hebrew language became one of the most important and unifying forces in the rebirth of Israel. Yet, for many newcomers, the matter of language also has negative repercussions. Practically without exception, children learn rather fast simple Hebrew, which is only sufficient, however, for them to be able to converse in a common language, whereas their parents—particularly those who are not educated—find that it is not at all easy to learn the language. Thus, children frequently become the main interpreters for their parents of habits and customs prevailing in the new environment. In the traditional family structure, it is inconceivable that children, and particularly small children, should gain such an important status—equal in a way to that of the parents.

Loss of parental control has often coincided with maladjustment in children. When parents were able to give their children sufficient security and adequate freedom in the new environment, and when they tried—not too forcibly—to assimilate new values, families were spared the process of disintegration. If, on the other hand, parents were hostile towards the new environment, if they were unable to protect their children from outside pressures, or if they tried too eagerly to accept new values, then the breakup of the family unit was more likely and there was more likelihood of delinquency.

The children of these Oriental Jewish families become deeply disappointed in their parents, even if unconsciously in most cases, when they cannot get support, help, and security at a time when it is most essential to them. Let us consider, for instance, the simple matter of school attendance. The child often finds it difficult to keep pace with the ordinary school curriculum, particularly when the subjects to be studied involve abstract thinking, but he cannot get the necessary help from his parents, because they themselves lack basic knowledge. The difficulty is increased by the fact that these parents usually do not share a common language with the teachers and by the fact that the teachers demand of the child conformity to accepted norms in Western society, norms which are quite foreign to the parents. Consequently, the child feels let down by his parents because they cannot help him and by his teachers because he cannot fulfill their demands. For many of these children, completion of eight grades of elementary school means attainment of social status. But even twenty-three years after the introduction of compulsory elementary education, there are still large numbers who do not complete the eight grades of elementary school. In a competitive society like that of Israel, those children who have not been trained in systematic thinking and learning will find it very difficult to obtain even a semiskilled job. This is likely to be detrimental to their future behavior, and the danger that the family pattern, with its attendant difficulties, may be repeated is present even at this early stage.

The interests and needs of the children make it necessary for them to conform to the values of the new environment, for they sense that in such conformity lies the key to their future advancement. Apart from this, there is their strong desire to be equal to their playmates and to be accepted on the same footing. On this issue a clash of interests has developed between the traditional values which the family wishes and tries to preserve and the pressures and trends in the new society, which have worked in the direction of establishing and fostering new relationships, mostly outside the family circle. Thus the basis for conflict has been widened and has often caused the disruption of the family.

It should be pointed out that, because of their heterogeneous backgrounds and traditions, the various Oriental communities do not necessarily have a uniform reaction to the impact of Western culture. Consequently, it is difficult to estimate how long it takes for the process of integration to be accomplished. Our experience has taught us that there are many who can adapt themselves to this entirely new environment fairly easily, while others adjust with much greater difficulty. Some communities try to safeguard themselves against this process and only reluctantly give way to the influences of the new environment; others are more submissive and manifest passive acceptance; still others try to assimilate the prevalent Western pattern rapidly. It remains to be seen whether this adoption of values, habits, and customs is only superficial and temporary, and if so, how long genuine and complete integration will take. The time factor seems to work in two diverse directions: many adjust to prevailing conditions in the course of time, but there are others whose problems only become manifest with the passing of time. The attitude of the parents usually has a direct bearing on the behavior of children and their ability or inability to conform to their parents' expectations in particular, and to those of the community in general.

The first step in the process of integration is the accumulation of material goods, which I consider to be a positive fact, to be welcomed. In an environment in which the possession of material goods plays an important role in conferring social status upon the individual, the desire to be on an equal footing with those who possess material effects is natural. In a prospering society like that of Israel, where there is no unemployment, it is relatively easy to acquire material goods, and apart from according social status, these acquisitions also make life and adjustment much easier .

The acquisition of knowledge, however, is an entirely different matter. It will take considerable time for those from Oriental communities to acquire the knowledge and sophistication that will place them in positions of leadership. This necessarily leads to frustrations, but shortcuts are almost an impossibility in a technological society.

Another important phenomenon which has been observed is that juvenile delinquency among newcomers is usually manifested only a number of years after their arrival in Israel. During the first few years the child feels insecure in the new environment, and for a time his inhibitions work in the direction of deterrence. It takes time for the influence of the new environment to penetrate the family structure, and it also takes time for identity conflicts to reach the point at which they disrupt the family unit. If this is a rapid process, juvenile delinquency is more likely to result. In addition, as time goes on, failures and frustrations increase, and in many instances these result in negative behavior.

Parents frequently complain in the juvenile court that the influences of the new environment and the hitherto unknown habits and customs are to blame for the delinquent behavior of their children. Some may admit their inability to take better care of their children in this unfamiliar environment and request the court to find an appropriate solution; others may try to protect and shelter their children. Many a parent is on the verge of a breakdown because he regards it as a disgrace for the family to have come to court. In these situations it is sometimes the duty of the juvenile court to encourage parents, to comfort and inspire them with new will in their relationships with their children. The tolerance of the juvenile court and the attention paid to each individual offender have provided many parents and children with an opportunity of adjusting their disturbed relationships.

In our consideration of the function of the juvenile court in a changing society like that of Israel, the basic features touched upon in this chapter must be borne in mind, for they are essential to an understanding of the situation in this country.

2

Israeli
Jewish Youth
Within a
Changing Society

Israel, like many other countries, is confronted with the phenomena of changing behavior patterns among its youth. These changes have given rise to bewilderment on the part of the general public. The public is particularly astonished at the growing number of juvenile delinquents because this seems to contradict a widespread assumption that delinquency among Jewish youth, even in centers with large numbers of Jews, is only a minor problem. "How is it that in Israel," they ask, "where Jews live in their own state, there should be a growing problem of juvenile delinquency? What are the possible causes?"

A current belief has been that delinquency among Jewish children and juveniles is conspicuous by its absence, due to the well-knit cohesion of the Jewish family. One wonders, therefore, why the same should not also apply to Israel. The foregoing assumption makes it appropriate to examine—even if briefly—some of the characteristic behavior patterns of Jews all over the world. These include several features which may explain to a certain extent the low rate of juvenile delinquency among Jews.

1. Jews have lived as a minority group in various nations for about two thousand years. Merely by adhering to a different religion from the one prevalent in their countries of domicile, they have a special sense of belonging and of mutual responsibility toward coreligionists.

2. This sense of belonging and of mutual responsibility has been constantly nourished by their being exposed to discrimination and persecution of varying kind and degree. For many generations they lived in secluded areas, either by force of circumstances or by choice.

13

This secluded environment inevitably fostered meaningful relations among the Jews themselves.

3. One result of these conditions was that the family became a closely knit unit which was largely immune to outside pressures and influences. This led in turn to the development of identical values within the family, further strengthening the family as an institution.

4. One of the distinct characteristics of Jews, whatever the country of domicile, has been their avoidance of the attention of their gentile neighbors. Their experiences of persecution have led to suspicion and insecurity, and the almost inherent maxim has been to be constantly on guard. The result was a particular sensibility concerning their neighbors' opinion of them. With the possible reaction of their non-Jewish environment to their deeds uppermost in their minds, they developed minority reaction patterns, which, among other things, were expressed by inhibited behavior. Jews were rather timid when not among their own kind and usually preferred the company of their coreligionists, where they felt secure and more at ease. The result of inhibitive reaction patterns is clear in this instance: if inhibitions are effective, there is less likelihood of delinquent behavior.

Although there were individual Jews or even small groups to whom these general statements would not apply, or would apply only in part, this was the state of affairs for the majority. After the Second World War, great changes in this respect took place in many European countries and in the United States. Barriers between Jews and gentiles began to break down, often leading to an increase in mixed marriages, in the adoption among Jews of manners considered to be gentile behavior patterns, and in the lowering of the inhibitions that had prevented delinquent behavior. Although Jews had previously been preoccupied with acquiring social status mainly by excelling in the scholarly and professional fields, this was no longer the sole yardstick for gaining recognition. It could also be achieved in negative ways. Nevertheless, in whatever fields Jews have been active, or have excelled, their identity as Jews has continued to play a significant role when non-Jews have evaluated their behavior. Indeed, it is the non-Jewish environment which is conscious of the Jewishness of a compatriot, regardless of whether or not he himself adheres to religious customs or has ties—emotional or otherwise—with the Jewish faith or with the Jewish community in general. He is still regarded by non-Jews as a full-fledged Jew.

The situation in Palestine during the prestate period was similar to that which existed in other places where Jews were a minority group. Jewish society was very closely knit, since its members were striving towards a common goal—namely, autonomy, and ultimately, political independence. These Zionist aspirations, the fact that Jews were a minority ruled by the British Mandate and outnumbered by Arabs, and a strong sense of belonging to this place where Jewish nationhood had been born almost six millennia before impressed on Jews a feeling of mutual dependence and responsibility. There was a close identification between the older and younger generations, since both had the same ideological aspirations; as a result, there was agreement on basic values and modes of behavior. And during this period, there were only small numbers of Jewish juvenile offenders as compared to their gentile counterparts.

A characteristic feature during the prestate period was the personal and even intimate social relationships which had developed over many years among various segments of the Jewish population. The origins of these relationships can be traced to membership in parties and ideological discussion groups, in underground defense organizations, and in youth movements, or even in all three of these. The common denominator of all three was the strong bond of comradeship which developed among members, which was further cemented by the feeling of a common destiny.

The youth movements are of special interest. Jewish youth movements patterned on the German *Wandervogel* started in Western Europe at the beginning of the twentieth century. Their goals were to develop a sense of mutual respect and responsibility and to communicate as equals; the members also shared a general attitude of protest toward parents and the older generation. An atmosphere of romanticism and *Weltverbesserer* pervaded many of these groups, and this helped bridge differences and overcome difficulties. At first the Jewish youth movements engaged in sports, hiking, and discussions. Later the Zionist idea caught their imagination, and many youth movements with the sole purpose of advocating this ideology appeared on the scene. Some were established and affiliated with political parties. These youth organizations created among their members a sense of purpose, of achieving goals, and of promoting definite values. Their main object was to contribute as much as possible to the renaissance of the Jewish people.

The Zionist youth movements played a vital role in creating a special social climate. On the one hand, they developed a philosophy of life which had great appeal to young people; and on the other, they were actually implementing the ideals they represented. Any observer of Jewish life since the beginning of the twentieth century cannot but take into account the role of these movements, nor can one discuss Israel, a new society in the making, without considering their major contribution to this process, mostly during the prestate period.

Since the founding of modern Israel, the situation has altered considerably. In the first place, the majority of Israel's population is Jewish, and the state is managed by Jewish leadership in all spheres of life. Israeli Jews have a definite feeling of power, of security, and of freedom from discrimination and persecution. Since Israel is a small state, one has the feeling of being at home and yet of being a citizen of a state equal to other states. As a result, Jewish youth in Israel do not feel the necessity of governing their behavior according to reactions of non-Jews. Having grown up in a secure environment, they have developed self-confidence and a straightforward behavior pattern which is unique to Israeli Jewish youth, as compared to their peers abroad. This basic feeling of security has become a very important factor in their character formation.

Secondly, the family, whose structure and unity had previously been, among others, a major factor in the prevention of juvenile delinquency, is undergoing great changes. This is particularly the case among Jewish groups originating from Moslem countries, as Chapter 1 indicated. The common denominator of all these groups, the patriarchial family structure, has been severely shaken in Israel. Moreover, in their attempt to assimilate rapidly the manners of Western society, young people from these communities have developed relations with people outside their own family circle, which was not previously customary. This has also led to serious changes in the traditional pattern of the family unit.

A negative repercussion can be seen in the high percentage of juvenile offenders among these groups; over 92 percent of all juvenile offenders in Israel come from Oriental Jewish groups, although young people from these communities constitute only 57 percent of their age group in the total population.[1] Apart from individual factors which may account for the preponderance of juvenile delinquents from these communities, various general aspects are evident: these include a large number of problem families, a low educational standard, many emotional and health problems, and feelings of inadequacy. Many of these problems are concentrated in the Oriental communities, which also has a negative effect on the image they present to the public. In view of the continuous influx of new immigrants, it is also difficult to evaluate factors which may have either a stabilizing or a disrupting effect. For example, practically nothing is known about previous social or antisocial behavior of new

---

[1] The compilation of these figures is made according to the father's place of birth.

immigrants, and no prediction can be made as to their future behavior under the new conditions of Israel.

Experience in Israel has shown that the family in which all members observe religious duties is a stronghold against juvenile delinquency, provided that religion is the basis of family life. If this is the case, religious customs become meaningful and enrich life. There has also been a contrasting development, however. A large number of Jews from Moslem countries keep religious observances to find this a particular obligation in Israel. But many of their children greatly desire to be regarded as equals by their peers who do not observe religious duties. Their protest against their parents and against the general difficulties faced by the family finds its foremost expression in the giving up of religious observances. This is always a highly emotional issue, giving rise to tension, anxiety, clashes between parents and children. In these instances, religious observance does not prevent delinquent behavior, but rather increases its likelihood, because conflict situations are enhanced.

Of special significance is the existence in Israel of a considerable number of problem families, a result of the government's policy of unrestricted Jewish immigration, or "ingathering of the exiles." The manifold social and cultural problems of these families have become conspicuous and even aggravated in Israel, because of the confrontation between entirely different concepts and modes of living. Many of these families are unable to benefit from existing social services. Witness the simple matter of school education: even now, almost twenty-three years after elementary education was made compulsory, there are thousands of children who do not finish all the prescribed grades in elementary school each year. Although many reasons account for this, an important one concerns their parents. A large percentage of parents from Moslem countries did not themselves attend a regular school and are therefore unable to provide their children with the necessary stimulus to complete their schooling.

In summary, there is a breakdown of old customs and of traditional family ties in Israel. The small family units of Jews who were scattered throughout the large gentile world are replaced by the large and independent Israeli Jewish society. For many this has become the large family, with all its implications. There is no longer any fear of persecution or a need to orient oneself according to the possible reactions of a gentile world. The inhibitions which worked to prevent delinquency outside Israel are no longer operative in Israel. On the contrary, it can be assumed that the absence of inhibitions may be a contributing factor in the development of delinquent behavior among Israeli youth.

In recent years there have been repeated remarks that Israeli Jewish youth have changed, that they are less idealistic and less purposeful than the youth of previous generations. Time and again the opinion has been expressed that Israeli youth no longer volunteer for pioneering missions, but have instead become preoccupied with furthering their personal ambitions. Supposedly, they lack identification with those values which were central to the prestate period. Whereas at that time individual ambitions and aspirations were superseded by those of general and national interest, it is said that this is no longer the case. It is further maintained that youth have become overly interested in leading an easy and comfortable life, which is not in keeping with the ideas and ideals of a society still in the process of molding itself. These attitudes are seen as contrasting with those prevailing among the youth of this country several decades ago.

Such remarks, however, do not do justice to reality. What must be taken into consideration is that the structure of our society as a whole has changed considerably since the prestate period. It is sometimes not realized that what was called Palestine was an economically impoverished society; this continued to be the case during the early years of Israel's independence. A very simple way of living was the established norm for the large majority of the population. In 1933, when many thousands of Jewish intellectuals, professional people with financial means, came to Palestine from Germany and Central Europe, industry and commerce were just beginning to develop. The economic structure did not allow very many of them to be absorbed into their own professions, so they were forced to look for other employment. At that time, the major emphasis was on agricultural work—a reflection of the Zionist idea that a return to agriculture was the most important step in returning the Jewish people to nomal life—and the highest social prestige was bestowed on those who were engaged in such work and living in rural areas. As a result, large numbers of these immigrants were channeled into manual and agricultural work. All of them invariably had to lower their standard of living, a very difficult adjustment. But their desire to be an integral part of the Jewish community in Palestine and their Zionist aspirations were important driving forces. Furthermore, the concept of an egalitarian society was widespread, and together with the limited economic possibilities, had a decisive impact on people in all walks of life. One result was the marked absence of distinctions and differences characteristic of a materialistic, competitive, and technological society.

In contrast, the changeover to an independent state coincided with the onset of technological development, which produced different modes of life and different values. Naturally, this complete change in the economic structure of Israel is being felt by adults and juveniles alike. Nevertheless, although adults are aware of the great changes which have occurred, and although they benefit from the achievements of the technological age, theirs is a nostalgic attitude concerning the "good old days," particularly so far as the behavior of youth is concerned. The question is whether such an attitude is not an expression of bewilderment and confusion because of an inability to cope with the changing habits of young people.

The rapid advances in science, technology, and industry in Israel within the last fifteen years or so have changed the country into an economically vital society. Because of these advances, the demands of contemporary Israel on its youth changed considerably. Young people became aware of the need to prepare themselves to cope with the requirements of a rapidly developing technological society. Thus, today one can find a very large number of young people in quite complicated jobs, including the sciences, technology, industry, research, and administration. There is a drive to acquire the tools for understanding the wide range of information which has become a necessity in present-day society, and one cannot but be deeply impressed by the great effort put forth by large groups of youth who are engaged in furthering their studies. Indeed, the desire to attain more knowledge exists on an unprecedented scale.

Israel's needs as an independent state, with its responsiblility of providing the population with state services, also opened up new possibilities for young people. Those who were gifted were naturally chosen to fill the gap during the changeover period, although appointments were sometimes made because of political affiliations or in recognition of veteran services. The great contribution which young Israelis are making in the Israeli Defense Forces deserves special mention. Although military service is regarded as a necessary evil forced upon Israel by neighboring enemy countries, there is great dedication to it, because military service is the embodiment of Israel's very existence. As a result, personal prestige and high social status are attached not only to those who fulfill the compulsory conscription of three years but also to those who choose to remain in the army for a further period. Those who belong to the armed forces display a very high degree of comradeship and a readiness to make personal sacrifices for the well-being of the general community. In a sense, the army perpetuates the ideals of the prestate period—the comradeship of the youth movements, the pioneering enterprise of the kibbutz founders, and above all, the fight for survival.

The creation of statehood brought an enormous influx of newcomers from many countries, as we have already seen. The absorption of these large masses of people within a brief period and within a small territory has entailed a heavy strain on the economy, as well as made more difficult sociocultural integration. Existing cities grew fast, and towns with the goal of someday becoming cities became cities almost overnight. The result of this rapid growth and urbanization was that those intimate social relationships which were so satisfying during the prestate period lost much of their significance or disappeared entirely. The focus of interest switched from common and identifiable goals to more diffuse objectives and individual ambitions.

While considering changes that have occurred among Jewish youth in Israel, one must mention the kibbutz, because of the enormous impact the kibbutz movement has had on Jewish youth in this country, and on Zionist youth groups abroad. The kibbutz is an agricultural settlement in which there is communal ownership of property and the pooling of labor. Its social structure is based on voluntary membership and equality of all members. In other words, a member of a kibbutz places at its disposal his work capacity, energy, and time, while the kibbutz provides him with all necessities both material and spiritual, and is responsible for the upbringing of his children.

The kibbutz has undergone tremendous changes since the establishment of the state of Israel. The most conspicuous of these is that the egalitarian concept of life has given way to the influences of a materialistic society. A prospering society has its impact on the kibbutz as anywhere else, and differences between the behavior patterns of kibbutz youth and urban youth are increasingly disappearing. A growing number of kibbutz-born youth find city life so agreeable and comfortable that many prefer it to the life of the kibbutz, which they leave if any opportunity arises. At the same time, the kibbutz has also lost a great deal of its appeal for Jewish youth growing up in this country and abroad; and the large influx of newcomers to Israel did not proportionally enlarge the membership of the various kibbutz movements, since only a small percentage of these immigrants joined a kibbutz. Three major factors account for this. First, the primary motivation for joining the kibbutz was based on its original image as the pioneering force in the renaissance of the Jewish people. Those who joined were dedicated to the upbuilding of the country under adverse circumstances and shared an esprit de corps and common values. Their special way of life set them off from their peers. Secondly, Israel's requirements as an independent state now provide ample opportunities for varied pioneering activities—for example, in engineering, medicine, university teaching and research, and in administration and planning, as well as in the professional army and the security agencies. Finally, employment in these fields now confers the high social prestige which was previously given to those who joined a kibbutz, and young people nowadays direct their ambitions almost entirely to achievements in these fields instead of joining a kibbutz. A new value is the great desire for material gain.

Whereas there was previously only the kibbutz to capture the imagination, enthusiasm, and pioneering spirit of youth, there are now many vital professions open to them in which they can make a contribution toward building the country. Therefore, instead of joining a kibbutz, a young person can engage in one of the professions without feeling guilty about it and without losing social status. Furthermore, it is now much easier for kibbutz-born children, who were once expected to continue in their fathers' way of life, to leave the kibbutz permanently. Whereas previously, such a step was rarely taken and was then regarded as a betrayal of the ideology, it now occurs frequently, with bad feelings rare. This new tendency is, of course, a reflection of technological development in contemporary Israel. The impact of technology can also be seen in the increasing demand by gifted members of kibbutzim, particularly among the younger generation, to be able to study at the universities on behalf of the kibbutz. This poses difficult problems for each kibbutz, but it also points to a fundamental change going on among youth in the kibbutz.

Nonetheless, the kibbutz still has a role to play. For many boys it remains an ideal—even if the fantasies they weave about kibbutz life have little relation to its reality—and the image of rescue that it offers is a very powerful one, both for the offender and for those who must in some capacity or other deal with him. This is especially the case with children and juveniles whose homes are not in a kibbutz to begin with. Some, particularly children, but including all ages up to sixteen or seventeen, are sent to a kibbutz by parents or by a social welfare agency as to any other residential placement facility. Some youth movements have special arrangements with a kibbutz, whereby their members can spend a training period of a year or so in a kibbutz. There are also juvenile offenders, mostly above the age of fourteen, who, in fear of the consequences of their offense, decide, on the spur of the moment or on the advice of parents, to join a kibbutz. Some of them may genuinely desire to break with unwarranted associations. For others, joining a kibbutz is an obvious maneuver, a bid for time. They remain in a kibbutz until their case is tried in court, because they figure—quite rightly— that the mere fact of their being in a kibbutz may sway the issue in their favor, and will almost inevitably lead to a mitigated sentence. Once the verdict is announced, they leave the kibbutz. For them it is a kind of provisional shelter, and they do not even find it worthwhile to "suffer" the adaptation to modes of peer group behavior in the kibbutz. There are only a few who have the endurance to stay at the kibbutz for a few weeks or more. Most leave within two weeks or so after arrival. Shlomo, aged fifteen and a half years is a case in point.

Shlomo was caught twice within four months while stealing a motor-cycle. The first time, he was released on a bond of recognizance, but he realized that it would be different the second time. About two weeks before trial began for the second offense Shlomo went to a kibbutz, and the probation officer requested an adjournment of the case until she could find out whether or not he was going to settle down there. Accordingly, I adjourned the hearing for three months, taking into account the facts that Shlomo was obviously afraid to stand trial and might therefore make a real effort to remain at the kibbutz; and that if sufficient time were allowed for his adaptation to kibbutz life, he might perhaps stay there longer.

When the trial eventually started Shlomo was in good form. The in-structor of the kibbutz came especially with him to court and she, as well as the probation officer, had only positive reports about him. He had twice been on leave over the weekend and came back on time to the kibbutz. He reported proudly to the inspector that during leave he had not been seeing his previous friends. I had certain doubts about his genuine-ness and adjourned the case for another two months, to his great displeasure; he pleaded to have the trial over there and then, because, as he put it, he had proved to all that he was a different person. It was quite clear to me, however, that Shlomo was very manipulative, and I wanted him to realize that although the reports were in his favor, I was not quite certain of him.

When he came next time, the reports about him were still favorable, and I put Shlomo on probation on condition that he reside in the kibbutz. He readily agreed to this, and he left the court happily with his instructor. The idyll which had prevailed for about six months came to a sudden end only five days after the case was finished in court. For no obvious reason and to the great disappointment of the kibbutz instructor and the proba-tion officer, he suddenly left the kibbutz. Back in the city, Shlomo again started to frequent the company of old friends who had delinquent records. He defied the probation officer and his parents alike. The probation officer, who saw his pattern of reaction, summoned Shlomo to court on breach of probation. Again Shlomo reacted in the same way, by finding himself a job before trial started on the matter of the breach of probation.

To my mind this fact could be seen as evidence that Shlomo still cared what might happen to him, and that he was not yet set on a criminal career. It was therefore worthwhile to go along with his manipulations and keep the court case open, because it had, for the time being, a salutory effect, even if limited. I adjourned the case another three times, stipulating that he continue to work and that he see the probation officer regularly. During these sessions in court he never mentioned the kibbutz again, and it was quite clear that he would not return there. I did not insist on this, but I made it clear to him that a further breach of probation might lead to a prison sentence. There was no doubt in my mind that he would try to avoid such a sentence.

To a somewhat different category belong those, on probation, who join a kibbutz according to a plan devised by the probation officer. If the latter thinks that it might be beneficial for the probationer were he to join a kibbutz, he will also take appropriate steps to make sure that at the kibbutz the probationer joins a training group which enables him to be under supervision and in the company of a peer group suited to him. There is the advantage that the probation officer usually has close contact with the instructor of this youth group and, of course, with the probationer himself. Such a measure is felt to be of vital importance in insuring a smooth integration into the difficult pattern of kibbutz life.

Yet although much effort, energy, time, and money have been spent to make this method of treatment a success, it has been proved that only a negligible number can really adapt to the requirements of a kibbutz. There, constant demands are put forward patterned on the normative behavior of kibbutz children, which is on an entirely different level from that to which those who join a training group are used. These are constantly under stress because of the effort they have to make. There is still another great difference, particularly among children and juveniles. Kibbutz children are given care and attention from early childhood by their parents and by the kibbutz. The common denominator of those who join a kibbutz under circumstances as above is the emotional and material deprivation which they have experienced from early childhood. This distinction is such a striking one, especially in a small, closed community such as the kibbutz, that it is very difficult indeed to control envy and frustrating situations.

Last but not least, city children are drawn to city life, unless there exists a special motivation, which they have emotionally and intellectually integrated into their personality, to live in a rural district or in a kibbutz. Time and again, in our experience, the most wretched living conditions in urban districts have more attraction for them than a comfortable life in a rural district. Those who join a kibbutz without sharing the ideological motive will usually not settle down there.

Whenever a child or juvenile who is a temporary resident in a kibbutz is caught while committing an offense, he is inevitably and immediately sent away. Sometimes, but not always, the police are informed. At times this is not done because the major consideration of the kibbutz is to get rid of that person as quickly as possible. In several kibbutzim, where a pioneering spirit and a fund of goodwill exists, one can find instructors who are willing to include some problematic children and juveniles in a group under their responsibility. They regard it as a challenge and are not easily discouraged in spite of repeated disappointments. Furthermore, there are several kibbutzim that have developed a system of monthly payments to those juveniles who are mainly engaged as temporary laborers. Such an arrangement helps to solve the manpower shortage for the kibbutz, and does not usually raise ideological conflicts because such payments are regarded as pocket money and not wages. (Kibbutz ideology forbids wage-labor by nonmembers.) Those young people who have the endurance to stay at a kibbutz for a reasonable length of time may benefit. Sometimes a change is felt soon after a youngster has left the kibbutz, although at other times the positive results appear only later. If the stay in the kibbutz was reasonably successful, those involved will mention this fact with pride.

In summary, the different needs of Israel today as compared to those of the prestate period and the technological development of the last fifteen years have produced new trends that have their impact on the whole population. A different social climate has developed, and the yardstick for ideals, values, ambitions, and achievements has undergone a radical change. It seems that there is less interaction between parents and children and less communication between members of a family. The interests of everyday life are scattered over wide areas, and the identification with and the concentration on common ideals and goals is decreasing. That children are nowadays better able to defy customs and traditions than their own parents were able to do at the same age may be part of a general process. Children and young people are much more competitive, and a realistic, down-to-earth attitude is prevalent.

These changes are significant in a society which was previously famous for its ideological discussions.

Children and youth in Israel have developed a feeling of superiority toward their parents, teachers, and the older generation in general, because technological developments and mass media have made them sophisticated. They look at the older generation with pity, disappointment, and sometimes contempt, refusing to accept their values as worth imitating. Their elders are no longer those who have the know-how. The widespread use of television has particularly changed the outlook of the young. Even village children know what their contemporaries the world over are thinking and doing, and there is a desire to identify with and imitate them.

In addition, parents are less certain of their own attitudes and ideas and often find themselves questioning traditional customs and habits. This leads to insecurity on their part as to what is right and wrong, and almost necessarily, to a critical attitude on the part of their children. From this point it is only a small step to losing control over their children. Moreover, the high standard of living exerts its influence on parent-child relationships. Parents who are preoccupied with increasing their material wealth, invariably have less time to take care of and to establish emotional ties with their children. Their children often regard this as indifference. For them, it has no real meaning if parents plead, in critical situations, that they have not spared expense to satisfy their children's material needs; in fact, it often has an adverse effect. Under these circumstances, children may become less discriminating in their choice of friends and acquaintances, perhaps in protest against their parents.

In a prosperous society like that of Israel, there is a great desire to make use of the wealth of available commodities. This desire is enhanced by the fact that within the last twenty years Israel has had to fight three wars; among the repercussions, one can observe an inclination to take life in stride and not to postpone pleasures for a better time to come. There is a desire for immediate gratification, which is foreign to the patterns that once prevailed here. This affluence also brought in its wake a different attitude toward money. In contrast to the previous tradition of saving money, there is now a widespread tendency to spend it.

Israel is no longer the small, isolated country it was. Young people from all over the world come to Israel for long or brief periods, and increasing numbers of young Israelis travel abroad. Inevitably, this brings about changes in modes of behavior. Israeli youth imitate the fashions, fads, and behavior and share the interests of youth today; they wear youthful clothing and hairstyles, use drugs, enjoy light entertainment and light music, have a special interest in popular songs—in brief, there is an admiration for everything which is beyond what was once customary in Israel. These tendencies are constantly nourished by industries which specialize in products for young people. Commerce has realized that it is worthwhile to cultivate this particular market.

Although one gets the impression that today's youth are purposeful and straightforward, that they condemn the concepts and ways of the older generation, one can also observe a great deal of confusion and bewilderment. This mixture has, in turn, an irritating effect on parents, teachers, and adults in general. It is largely because of these new customs that the older generation in Israel often feels estranged and sometimes takes an unfriendly attitude towards youth, maintaining that the new patterns of behavior are out of place here. They fear that these new manners and interests may imperil the ideals and the pioneering spirit which have been salient features in the building of Israel.

Against this background one must evaluate recent developments among certain groups of Jewish youth. We have witnessed repeated outbreaks of violence organized by young people from Oriental Jewish communities. The first group was organized in Jerusalem, and since then, other groups have been formed. Although these groups are only loosely organized and lack common leadership, they have tried to coordinate some of their activities, particularly protest demonstrations. So far, however, the most militant group is that of Jerusalem.

The common goal of all these groups is what they call the "abolishment of discrimination against Oriental Jews." In order to bring home to the Israeli public their viewpoint and to indicate how their situation is analogous to that of American Negroes, they call themselves Black Panthers. Among their demands are eradication of want and poverty among Oriental Jewish groups, better educational and housing facilities, job opportunities, and appropriate representation of Oriental Jews in all governing bodies. They maintain that it is only by using violence that they can achieve redress of discriminatory conditions.

Within a brief period of time these young and inexperienced groups have succeeded in bringing to public attention the dearth and misery which is the lot of many people, particularly those who belong to Oriental Jewish communities. In fact, the leadership of Israel was apparently so shocked that it has met with representatives of the Jerusalem Black Panthers and discussed with them ways of improving existing conditions. Overnight, as it were, a new group of experts in solving social problems was formed to advise the country's leaders. The prestige bestowed upon the Black Panthers by this fact alone enhanced their importance in the eyes of the public. Furthermore, they in fact achieved more than professors of social work, social administrators, and professional field workers, who have been trying for years to convince the establishment of the needs of underprivileged groups within the general population. Suddenly, money was made available regardless of whether or not appropriate plans for meeting actual needs were in existence. The sudden availability of large sums of money can be regarded as an expression of guilt by the leadership, who were apparently only made aware by the violent behavior of these young people of prevailing deficiencies in Israel's flourishing society. It is obvious that, because poverty and want are particularly present among Oriental Jewish groups, the feeling of discomfort is enhanced. The giving of money under such circumstances is identical with the paying of reparation, and in this context it may have special meaning.

The Black Panthers and the aims they stand for enjoy a considerable amount of sympathy among the general public. This in itself is an interesting phenomenon, because the spokesmen for the groups do not have a good command of the Hebrew language and cannot, therefore, adequately convey the state of affairs among the underprivileged. For the time being the sympathy has been of a passive nature, finding its expression mainly in newspaper articles, radio discussions, drawing-room conversations, and public opinion polls. The real test will be whether or not active support will be forthcoming.

Many have posed the question: How can one account for such a development in Israel? For, on the face of it, there has been a remarkable and constant rise in the general standard of living among a large number of Oriental Jewish communities. Job opportunities are increasingly available, as well as training projects; there are more and better educational possiblities for those who are gifted and for those who need special instruction; even housing facilities are greatly improved, although many are still substandard.

The answer may be that in a society like that of Israel, in which there is prosperity and in which social status is allied to material wealth, mounting bitterness is felt by those who cannot keep pace with such fast developments. In our competitive society, in which specialized knowledge is in high demand, many feel frustrated because they are unable to compete. Their constant confrontation with a demanding, sophisticated society leads to repeated failure. The difficulty or impossibility of conforming to the standards of this society may easily lead to the conviction that there are no equal opportunities for Oriental Jews. Under such circumstances, no amount of reasoning or counting of facts will yield results, because the issue is emotionally overcharged.

Furthermore, Israeli society is polarizing. Distinctions between the different income groups are growing and crystallizing. Active participation in the policy-making and top-level decisions which determine the way of life of all inhabitants is still confined to the old guard. They have by and large proved to be reliable and efficient, and they can further reckon with general public support. But only a small number of Oriental Jews are among these high administrators, which, argue the Black Panthers, is also the result of discriminatory manipulations. Grudges have therefore accumulated over many years, and are now canalized on a target, namely, the abolition of this very system.

The governing system, however, is not identical with personal achievements or failures. In a technological and competitive society, an education and an intellectual understanding of the mechanism of society are necessary for obtaining key positions. Lack of these assets leads almost inevitably to less well-paid jobs and to a lesser social status.

All things being equal, it can be maintained that the system has not done enough to improve social conditions. Such improvement cannot be achieved, however, by sporadic and uncoordinated actions of various government departments. The issue is a very complicated one and is not confined to budgetary considerations only, but is also a matter of the appropriate distribution of manpower and of priorities. It can be said with certainty that individuals who are unwilling or unable to continue to acquire knowledge and to develop their potentialities are going to remain in inferior positions. Sporadic outbreaks of violence like those of the Black Panthers may continue to occur, but they will not change fundamental conditions of deprivation.

For Israel, as a society in the making, must be interested in furthering knowledge and in making provisions to assist those engaged in such endeavors. In order to survive, it must be in a position to compete with other nations on a qualitative basis of the highest order.

II
Delinquency
and Its Problems

3

Delinquency
Among Jewish
Youth

CHARACTERISTICS OF DELINQUENCY AMONG JEWS

An analysis of the conditions described in the preceding chapters indicates that three major factors contribute to juvenile delinquency among Jews in Israel. These are (1) the breakup of the family unit, (2) the clash of cultures in a melting-pot setting, and (3) the rapid development of a technological society. Each of these factors alone is of sufficient magnitude to create situations which can lead to delinquent behavior. For many individuals, however, they are present simultaneously, and naturally in such cases the delinquent behavior tends to be more serious.

There are also, of course, emotional factors which may result in delinquency; however, our experience over many years has shown that emotional disturbances by themselves are seldom the determining issue but rather a by-product of the factors mentioned above. In those instances of juvenile delinquency where a major contributing factor was of an emotional nature, it could be observed, particularly among adolescents, that there was some kind of behavior disorder that was manifest in different ways, one way being delinquency. When such individuals are placed in a benevolent, supportive environment, these manifestations often either disappear entirely or greatly diminish; such placement is indeed the remedy most often suggested by psychiatrists and psychologists.

Time and again one is impressed by the strong emotional repercussions seen in children and young people exposed to long-standing stress and conflict situations. To this domain also belong the possible effects on children and young people of the long war in which Israel

31

has been involved since its establishment. It is sometimes overlooked that the majority of them either were born and grew to adulthood under permanent war conditions or were born abroad but spent their formative years under these conditions. Sometimes these conditions made themselves felt to such a degree that they determined all aspects of life, while at other times they did not affect all individuals so strongly. Nevertheless, during all these years—almost a quarter of a century—the personal safety of everyone was imperiled. The mere fact of living under the stress of war could therefore be expected to affect behavior patterns of children and young people, including the incidence of delinquency.

In spite of adverse circumstances, however, juvenile delinquency is neither quantitatively nor qualitatively a serious problem in Israel. The figures which will be analyzed in this chapter do not indicate a rapid growth in the number of juvenile delinquents. The quantitative aspect is even less serious than a superficial glance at the figures would suggest, because offenders are counted anew each year (this is explained later in this chapter). What is serious, however, is the large number of recidivists, for this points up society's failure to provide adequate treatment facilities and to develop and implement preventive measures and methods of treatment. Although recidivism can, to a certain extent, be attributed to personal factors, the high percentage of recidivists in all age groups points to insufficient and inadaquate special community services.

So far as the types of offenses committed by juveniles in Israel are concerned, serious crimes are infrequent. There are almost no cases of robbery, murder, arson, or extortion. Rape is virtually nonexistent, and even minor sex offenses occur only on a small scale (see Chapter 5). All these offenses can be regarded as violent delinquent patterns. It is this particular type of delinquency, of "acting out," which could have been expected to be present on a large scale if one accepts the hypothesis that aggressive behavior is the personal expression of frustrations.

Large numbers of children and young people in Israel not only often find themselves in frustrating situations, but also in an accumulation of frustrating situations. It is this accumulation which is, in my opinion, of major importance. For instance, many children who belong to Oriental Jewish communities find it difficult to keep pace with the ordinary school curriculum, although they are not mentally backward. Many eventually drift away from school without finishing the prescribed grades, but they continue to hold a grudge against the school, which, as they see it, prevented them from gaining the social status of their peers. They early become aware, albeit not intellectually, that their failure to finish school hampers their integration into Israeli society. Many children who are charged in juvenile courts with having wilfully broken windows in school buildings have this background. Such children and young people, who have difficulty expressing themselves verbally, and who feel inferior because their status is not equal to that of their peers, often resort to the use of force in lieu of words. By using force they can not only compete with others on an equal footing but can also give vent to their frustration. Yet, despite all these factors, violence as a delinquent behavior pattern or as a by-product of a particular offense is an irregular occurrence.

Another phenomenon is that there are practically no gangs among delinquents.[1] There are juveniles who commit offenses together, but they do not constitute a gang. The basic elements of a gang—an offender with leadership qualities exercising his influence on a group of others for the purpose of committing delinquent acts—are conspicuously lacking.

In short, the general picture of delinquent behavior has remained the same for approximately the last ten years. In fact, the Central Bureau of Statistics has recently published figures for 1969 and 1970, there has, accordingly, been no serious increase in delinquency. Nevertheless, the public continues to be alarmed about its growth, and many think that something drastic should be done to curb further negative developments in this area.

This discrepancy between public assumptions, which are also expressed in newspaper reports, and actual fact requires an explanation. The public usually does not differentiate between juvenile offenders who are tried in the juvenile court and young people who are tried in a court for adults. The juvenile courts in Israel have jurisdiction over male juvenile offenders from nine to under sixteen years of age, and over females from nine to under eighteen years of age. This means, in effect, that those over the ages of sixteen or eighteen, respectively, are tried in a court for adults (although there are a number of cases in which the prosecuting authorities refer a trial at these ages to the juvenile court).

What goes on in adult courts usually receives wide publicity, because such courts are open to the public, and the proceedings there are published in newspapers. For the sake of sensation, more publicity is

---

[1] Israeli Police Force, *Annual Police Report for 1968*, p. 109.

given if young offenders of middle-class background are being tried. Even if such cases account for only a few extreme instances, the reports published are geared to catch the public eye, and thus lead to wrong impressions.

Such reports also give support to the general assumption that crime is spreading among the well-to-do. At the same time there is an undercurrent of fear among the middle class that their own children may get involved in unlawful activities. Middle-class offenders also encounter resentment because they probably wear long hair and are slovenly dressed. Many adults therefore project onto these young people an image which is not necessarily in accordance with reality. Furthermore, they generalize, maintaining that these instances reflect the general condition of today's youth. In fact, among the general group of delinquents there have always been small groups from a middle-class background. Some of them become hard-core delinquents, but for the majority delinquent behavior has been nothing more than a passing phase in their development.

STATISTICS ON DELINQUENCY

In a discussion of juvenile delinquency it is common to compare statistics with those available from other countries. Such comparisons, however, are often inconclusive and may even be misleading, because there is no uniform method of compiling criminal statistics. Furthermore, as a result of differences relating to the age of criminal responsibility, distinctions as to what is regarded as a criminal offense, variations as to the judicial competence of a juvenile court and so on, there are often no uniform basic items that can be compared. Consequently I will attempt no such comparison.

In Israel, there are three different sources of information about juvenile offenses: police statistics; statistics of the juvenile probation service, compiled by a different system; and data of the Central Bureau of Statistics, which is the government agency for compiling statistical information. The statistical material from these three sources has one feature in common: both each offense and, if he again offends, each offender, are registered anew for a particular year. A person prosecuted or convicted several times during a particular year is counted each time he was prosecuted or convicted. The juvenile probation service, however, also keeps a record on an individual basis, according to which an offender is counted only once a year, regardless of the number of offenses he may have committed during that year. In addition, during the "lifetime" of a juvenile offender—i.e., the period during which he may be adjudicated by the juvenile court—he is counted anew each year as a first offender, but he also appears in the list of recidivists. One further has to differentiate between the number of offenses which were committed and the number of offenders who have committed these offenses.

TABLE 3.1
PERCENTAGE OF OFFENSES
COMMITTED BY JUVENILES
AND ADULTS, 1960–70

Year	Offenses by juveniles	Offenses by adults
1960	21.1%	78.9%
1961	24.1	75.9
1962	27.1	72.9
1963	28.7	71.3
1964	29.8	70.2
1965	30.7	69.3
1966	30.1	69.9
1967	29.4	70.6
1968	33.0	67.0
1969	32.4	67.6
1970	31.5	68.5

Source: Israeli National Police, *Annual Police Report for 1970*, Table 34, p. 53.

Note: Police statistics do not register females above the age of sixteen and under eighteen as juvenile offenders, although according to law they are adjudicated by the juvenile court.

Table 3.1 lists the percentage of offenses committed by juveniles as compared to offenses committed by adults. These figures show clearly that over the years there has been an increase of *offenses* committed by juvenile offenders. Three major reasons may account for this: juvenile offenders are more easily apprehended than adult offenders; juvenile offenders, once they are apprehended, often admit to having committed offenses previously unknown to the police (in these instances the police obtain initial information from the offender's voluntary admission); the percentage of recidivists has constantly increased over the years.

A number of these juvenile offenders are never brought to trial, however. By administrative arrangement, there is a waiting period of two months during which the juvenile probation service can recommend to the police the closure of files, if this seems expedient. The final decision concerning such closure rests with the police. The percentages of files closed by the police for true offenses from 1960 to 1970 were as follows:[2]

Year	Percentage	Year	Percentage
1960	30.8	1966	28.1
1961	33.4	1967	27.2
1964	28.5	1968	29.5
1965	28.9	1969	23.8
		1970	22.2

As these figures show, a rather high percentage of files are closed by this procedure each year. Such a decision is based on the following considerations: whether or not a first offender is concerned; the type of offense; the age of the offender and his home background; and whether or not it is in the interest of the public to proceed with a trial. An investigation carried out several years ago revealed that less than 20 percent of those whose files were thus closed committed another offense and had proceedings started against them for the second offense. Yet, the police and the juvenile probation service keep a record of offenses not proceeded against.

TABLE 3.2
RATES OF JEWISH JUVENILE OFFENDERS
PER 1,000 OF THE CORRESPONDING
POPULATION GROUP, 1960–70

Year	Males	Females	Both sexes
1960	14.7	1.9	8.1
1961	15.7	1.5	8.1
1964	18.2	1.8	9.4
1965	19.1	1.9	9.8
1966	18.8	2.0	9.8
1967[a]	12.5	1.2	6.4
1968	16.2	1.5	8.0
1969	18.3	1.7	9.2
1970	19.1	1.8	9.6

Source: Israel, Central Bureau of Statistics, Special Series, No. 168, 244, 322, 370, 408, Table B. No figures published for 1962-63.
[a]Decrease in offenders during this year due to an amnesty.

[2] These figures are derived from those published annually since 1960 by the Central Bureau of Statistics (no figures were published for 1962–1963).

Table 3.2 gives rates of Jewish juvenile offenders, computed according to the corresponding age group in the general population. The criminality rates here reveal that in 1964 there was an increase in the total rates of juvenile offenders. These rates remained about the same for the next two years. During this period the economic development of the country was curbed by special government policy, and unemployment reached rather great dimensions, which naturally affected young people as well as adults. The increase of juvenile delinquency during this period was a direct result of that economic depression.

On the other hand, the decrease in rates for 1967 was due to the amnesty that was passed by the Knesset on July 12, 1967, following the Six Day War. This law applied to offenses which were committed by any person before June 5, 1967, and for which a prison sentence is prescribed. It was applicable to all instances, whether an offender had already been sentenced, or whether the case was still under investigation. There were a few exceptions, however. The law did not apply, for example, to a prison sentence of more than ten years, or to instances of burglary, housebreaking, and the like in the event that the offender had been previously convicted for such an offense; nor did it apply to an offense according to the Penal Law Amendment of 1962 (Prostitution Offenses).

As a result of this law a large number of files were closed by the police. The law applied to juveniles and adults alike, but the greatest beneficiaries were adults, because only a small number of juvenile offenders were then actually in prison or had a conditional prison sentence.

All who were engaged in studying and observing developments in the field of delinquency knew that there was again bound to be an increase in delinquent behavior, and this can be seen in Table 3.2 in the rates for 1968, 1969, and 1970 when things, so to speak, went back to normal. It can also be seen in the absolute numbers of those convicted in juvenile courts during these years (Table 3.5). Those who assumed that the tendency toward increase was going to continue, however, are confronted with opposite findings. According to police statistics already available, there was a decrease in juvenile offenses in 1969 and still a further decrease in 1970.[3] The decrease can be attributed to the greater employment opportunities resulting from the growing economic prosperity after 1967. Although many factors have to be taken into account,

[3] Israeli Police Force, *Annual Police Report for 1970*, Table 33, p. 51.

it can safely be said that the statistical data in Table 3.2, together with the figures in the *Annual Police Report for 1970*, point to the importance of the economic factor in the occurrence of juvenile delinquency. The increase during 1964–66 can to a large extent be attributed to unemployment, whereas the slight decrease in 1969 and 1970 was, in turn, largely due to full employment. A salient feature has been the rather high wages paid for unskilled jobs, even in cases of irregular attendance.

Yet another important feature has to be mentioned. A decrease or increase of juvenile offenders and offenses depends to a considerable extent upon whether or not there is sufficient police manpower available for the detection of crime among juveniles. If such manpower is scarce, considerably fewer offenses will be detected. Furthermore, the police may dismiss minor offenses and not report them, because they are engaged in more important cases. In other words, circumstances may compel the police force to adopt a selective approach to offenders and offenses alike. In these instances, statistics will necessarily show a decrease. If, the other hand, there is sufficient police manpower available, and if such manpower is geared to the detection of juvenile crime, reports will be made accordingly and the statistics will show an increase.[4] After the Six Day War of 1967, the Israeli police force shouldered additional duties in Israel as well as in occupied areas, and a diffusion of available manpower resulted.

Table 3.3 gives the total number of Jewish juvenile offenders brought to court each year from 1960–70 and indicates the age groups of these offenders. As can be seen, the percentage of those from the age group nine to twelve has decreased constantly over the years, from 31.5 percent in 1960 to 20 percent in 1970. The age group thirteen to fourteen has remained more or less constant. The youngsters in this age group are in a very precarious situation. Many of them no longer attend school but are not allowed by law to be engaged in any kind of work. Circumstances force them, therefore, to be idle and roam about the streets, making them prone to delinquent activities.

In line with expectations, there was a constant increase in the representation of those aged fifteen to sixteen: 34.2 percent in 1960, 45.5 percent in 1970. It is among this age group that one finds the more

---

[4] I would differentiate between offenders and offenses. It is my impression that, while offenders are most likely to be caught sooner or later, not all offenses which are committed by them are duly recorded. The more experienced or more shrewd juvenile offenders, when apprehended by the police, withhold information as to the number of offenses which they have committed.

TABLE 3.3
JEWISH JUVENILE OFFENDERS CONVICTED IN JUVENILE COURT,
BY AGE GROUPS, 1960–70

Year	Total no. of offenders	% by age groups					Median age
		9–12	13–14	15–16	17–18[a]	Total	
1960	4,858	31.5	29.7	34.2	4.6	100	14.2
1961	4,845	31.6	28.1	36.7	3.6	100	14.4
1964	5,391	30.5	31.1	34.0	4.4	100	14.3
1965	5,616	29.7	30.2	35.8	4.3	100	14.3
1966	5,740	24.5	29.6	41.6	4.3	100	14.7
1967[b]	3,861	20.9	28.7	46.2	4.2	100	15.0
1968	4,623	23.8	28.1	44.2	3.9	100	14.9
1969	5,125	20.8	28.2	45.7	5.3	100	15.0
1970	5,697	20.0	28.8	45.5	5.7	100	15.1

Source: Israel, Central Bureau of Statistics, *Special Series*, No. 244, 322, 370, Table D, and 370, 408, Table 1 (p. 5). No figures published for 1962–63.

[a] Females only.

[b] Decrease in offenders during this year due to an amnesty.

serious offenses. The situation in 1967 illustrates this point. Because of the amnesty, the figures relating to juvenile delinquency decreased. This can be seen in absolute numbers, as well in percentages and rates. Yet the salient feature in Table 3.3 is that, despite the general decrease in figures, there was an increase in the percentage of delinquents aged fifteen to sixteen, from 41.6 percent in 1966 to 46.2 percent in 1967. This means that these offenders committed a large number of offenses which were excluded from the amnesty law.

Another relevant factor is the age of juvenile offenders. The group aged fifteen to sixteen are close to the lower age group of young adult offenders, who are tried in a court for adults. More often than not young people from these two age groups know each another and may be friends. The younger ones—i.e., those fifteen and sixteen years old—try to imitate the delinquent behavior patterns of their older friends, those aged seventeen to eighteen years. Often it is the best way to prove their know-how, to be accepted by the older and more experienced ones. This aspect is of sufficient importance to be taken into account while planning treatment methods.

Table 3.4 presents a complementary picture concerning age groups and recidivism. (Females aged seventeen to eighteen years were not included in the data on which this table is based probably because they never reached 5 percent of all juvenile offenders and were not statistically

TABLE 3.4
RECIDIVISM AMONG JEWISH JUVENILE OFFENDERS ACCORDING
TO AGE, 1960–70
(RATES PER 1,000 OF THE CORRESPONDING POPULATION GROUP)

Year	9–12 yrs.		13–14 yrs.		15–16 yrs.	
	No. per 1,000	Recidivists	No. per 1,000	Recidivists	No. per 1,000	Recidivists
1960	5.3	. . .	10.8	. . .	16.0	. . .
1961	5.2	1.7	9.5	3.4	15.0	5.9
1964	6.2	2.6	12.8	6.1	15.0	7.9
1965	6.6	3.1	12.5	6.2	16.4	8.6
1966	5.5	2.7	12.4	6.8	17.9	9.5
1967[a]	3.1	1.7	8.1	5.2	12.5	7.4
1968	4.4	2.2	10.1	6.3	15.0	8.0
1969	4.4	2.3	11.8	7.4	18.2	10.4
1970	4.4	2.2	12.4	7.1	19.3	11.3

Source: Israel, Central Bureau of Statistics, *Special Series*, No. 168, Table D, No. 244, 265, 301, 322, 370, 408, Table C. No figures published for 1962–63.
[a] Decrease in offenders during this year due to an amnesty.

significant.) In the age group of nine to twelve years, an increase in the rates can be observed from 1961 to 1965, but a reverse tendency can be seen in 1966. Because of the amnesty, 1967 is not representative and cannot be taken into account, but in 1968 an increase can already be noticed. The same observations apply to the figures for recidivists. The outstanding feature, however, is that during 1965, 1966, 1968, 1969, and 1970 the rate of recidivism among nine- to twelve-year olds reached about half of the total rate during each year. This fact is certainly of considerable importance, as it points clearly to a failure of our social services to cope adequately with delinquent behavior patterns, even among the younger age groups.

A different picture is presented by the age group of thirteen to fourteen years. After a sharp increase from 1961 to 1964, the total rates for 1964, 1965, and 1966 remained almost unchanged, with a slight decrease. The precarious situation of this age group has already been mentioned. It is possible that the high figures of recidivists in this age group are accounted for by the failure to provide appropriate preventive and treatment facilities for them. As can be seen, the number of recidivists increased from nearly half the total tried in 1964 to exactly half in 1965, and to considerably more than half in 1966, 1967, 1968, 1969, and 1970.

The age group of fifteen to sixteen years presents a more serious problem. This is indicated by the total figures and the rates of reci-divists in Table 3.4. From 1964 to 1966 there was a considerable increase in the total rates, with a reversed trend for 1967, as a result of the am-nesty. For 1968, 1969, and 1970 there is already a real increase. And from 1964 on, recidivists constitute more than half of the total.

From Tables 3.3 and 3.4 it is evident that provisions for the different age groups merit special consideration. While children in the age groups of nine to twelve and thirteen to fourteen need special projects within the elementary educational system, those aged fifteen to sixteen years need special provisions in the field of employment. Experience has shown that projects for the first group must provide a selective curri-culum and special teaching methods geared toward preventing drop-outs. The problem of dropouts has to be tackled in the lower grades, as soon as the first signs of learning or behavior difficulties appear.

If sufficient attention is paid in the lower grades, and if preventive measures are adopted before crises arise, the number of dropouts in the higher grades might diminish considerably.

As far as those in the age group of fifteen to sixteen are concerned, many lack the appropriate qualifications to apply for those general employment projects which are available in the community. In fact, they cannot fulfill requirements for even semiskilled jobs. Furthermore, they are not used to working habits, nor do they have sufficient ele-mentary knowledge, which is now a requirement for getting and keeping a job. It is therefore imperative that training (including on-the-job training) and special job opportunities be provided.

As Table 3.5 indicates, there have been only minor changes in the types of offenses over the years. The one exception is offenses which belong to the category labeled "against property." This category shows a considerable increase, from 77.6 percent in 1960 to 86.2 percent in 1968, and a slight decrease to 84.8 percent in 1969 and 85.4 percent in 1970. The category of offenses against property includes breaking and entering, which is considered a felony. During the period indicated in Table 3.5, convictions for breaking and entering fluctuated between 25 and 31 percent. Among the offenses which belong to breaking and entering, there is one which is of special interest to the juvenile court, namely, that of "breaking into a dwelling." This type of offense ac-counted for 6 to 7 percent of all offenses listed in the category "against property." This is rather a low representation, which may indicate an offense of less serious character. A person who steals something from a room merely by putting his hand through a window is charged with having committed a felony. This includes a young child who is completely

TABLE 3.5
OFFENSES COMMITTED BY CONVICTED JEWISH JUVENILES, 1960–70

Year	% of total convictions						Total no. of offenders
	Against public order and lawful authority	Against persons[a]	Against morality	Against property	Traffic offenses[b]	Miscella-neous[c]	
1960	6.2	7.8	0.9	77.6	5.2	2.3	4,858
1961	7.1	7.9	0.6	79.3	3.5	1.6	4,845
1964	6.2	6.1	0.6	84.8	0.7	1.6	5,391
1965	6.9	6.6	0.8	81.5	1.2	3.0	5,616
1966	7.4	7.4	1.0	81.3	1.1	1.8	5.740
1967	7.8	7.2	0.8	82.1	1.0	1.1	3,861
1968	4.9	6.6	1.0	86.2	0.3	1.0	4,623
1969	6.5	6.2	1.1	84.8	0.4	1.0	5,125
1970	5.3	6.7	1.3	85.4	0.4	0.9	5,697

Sources: For 1960–65, Israel, Central Bureau of Statistics, *Special Series*, No. 168, 244, Table 2; for 1966–70, ibid., 265, 301, 322, 370, 408, Table 3. No figures published for 1962–63.

Note: The figures in this table do not include offenses tried in municipal courts.

[a] Includes drug offenses.

[b] Includes only those traffic offenses involving an accident.

[c] Includes fraud, forgery, defamation, and offenses against control regulations.

unaware of the seriousness of such an offense. For him it may be a moment's temptation, with no previous intent or planning. According to law, he will have to bear the consequences of having committed a felony. Different circumstances exist if a kiosk or stand is broken into, either by breaking open a door or a window, by opening a lock by force, or by lifting a shutter by force; in these instances, physical force is used, and the juvenile offender, even if very young, is aware of the seriousness of the offense.

The category of traffic offenses also requires a brief explanation. The figures in Table 3.5 refer only to those offenses in which an accident was involved. These are mostly contested cases. The discrepancy in figures between 1961 and 1964 is due to a new registration policy adopted in 1964. Statistically, there has been a considerable increase in the stealing of cars and motorcycles, but these are not registered in a unified system, so statistics need to be compiled from different sources. If a motor vehicle is stolen and driven without a license, the offender, if apprehended, is brought to court on two charges: stealing, and driving without a license. The theft is registered with other stealing offenses.

With the increase in these offenses it became necessary to amend the existing law so as to clarify the legal issue—conviction on the charge of theft had often proved difficult. The amendment says on this point: "A person who uses a vehicle [including a boat or carriage] for a journey without obtaining permission from the owner of the vehicle or from the person lawfully in possession thereof shall be liable to imprisonment for a term of three years." [5]

If a juvenile offender is apprehended after an accident, the police statistics register the fact in the category of "road accident." This is the major issue, and the fact that the vehicle was stolen may often be disregarded, although not the fact that the offender was driving without a license. If no accident precedes arrest, the juvenile offender is charged under the new amendment.

A few social aspects which are typical for this kind of offense also need to be mentioned. The stealing of a car or motorcycle is often looked on by parents as a kind of sport. Indeed, many parents differentiate between this type of offense and any other offense, viewing theft of a motor vehicle with indulgence, even though they would object strongly to their child's being involved in other offenses. Such an attitude has direct repercussions on the commission of that offense, since children are very much aware of their parents' attitudes.

Time and again one is also struck by the feeling of omnipotence which many young offenders manifest in driving a car or riding a motorcycle. For many boys it is an opportunity to make contacts with girls, which they find much easier to accomplish once they have a motor vehicle at their disposal. There are others who show deep satisfaction in being able to show off while in possession of a motor vehicle. A rather high proportion of car and motorcycle thefts are committed by two or three boys together. Many of them initially get together for the sole purpose of committing this offense. Some later on become involved in other offenses as well. There is also a high incidence of recidivism among them. Some boys may take as many as twenty cars or so during one night, trying out the speed of different models. One is often impressed by a kind of obsessional pattern found in this particular offense. Furthermore, stealing a motor vehicle for joy rides has become an offense in which juvenile offenders of middle-class background are highly represented.

[5] Penal Law Amendment (Use of Vehicle Without Permission) Law, 5724–1964, in *Laws of the State of Israel*, Vol. 18, p. 66.

The minimum age for receiving a driver's license for a motorcycle is 16, and for a car is 18; examinations are required.

In recent years driving cars in a way which, by its very nature, expresses opposition to law and order has become more frequent. This is done with the definite intention of antagonizing the police. It is characteristic of such instances that the stolen vehicle is brought to the quarter where the offender lives and where he is well known, and is there driven in a reckless and dangerous way. By such boastful and flagrant delinquent behavior the offender hopes to earn social prestige in his own neighborhood. And it is true that by openly demonstrating his resistance to law and order, many an offender has been applauded for his bravery.

DELINQUENCY IN KIBBUTZIM

In discussing delinquency among Israeli Jews, we need also to consider delinquent behavior among juveniles in kibbutzim. There is a widespread and rather unfounded belief in Israel that inherent in the kibbutz is a magic power to rectify behavior disorders of any kind. Invariably, one encounters people, particularly parents, who assume that once a child has shown symptoms of behavior disorders, including delinquent behavior, placement in a kibbutz can modify or change this behavior. They argue that the values on which a kibbutz is based and its social structure have a salutary effect. It is also maintained that in a kibbutz there is less likelihood for antisocial acting-out, because this particular environment impresses—directly and indirectly—a high social and moral code of behavior on those who live there.

Possibly for exactly these reasons, however, it may be very difficult for juvenile offenders and young people with behavior disorders to adapt themselves to the way of life of a kibbutz. In regard to juvenile delinquency, one finds two different phenomena in kibbutzim: delinquent behavior among kibbutz-born children and delinquent behavior among children and juveniles who are temporary residents there.

Kibbutz-born children and juveniles are seldom charged in court with criminal offenses, even though delinquency does occur among these youth. The following reasons account for this:

1. If a child or juvenile of a kibbutz commits a delinquent act, the kibbutz regards it as an internal matter which does not need outside intervention, so that the police are not called in to investigate.
2. If damage is caused to property which does not belong to the kibbutz, the complainant will receive compensation from the kibbutz, and the matter will be settled in this way, so that again there is no referral to the police for investigation.
3. If a child or juvenile of a kibbutz repeatedly commits delinquent acts, one or more of the various committees empowered to deal

with such matters investigate, focusing, however, on what sort of treatment can be initiated for the child. There are treatment facilities available to every kibbutz, including child guidance clinics, residential homes for kibbutz children, and other facilities available to members of the general trade union *(Histadrut)*. The kibbutz also uses, and pays for, private treatment facilities. In these instances, if necessary, referral will be made by the kibbutz committee, but no police action will be requested.

Prosecution against a juvenile of a kibbutz is more likely to be initiated if he has committed an offense outside the kibbutz and if the complainant lodges a formal complaint with the police. Prosecution is almost inevitable in instances involving the theft of a motor vehicle and driving without a license, particularly if damage is caused. This applies even if the vehicle is stolen from the kibbutz itself, and an accident occurs outside the kibbutz. In these cases, informing the police is mandatory.

It should be noted, however, that delinquent behavior in rural districts is considerably less frequent than in urban districts. The fact that practically all kibbutzim are situated in rural districts also accounts, therefore, for the low number of juvenile offenders. The sheltered environment of the kibbutzim and their ability to deal effectively with different forms of maladjustment are additional factors; deliquent behavior is dealt within the kibbutz family, the police are not called in, and there is no court action.

Where the second group—i.e., temporary residents of a kibbutz— are concerned, the situation is much simpler. The kibbutz has no moral or other obligation towards them if they do not comply with the standards set by the kibbutz. Although some kibbutzim make special arrangements for them and are willing to apply a different, more lenient yardstick to their behavior, there is usually a rigid attitude with regard to delinquent behavior. Sometimes the kibbutzim say that they do not have the facilities to deal effectively with such behavior problems; sometimes they maintain that these problems are a matter to be dealt with by the government; and often they openly admit that they are afraid of possible negative influences on their own children.

DRUG ABUSE

There is no more striking illustration of the change in the behavior patterns of Israeli youth than that of increasing drug abuse and addiction. Although drugs have always been used to a certain extent in Israel and previously in Palestine, their use was on a rather small scale and then was almost completely confined to delinquents. Moreover, there was a widespread social taboo against drug taking. Now, however, the use of drugs has become one of the most talked-about topics and a social problem. It is maintained that wide circles of people from middle-class backgrounds, university students, and pupils from secondary schools are joining the ranks of drug users. Here, one is confronted with a new type of delinquent behavior which is spreading rapidly and which also involves a new stratum of society.

As the use of drugs has become widespread among people of middle-class background, and as it is no longer confined to the lower stratum of society and to delinquents, it has ceased to be a matter of taboo. Moreover, protagonists are propounding the virtues of various drugs and have started a campaign to legalize their use. The underlying motivation for this is that people from the middle class usually do not like to conduct themselves in a way which is a flagrant transgression against the law. The best way to avoid such an unpleasant state of affairs is to legalize what has been illegal.

Much has been published about drug abuse and addiction; it is therefore not my intention to go into details concerning the manifold aspects of this topic. But because juvenile courts are nowadays more often than ever confronted with juvenile offenders who are drug users, a few remarks are appropriate. One of the most common drugs in use in Israel (and previously in Palestine) is hashish. Hashish is taken in secret, in the company of other users. There is a sort of induction ceremony, whereby the novices are led into the secrets of how to smoke and how to get the maximum pleasure from it. After they are knowledgeable, they usually continue to smoke in company of other smokers. The user of the drug is an offender, but at the same time he is also a victim.

It is therefore very difficult to estimate the magnitude of the drug problem. Police statistics reveal the following figures on juvenile offenders charged in juvenile courts with drug possession: 1960, 9; 1964, 24; 1966, 36; 1969, 48; and in 1970 the figure almost doubled, to 92.

In most of these instances the use of hashish was involved. It is presumed that to be in possession of drugs is equal to being a user of the drug. In recent years, however, apart from those brought to juvenile court on the specific charge of possession of drugs, there have been others charged with another offense, but whose major problem was drug use. This was frequently the case with young girls charged with prostitution, a large number of whom are drug users, or have had at least some experience in this field. Our experience so far has shown that the difficulties in rehabilitating these girls have been increased by their use of drugs.

That rehabilitation has become a more complicated matter because of the use of drugs is equally true for male juvenile offenders who are placed in one of the educational establishments. There, the use of drugs has become rather widespread, and although one is not necessarily confronted with addiction proper, the process of reeducation and rehabilitation is greatly hampered by the detrimental effects of drugs. It is no great solace to maintain that in both instances one is concerned with emotionally unstable young people.

As the use of drugs is no longer confined to the delinquent subculture, the stigma which was previously attached to it is diminishing rapidly. Nowadays, the taking of drugs has become for many young persons the embodiment of protest—protest against parents and adults in general, protest against public order, and protest against the establishment. The mere fact that the use of drugs is an offense according to Israeli penal law may be sufficient reason for young people "in protest" to use drugs.

There are, however, more aspects involved. Take, for instance, the inclination of many young people to try drugs out of curiosity or in imitation. This desire to imitate, together with the tendency to conformity, is particularly known among university students and pupils of secondary schools. Drug use is also a way of showing courage and defiance, both of which are important in obtaining social status. This leads necessarily to some pertinent questions:

1. Is the use of drugs among adolescents increasing as a result of a more tolerant attitude among adults?
2. Is the use of drugs by adolescents a way of acting-out, by using the very illegal method used among adults?
3. Does rationalization or genuine sentiment account for the belief that the use of drugs is due to desperation arising from fear that an atomic war is imminent?
4. On the other hand, can drug abuse be nothing more than a contemporary phenomenon, caused mainly by the fact that drugs are more easily available?
5. Are emotional and pathogenic factors of major importance in the use of drugs by adolescents?
6. To what extent do sensational press reports have a contagious impact in promoting the use of drugs among adolescents?

The small number of drug users charged in the juvenile court can be no yardstick of the seriousness of drug abuse, and there is great public concern over the matter. There is evidence that the use of drugs has become widespread since the Six Day War in 1967, for three major reasons. (1) Volunteers and students from abroad who were accustomed to using drugs in countries they came from continue to use drugs here as well. (2) Israel is situated on the crossroads between the great hashish producers. Since the Six Day War and the breaking down of many barriers, illegal traffic in drugs has increased considerably. Drugs have become rather cheap and easily accessible. (3) The two afore-mentioned points have had their impact on Israeli youth. In addition, the urge to imitate, the easing of stress situations, and the desire to conform to cosmopolitan ideas were responsible for an easy penetration of drugs.

In summary, juvenile delinquency has not actually increased during the years 1960–70, except for 1964–66. Figures can be regarded as particularly small, if the complexity, magnitude, and many-sided nature of the problems involved are considered. The fact that offenders are each year counted anew if a new offense occurs is further proof that juvenile delinquency is as yet no serious problem.

More important still, the types of offenses are of no serious character. The largest contingent commits offenses against property, a type of offense in which many children become often unintentionally involved. Such offenders outnumber by far the small group of youngsters who represent the hard core, and who commit severe offenses. Fortunately, we have no gangs of juveniles. We have almost no violence, there are no robberies, and no holdups among juvenile offenders. There are few sex offenses committed by juvenile offenders, and rape is conspicuous by its absence.

Yet the large number of recidivists is a most disturbing feature, indicating severe deficiencies in planning and in implementing appro-priate social services for those whose need is great. This is a matter of great public concern. Furthermore, over the last few years there has been an increase in delinquent behavior patterns that were nonexistent here, but known in some affluent societies, where they cause great concern. This coincides with the increase in youngsters from econo-mically secure backgrounds who drift into asocial behavior. Some adopt delinquent behavior patterns, and their intelligence brings them to positions of leadership. The motivations involved are not yet clear, but one receives the impression that a new form of social pathology is gaining ground, and that new forces with negative implications, specific for an affluent society, are at work.

4

Delinquency Among Israeli Arabs

The problems of juvenile delinquency among Arabs in Israel differ in several respects from those among Israeli Jews. The special features which merit examination will be dealt with briefly in this chapter.

THE ISRAELI ARABS

Strictly speaking, the term "Arab minority" does not accurately describe the composition of the minorities in Israel because of the great differences among them in religious beliefs, traditions, and habits of living. There are now close to 440,000 non-Jewish inhabitants in Israel —approximately 14.7 percent of the total population. This figure includes the non-Jewish population of East Jerusalem. Of the non-Jewish population, approximately 74.7 percent are Moslems, 17.1 percent are Christians (Arab and non-Arab), 8.2 percent are Druze and others. Before the Six Day War in 1967, 18 percent of the then-existing Arab population (in 1948 practically the whole Arab leadership in all fields had fled from Palestine to neighboring countries) was allowed to return to Israel on compassionate grounds, under the plan to reunite families. [1]

Among Moslems there are two major religious sects; in Israel, however, the Sunnites have an overwhelming majority, resulting in a comparatively uniform religious base among them. There are several Christian sects—Greek Catholic, Greek Orthodox, Maronite, Roman Catholic, Baptist, and other Protestant denominations. Among the Druze there is only one uniform code of religious observance. [2] I do not propose,

[1] Central Bureau of Statistics, *Statistical Abstract of Israel*, 1971, No. 22, Table B/1, p. 21.

[2] The religious rights and privileges of Israel's minorities are protected by law. In addition, the Druze were officially recognized as an independent religious community

however, to dwell on the features making for uniformity on the one hand, or heterogeneity on the other; my focus here is limited to the special problems of juvenile delinquency. For the same reason, I will use the word "Arab" to refer to the minorities, although it should be borne in mind that the term is subject to qualification.

Since 1948, when large numbers of Arabs left for the surrounding Arab countries, the demographic pattern of Israel has altered considerably. Cities such as Jaffa, Haifa, Acre, Ramleh, and Lydda, which once had a moderately large number of Arab inhabitants, now have very few. In cities such as Tiberias and Safed there are no longer any Arabs at all; Beersheba, once a little oasis on the fringe of the desert, populated mainly by Bedouins, has become a busy center of industry and commerce with over 80,000 Jewish inhabitants. On the other hand, the Arab population of Nazareth has risen considerably, owing to Arabs who moved there from surrounding villages.

In spite of these enormous changes, the overall rural and urban distribution of the Arab population remains roughly the same as it was during the mandatory period. About 23 percent of the Arabs now live in cities and the remaining 77 percent live in rural districts, whereas during the last few years of the British mandate, about 25 percent of the Arabs were city dwellers. On the other hand, the distribution over the country has altered. Nowadays, 50 percent live in the Galilee area, 20 percent live in the Triangle,[3] about 11.5 percent are Bedouins who live mostly in the desert south of Beersheba, and the rest are scattered in cities all over the country.

All the social services available to Jews in Israel—education, health care, welfare, national insurance, etc.—are also available to Arab citizens, and the standard of living among both urban and rural Israeli Arabs is much higher than that of citizens in surrounding Arab countries. This fact is best illustrated by the steadily decreasing infant mortality rate and by the longer life expectancy. There is a growing awareness of the importance of cleanliness and hygiene. Compulsory school education is visibly gaining ground, and there are also fewer objections nowadays to sending girls to school. As a result, approximately ten times as many Arab children now attend school as did so by the end of the British mandate period.

---

by laws passed in 1957 and 1962. The Druze community now has its own religious courts, which are no longer within Moslem religious jurisdiction. These courts are along the same lines as the courts of the other recognized religious communities: the salaries of the cadis are paid by the state, and the verdicts of such courts are binding.

[3] Roughly between Netanyah and Hederah.

The family structure of Arabs has been the stronghold of the patriarchal system, and this system is being shaken to its roots. During the period between the two world wars, and with dramatic effect since the establishment of Israel, new ideas and ways of life have begun to penetrate. Particularly during the immediate past few years have Western ideas, so different from the patriarchal family structure, made themselves felt. Arab nationalism has also contributed to the breakdown of old traditions, values, habits, and customs. The extent to which a growing number of Israeli Arabs have changed their outlook and behavior, in contrast to those Arabs who lived in the same territory twenty years ago during the British mandate, became particularly evident after the Six Day War, when the frontiers to East Jerusalem, to the West Bank, and to the Gaza Strip ceased to exist. For twenty years Israeli Arabs have been living and have taken part—actively or passively—in a dynamic society, in which Jews with modern Western ideas provided the leadership and constituted the majority of the population. Here is a living example of the extent to which far-reaching changes can be achieved within a comparatively brief period of time. For there can be no doubt that these changes in the Israeli Arab life have been due to and accelerated by the example of their Jewish counterparts.

A few examples may illustrate the character of some of those changes. Up through the period of the British mandatory government, political sympathies and loyalties and party membership among Arabs were determined by the elder members, or an elder member, of the *hamula* (clan), who enjoyed undisputed status as its leaders. The hamula leaders decided matters of general policy, and their decisions were binding on all members of the hamula—sometimes hundreds of people. They also decided issues of a more personal character, which the individual member again had to obey. This way of living was particularly pronounced among the rural population, but to a considerable degree it was also adhered to by those who lived in urban centers. It was comparatively easy to rule through the leaders of a hamula, who knew how to benefit from the special privileges granted them by the ruler.

The most important hamula leader also decided who would be the *mukhtar,* a function equivalent to that of a mayor or village head. So long as important jobs could be secured only with the help of a mukhtar or hamula leader, not much change could be anticipated. In Israel, however, the hamula has lost a great deal of power, and the institution of the mukhtar has become devoid of importance. The mukhtar no longer recommends positions, nor do promotions or appointments depend on his good will. Everyone can now enroll at the labor exchange, a fact which is greatly appreciated by the younger generation. In addition, the mukhtar's function as a mediator and as an agent of the authorities has ceased to exist.

Another example of change is the trend among young and more intelligent Arabs toward abolishing the *mohar,* the custom of payment to the bride's parents. Because of this trend, the mohar is often given in a disguised form, similar to the dowry system in parts of Western society. Nevertheless, it may still take a long time before the mohar is completely abolished, because it has become part of a national tradition, which many maintain is worth preserving, particularly in a changing society. Therefore, for the moment, social intercourse between young men and women outside the family circle is not encouraged, and in fact, is hardly possible, particularly among Moslems living in rural districts and also among Druze. Thus, although many of the younger generation may theoretically be against the mohar as an institution, when it comes to practical application they tend to want it preserved, an indication of an ambivalent attitude. It is one of many examples of how difficult deep-rooted customs are to abolish, and of what role prejudice plays in such matters.

Owing to such changes, there is great confusion, much irritation, and a great deal of anxiety. The older generation is trying to oppose the new tendencies, or at least trying to delay further development as much as possible, so as to avoid a complete breakdown of old traditions. The interests of the younger generation are in opposition to those of the older. Whereas the older Arabs try to keep aloof from new influences, the young feel that the social structure prevailing among the Jewish population has great advantages. They realize that the key to their own advancement lies in accepting and adapting to new modes of life. These issues provoke growing tensions and conflicts which concern practically every Israeli Arab.

There also have been great transformations within the Arab economic structure in Israel. Agriculture is no longer the most important source of income and is therefore no longer the most frequent occupation. Three major factors are responsible for this development. (1) Over the last few decades farm plots have become smaller and smaller because of distribution to many members of the family, and a large family cannot make a living on the small plots; it has therefore become necessary to look for other employment. (2) In approximately the last ten years a minor revolution has taken place in Arab agriculture owing to the introduction of mechanization and planning. (3) The Jewish-created labor market in industry and the crafts, as well as in agriculture, has opened up hitherto unknown opportunities, which usually pay well and are a great attraction. As a result of these developments, a considerable number of young people from rural areas now acquire new professions or are employed in new jobs. They work away from their villages, although they may continue to live there. Over two-thirds of the Arab village labor force is employed in Jewish settlements, villages, and cities. The mere fact that a large number of village people no longer till their own land, and work in other places and at other occupations, has had a major impact on village life. Many of the functions which traditionally belonged to men were of necessity transferred to the shoulders of women; this in itself constitutes a kind of revolution that will have far-reaching consequences for the family unit and for village life. Moreover, in recent years even Arab women have entered the Jewish employment market in ever-growing numbers, particularly in the field of agriculture, often far away from their villages. This process may have important repercussions, because it may lead Arab women to accept a different mode of life than was hitherto customary. While economic gain is now the primary motive for accepting employment within the Jewish labor market, this change in employment patterns may have more fundamental importance in the future.

There is now much more direct contact between large sections of the Jewish and Arab populations than had ever existed before. Whereas comparatively small numbers of Arabs were employed by Jews in the past, nowadays only a small number are not employed by them. This is important because these new places of employment are situated in a new environment and among people who have other habits of living. Thus, the Arab laborer is constantly confronted with habits and customs which represent for him the "new world," as it were, and which he is trying to imitate. There is a strong desire among most Arabs to be accepted into this modern environment and to be regarded as a progressive person who is trying to shake off the chains of tradition. Adaptation to and integration into the Jewish community is, however, very difficult indeed, making for a strong undercurrent of ambivalence and anxiety. The resulting vacuum enhances the possibility of many dangerous situations, including acts of a political nature and also juvenile delinquency.

JUVENILE DELINQUENCY AMONG ARABS

Most Arab juvenile offenders in Israel live in rural districts. There are, nevertheless, a disproportionately greater number of Arab juvenile offenders than Jewish juvenile offenders, the latter being concentrated in urban areas. Approximately 70 percent of the Jewish inhabitants of Israel live in urban districts, and about 75 percent of the Jewish juvenile offenders come from these areas. Among Arabs we encounter the exact opposite. About 75 percent of the Arabs live in rural districts, and about 80 percent of the Arab juvenile offenders come from rural areas. Moreover, a comparison between Tables 3.5 and 4.3 indicates clearly that the behavior pattern of juvenile offenders among Jews and Arabs differ greatly. This is particularly conspicuous in a comparison of offenses against public order and lawful authority and offenses against persons. Furthermore, no Jewish juvenile offenders commit the kinds of offenses committed by Arab shepherds.

The motivations for delinquent behavior among Arabs are of a special nature, and because of the preponderance of delinquency in rural districts, one can speak of a "rural delinquency pattern." Two types of juvenile delinquency are typical, and account for a high percentage of the offenses committed by Arab juveniles, although one can already observe changes in this pattern, largely due to the profound socioeconomic changes going on among Israeli Arabs.

The first of these offenses is what might be called the shepherdry offense and is concerned with leading cattle — cows, sheep, and goats — for grazing into any kind of cultivated land. The offenders are hired either by a farmer who owns a flock or by several villagers who have goats and sheep and share the hire of the shepherd. There are also children who look after the family flock. Sheep and goats are the most common animals kept by village inhabitants, since even a poor household can afford to keep a goat or two. These animals can feed on all kinds of forage, including that to be found in woodlands and bushy places. They provide milk, cheese, and butter, and eventually, also meat. Sheep have the additional advantage of providing wool. These flocks may even be a source of income.

In many instances, this offense is committed by young shepherds, sometimes not more than ten years old. Indeed, young shepherds are often employed precisely because they are very cheap labor, and because it is assumed that, should they be apprehended while herding, they are not likely to be brought to court for such an offense. If they are brought to court, it is reasoned that they most probably will get off lightly because of the wretched conditions they live in. These shepherds continue what was in fact the custom during the British mandate, namely, to lead cattle into young forests, newly planted woods, wheat fields, plantations, and other cultivated land, ignoring warnings against this. It was only in instances where the damage was serious that they were ordered to pay or brought before the juvenile court.

In recent years, however, a different policy has been adopted by the Israeli government. The government has ordered a strict enforcement of regulations against trespassing. In accordance with the new policy, fences have been built and signposts reminding shepherds that grazing is no longer allowed have been put up. These have turned out to be ineffective, for shepherds defy the new policy. Despite such defiance, however, the number of shepherdry offenses has decreased. Much more land has been made available for cultivation and for large-scale afforestation. This land includes areas which were once freely accessible to shepherds and their flocks. The Israeli Arabs have objected particularly to the cultivation and afforestation of those places which were preferred for grazing because of their proximity to Arab villages. Moreover, shepherds have often deliberately led their cattle onto these areas as a protest against the government's new policy. In this connection a political element might also be observed, particularly in relation to property which is now cultivated by the Custodian for Abandoned Property. Damage is also done to neighbors' land in the aftermath of a feud or as an act of revenge.

In 1965, the Israeli Knesset passed an amendment to the Criminal Code Ordinance of 1936, by which it is now possible to charge in court not only the shepherd but also the owner of the flock with trespassing on cultivated land.[4] The owner of the flock can no longer hide behind the young shepherd caught grazing cattle on cultivated land but is also held responsible for this offense, unless he can prove to the satisfaction of the court that he had taken precautions to prevent such an offense.

Although these shepherdry offenses may not seem serious, there is among the Jewish population much sensitivity towards such offenses because of the enormous efforts which have been invested in cultivating every available piece of land in afforestation. Apart from this, there is real damage done to public and private property. Afforestation suffers particularly if goats nibble at young saplings because they cease growing and new saplings have to be planted.

The decrease in shepherdry offenses can best be illustrated by the following figures. Of all Arab juvenile offenders, 25.9 percent were charged for that offense in 1958; this decreased to 18.9 percent in 1966, to 16.0 percent in 1968, and to 10.0 percent in 1970. With the decrease

---

[4] Criminal Law Ordinance (Amendment No. 24) Law, 5725–1965, section 385 A, in *Laws of the State of Israel*, Vol. 19, p. 51.

in this type of offense, there has been a constant increase in another type: offenses against property. Table 4.3 makes this abundantly clear.

The other kind of offense frequent among Arab juvenile offenders is assault by stone-throwing. Among Arabs, stone-throwing is a traditional form of attack, although it is often also used defensively. This form of aggression has its roots in ancient history. The story of David and Goliath is only the most famous of many incidents in the Old Testament where stoning was used for punishment or revenge: "Then they shall bring out the damsel to the door of her father's house, and the men of her city shall stone her with stones that she die." (Deuteronomy 22:21)

Even today the most frequent form of settling a feud among Arabs who live in rural districts is by throwing stones at the opponent. Repeatedly one is confronted with rivalry and quarrels between groups or members of a hamula, who fight one another to try to gain control in the village or to maintain positions which they have already gained. Injuries and even death are sometimes the result of apparently harmless quarrels. Children, for instance, curse one another with one of the famous curses with an erotic implication. Such curses, derogative of female members of the family, would be sufficient reason for serious clashes between rival members of a hamula. The same is true if female members or children of a particular group outsmart their counterparts, while bringing water from the well, for example. Incidents like these are sufficient reason for each hamula to defend its honor. Indeed, it is the duty of each member of a hamula to rally in defense of the good name of the clan, and by so doing, to demonstrate to all concerned that there is still leadership, and that this leadership is still powerful.

As recently as 1965, very severe clashes occurred between two rival hamulas in Kafr Kana, situated between Nazareth and Tiberias. There had already been severe clashes between them ten years earlier. At that time the feud was eventually settled after long negotiations in which renowned peacemakers among Jewish notables took an active part. But old resentments broke out again in 1965 because of a negligible incident, and hundreds of adults and children took part in the resulting clashes. Fighting continued for days, and resulted in many wounded and even in fatalities. In these instances, as in others, the dispute was largely fought out with stones. As an outcome of this incident, many children and youths were charged in juvenile court with having committed offenses.[5]

[5] After the court proceedings were finished, the juvenile court met with the hamula leaders of the village, together with high-ranking police officers and Arab probation officers, in order to make sure that children were left out of future clashes.

In this type of offense we must take into account the fact that the action is often motivated by tradition and by the duty to defend the prestige of one's hamula. Thus, the commission of this offense is determined by the particular pattern of the society, not by the personal inclinations of the offender. From the legal point of view, this motivation by societal pressures makes no difference when proceedings take place, but it may be an important factor when sentence is pronounced.

While a shepherdry offense is conspicuously absent among Jewish juvenile offenders, stone throwing does exist, although not with the frequency and in the manner customary among Arab village people. For many years, it accounted for 20 percent of juvenile offenders among Arabs, whereas among Jewish juvenile offenders it accounted for only 7 percent. There was, however, a sharp drop in this offense among Arabs from 1960 onwards—the same decrease as can be observed with shepherdry offenses. In both cases the decrease in offenses can be attributed to the fact that growing numbers of Arab children and youth move away from their villages in order to find better-paid employment with Jewish employers, or else with the Jewish labor market. They therefore have no opportunity to participate in these offenses. On the other hand, as was pointed out earlier, offenses against property are constantly on the increase among them.

Jewish and Arab juvenile offenders seldom commit offenses together. One must remember, however, that the possibility of joint offenses could in any event exist for only a small percentage of Arab juvenile offenders, since no Jews live in Arab villages, and the majority of Arab juvenile offenders come from rural districts. Their committing offenses jointly therefore can happen only in a few urban areas where Jews and Arabs live together. In these areas both groups live in substandard quarters, and usually belong to the lower income groups. Moreover, both encounter the same or similar social experiences with regard to deprivation. Yet these facts and the proximity of living quarters do not bind them together to commit offenses. Sometimes Jewish and Arab children who live in the same street are charged with having committed similar offenses at the same time, but each group was acting on its own. There are also no fights between these two groups. Conditions indicate, rather, a state of indifference and mistrust.

During the course of court appearance, 80 percent of Jewish juvenile offenders plead guilty to the charge at the first hearing, whereas among Arab juvenile offenders this is so in about 50 percent of the cases. The other 50 percent deny the charge even when circumstances point clearly to their guilt. Needless to say, in all these instances when the charge is

denied, evidence is heard in court. Evidently, those who deny the charge
do so to conform with the expectations of their families or villages, who
advise them not to plead guilty. It may also be typical of a pattern existing
particularly in villages; in any case, there is a strong tendency to prevent
authoritative agencies like the police and the court from interfering in
what the villagers regard as their own internal affairs.

A more detailed statistical analysis of delinquency among Israeli
Arabs is revealing. The year 1960 is taken as a starting point in the
tables presented here, because since that year the data assembled by the
Central Bureau of Statistics has been coordinated with that of the Juvenile Probation Service. It can therefore be assumed that these figures
are largely reliable.

TABLE 4.1

ARAB JUVENILE OFFENDERS CONVICTED IN JUVENILE COURT BY
AGE GROUPS, 1960–70

| Year | % by age groups | | | | | Median age |
	9–12	13–14	15–16	17–18[a]	Total	
1960	10.8	22.4	61.7	5.1	100	15.5
1961	19.8	23.4	51.3	5.5	100	15.3
1964	28.8	32.4	33.7	5.1	100	14.3
1965	24.7	35.7	36.4	3.2	100	14.4
1966	23.7	28.3	45.1	2.9	100	14.9
1967[b]	20.5	28.9	47.7	2.9	100	15.0
1968	20.6	32.2	44.9	2.3	100	14.8
1969	19.4	30.0	47.1	3.5	100	15.0
1970	25.8	29.5	41.3	3.4	100	14.6

Source: Israel, Central Bureau of Statistics, *Special Series*, Nos. 168, 244, 370, 408, Table D.
[a] Females only.
[b] Decrease in offenders during this year due to an amnesty.

The figures in Table 4.1, which indicates the percentage of Arab
juvenile offenders in each age group, reveal that for almost all age groups
there were great fluctuations over the period given. It is difficult to
speculate as to the reasons for these fluctuations. A certain degree of
stabilization can be observed in 1966 and 1967, again applicable to all
age groups, but no conclusions can yet be drawn from it. If we compare
the age distribution in Table 4.1 to that of Table 3.3 we find that the
median age in both is about the same over the years 1960–70. Yet there
are differences which relate to the various age groups. Whereas among
Arab juvenile offenders there is an increase in the age group nine to

twelve and thirteen to fourteen, among Jewish juvenile offenders there is a decrease in the representation of the first age group and more or less equal figures in the second age group. A reverse picture presents itself for the age group fifteen to sixteen. There is a definite increase among Jewish juvenile offenders, and a decrease among the Arab, except for 1964–65.

TABLE 4.2

RECIDIVISM AMONG ARAB JUVENILE OFFENDERS ACCORDING TO AGE, 1960–70

(RATES PER 1,000 OF THE CORRESPONDING POPULATION GROUP)

Year	9–12 yrs.		13–14 yrs.		15–16 yrs.	
	No. per 1,000	Recid- ivists	No. per 1,000	Recid- ivists	No. per 1,000	Recid- ivists
1960	5.3	...	10.8	...	16.0	...
1961	6.0	1.1	16.3	5.6	31.9	14.6
1964	8.0	1.9	22.0	6.5	29.8	12.9
1965	6.4	1.3	21.2	8.4	29.6	12.5
1966	5.5	1.1	15.2	5.4	28.3	10.9
1967[a]	3.7	0.6	12.3	3.8	22.2	8.2
1968	4.0	0.8	14.5	5.0	22.7	7.3
1969	3.6	0.7	12.0	3.6	23.7	7.6
1970	4.8	1.0	12.9	3.4	21.2	7.5

Source: Israel, Central Bureau of Statistics, *Special Series*, No. 168, 244, 322, 370, 408, Table C. No figures published for 1962–63.

[a] Decrease in offenders during this year due to an amnesty.

Note: The figures in this table do not include offenses tried under emergency laws.

A different picture is presented in Table 4.2, when we consider the rates per age group according to the relevant age group in the population. The table gives rates for all offenders and separate figures for recidivists. (Here we are concerned with offenders who have committed an offense during a particular year, and committed an offense in previous years as well. While figures are compiled according to one offense in a particular year, the same offender may be counted again during each consecutive year if he then also committed an offense.

After 1964 there was a decrease over the years in the total rates for each age group; this includes 1969 as well, if one disregards 1967, which is an exception because of the amnesty. The same applies to the rates of recidivists from each age group, with the exception of those aged thirteen to fourteen during 1965, but this may have no significance.

TABLE 4.3

OFFENSES COMMITTED BY CONVICTED ARAB JUVENILES, 1960–70

Year	% of total convictions						Total no. convicted
	Against public order and lawful authority	Against persons[a]	Against morality	Against property	Traffic offenses[b]	Miscellaneous[c]	
1960	32.3	13.6	0.7	52.0	0.5	1.0[d]	1,292
1961	35.0	15.0	0.9	47.1	0.5	1.5	1,138
1964	23.5	12.6	0.7	61.6	0.3	1.3	1,061
1965	18.2	14.5	1.8	60.0	1.5	4.0	974
1966	20.0	13.2	2.7	62.6	0.8	0.7	936
1967	20.8	14.0	0.8	62.2	0.7	1.5	743
1968	9.0	15.8	1.5	70.9	...	2.8	859
1969	11.4	11.2	2.9	69.7	0.7	4.1	913
1970	8.2	14.4	1.6	72.0	0.6	3.2	975

Sources: For 1960–65, Israel, Central Bureau of Statistics, *Special Series*, Nos. 168, 244, Table 2; for 1966–70, ibid., Nos. 265, 301, 322, 370, 408, Table 3. No figures published for 1962–63.
[a] Includes drug offenses.
[b] Includes only those traffic offenses involving an accident.
[c] Includes fraud, forgery, defamation, and offenses against control regulations.
[d] Percentages have been rounded.
Note: The figures in this table do not include offenses tried under emergency laws.

Table 4.3 indicates the types of offenses committed by Arab juveniles in Israel. The most important figures in this table are those of "offenses against property." As was pointed out earlier, this type of offense was previously quite infrequent, whereas other offenses, such as the shepherdry offenses (also included under offenses against property in the figures) and those causing bodily harm, were more frequently committed. This was due to the rural delinquency pattern typical for Arab juvenile offenders. The increase in offenses against property could be foreseen because of the ever-increasing number of Arabs, adults and juveniles alike, who have been streaming into cities to work there, while continuing to live in their villages. At the beginning many of the unmarried young men and juveniles return daily to their own villages; later, because it is cheaper and more convenient, they may remain at their places of work and go home only on weekends. Later still, they will come back to the village only for a special occasion. City life has many temptations to delinquent behavior, and the result is the steep increase of offenses against property shown in Table 4.3. In addition, as children and teenagers begin to work and live away from home, their parents' authority begins to dwindle and the restraining influence of the patriarchal family system is less felt. This factor undoubtedly also plays a role in the increase of offenses against property.

Also worth mentioning are the figures concerning offenses against public order and lawful authority. Table 4.3 indicates a definite decrease in such offenses over the years. The figures for 1968 (9.0 percent) may be an exceptional one, due both to the effects of the amnesty and to different methods of statistical registration issuing from the Six Day War, but the decrease over the years is still remarkable, which decreased further to 8.2 percent in 1970. It can, however, be assumed that a different interpretation of offenses in this category from that used previously is responsible for this discrepancy.

As far as the treatment of Arab juvenile offenders is concerned, the cultural pattern of Arab village life has to be taken into account. This applies to all those juvenile offenders whose homes are in a village, even though they may have been living in a city for months. Since the majority of Arab juvenile offenders come from rural areas, parents, without exception, hasten to take their children home once they have gotten into trouble. Sometimes this is done provisionally, until the court has finished the case. The parents' motive is always to regain control over their child, to bring him back into the family, and ultimately, also back into the village.

Consequently, it has been our experience that it is more feasible to have Arab probation officers look after Arab juvenile offenders and be in contact with their families than it is to use Jewish probation officers. It is naturally easier for them to understand and deal with conflict situations, as they are well acquainted with the generally accepted norms of behavior among Arab children and juveniles, and they also speak the same language and are aware of Arab mores. This last is of crucial importance if the probation officer is to deal effectively with the problems of Arab juveniles. It would, for instance, be a gross violation of good taste if a man were to enter a house when females are there without a male member of the family being present; this applies equally well to a professional visit. Moslem society is regulated by strong taboos regarding social contacts between males and females.

For the same reason there are educational establishments which cater only to Arab juvenile offenders committed to them by court order. These residential establishments also give religious instruction (Moslem, Christian, and Druze) and prepare customary food.

In summary, although both Jewish and Arab juvenile offenders share certain characteristics — e.g., there are no gang activities, robbery is practically unknown, and sexual offenses are infrequent — they differ in types of offenses. Among Arabs one finds a large percentage of shepherdry offenses, which are completely absent among Jewish juvenile offenders. Bodily assault is much more frequent among Arab juvenile offenders than among their Jewish counterparts. On the other hand, among Jewish juvenile offenders one finds a larger percentage of offenses against property, although these are becoming more frequent among Arabs. The striking point is that the incidence of juvenile delinquency among Arabs is higher than that among Jews. There are several possible reasons for this: at the pretrial stage, Arab probation officers use methods differing from those used by their Jewish counterparts, who much more frequently suggest dropping the charges; among Arabs complaints are much more frequently lodged than among Jews; one encounters among Arabs some types of offenses which, under prevailing circumstances and local conditions, tend to enlarge figures of Arab juvenile offenders; and the child population among Arabs is higher than among Jews. It is possible, however, that the constantly changing situation will present a different picture in years to come. And for Arab, as for Jewish offenders, one cannot too strongly stress the need for more effective agencies to counteract the high rate of recidivism.

5

Sex Offenses and the Protection of Children

Sex offenses in general, or offenses against morality, as they are sometimes called in law books, cover rather a wide range, including indecent acts committed on adults or on children, procuration for immoral purposes, living on the earnings of a prostitute, soliciting for immoral purposes, keeping of a brothel, and rape or attempt to commit rape. According to the circumstances and to the severity of a particular offense in this field, criminal codes make provisions related to the judicial provisions of each country to punish the offender.

There are three different ways in which a child may be involved in a sex offense: by committing such an offense, by being a victim, or by being a witness. When children themselves are engaged in a sex offense, such an offense may often be regarded as a sort of sex play, particularly when the children are under fourteen years old. Such sex play is often based on curiosity, without there necessarily being any criminal intent. The case may be different, however, if a child who seeks to commit a sex offense on another child is above the age of fourteen. Although in many instances it may also be a sort of sex play, one finds delinquent intentions more frequently.

Among the various types of criminal offenses, sex offenses do not play an important role in Israel, either for adults or juveniles. This is significant, because taking into consideration the changes and upheavals which are going on at present in our society, one would have expected more serious repercussions in this particular field. Moreover, a large number of the sex offenses in Israel are of minor character. There are not many instances of rape, and seldom is a sex offense accompanied by violence. Table 5.1 compares the number and percentage of offenses against morality with the total number of offenses committed during

63

TABLE 5.1

SEX OFFENSES COMPARED WITH OTHER CRIMINAL OFFENSES, 1958–70

Year	All criminal offenses (no.)	All sex offenses		Sex offenses against minors	
		No.	% of total offenses	No.	% of total sex offenses
1958	47,854	1,259	2.63	503	39.9
1960	55,919	1,475	2.63	602	40.8
1962	64,074	1,586	2.47	655	41.3
1964	79,002	1,915	2.43	912	47.6
1966	96,209	1,932	2.00	947	49.0
1968	101,056	2,107	2.08	814	38.6
1970	134,500	2,230	1.65	1,068	47.8

Source: Israeli National Police, *Statistical Year Books*, for the years indicated.

1958–70 and indicates the number and percentage of these offenses which were committed against minors. The category "sex offenses against minors" includes children and young persons up to the age of sixteen who were victims of a sex offense. There is, however, no information available concerning the particular age at which these minors were involved in such an offense. Not all of these were victims, since, for instance, these figures include girls who were caught soliciting. At a fair guess, approximately two-thirds of those in this category could be regarded as victims.

As the figures in Table 5.2 indicate, sex offenses committed by juveniles do not constitute a serious or special problem. Practically all these offenses were committed against other juveniles. The figures given in this table are those of juvenile offenders who were apprehended by the police but not necessarily brought to trial, even though they may have admitted the offense. According to an administrative decision by the Attorney General in 1952, many such juveniles are not brought to trial. In these instances, the children are under fourteen years, or the investigation has revealed that they were engaged in innocent sex play, or the young offender has shown great distress, and so on. Each case is decided on its merit.

In addition, of those who are brought to trial and found guilty of having committed a sex offense, very few are ordered by the court to reside in a juvenile institution. It is obvious to all who actually work with juvenile offenders that any kind of sexual digression is bound to be fostered in an institution and not hindered or solved.

TABLE 5.2
SEX OFFENSES BY JUVENILES COMPARED
WITH OTHER OFFENSES,
1958–70

Year	All juvenile offenses (no.)	Sex offenses	
		No.	% of total juvenile offenses
1958	7,479	77	1.02
1960	11,247	150	1.33
1962	14,834	206	1.38
1964	17,910	193	1.07
1966	18,906	222	1.17
1968	21,268	258	1.21
1970	22,222	194	1.10

Source: Israeli National Police, *Statistical Year Books*, for the years indicated.

SEXUAL CONFLICTS AMONG GIRLS AND PROSTITUTION

The most frequent charges brought against girls above the age of fourteen in Israeli juvenile courts are related to sexual misbehavior. Some of these girls are brought to court on criminal charges, whereas others are tried as minors in need of supervision and treatment, a provision outside the jurisdiction of criminal procedure.

Of those tried for a criminal offense, some are charged with soliciting or with disorderly behavior in a public place, but not with prostitution, for prostitution is not a criminal offense in Israel. Others are charged with stealing, disturbance of public order, or causing bodily harm, but during the trial it often transpires that the major issue is sexual misbehavior. Even in those instances in which the charge sheet does not mention sexual misbehavior, it is of paramount importance to take this matter into account at the stage of disposal if it is brought to the notice of the judge in open court, for the juvenile court cannot afford to adopt an "ostrich" policy, and to hide behind pure formality. (This by no means implies, however, that sentence will be passed for an offense that does not appear on the charge sheet, and for which the girl was not charged.)

The greatest number of girls brought to trial for criminal offenses are charged with loitering for an illegal purpose. These are girls, sometimes even under the age of fourteen, who loiter in the streets and on interurban highways for the sole purpose of prostitution. Apart from everything else, they are a nuisance to the public and cause discomfort and concern. From time to time they are arrested by the police, which also often leads to public disturbance. Many of them have fixed places where they can be found at specific hours. Others roam about from street to street, even from city to city, only to turn up again where they started.

The majority of girls are tried, not on a criminal charge, but as minors in need of supervision and treatment. This is a more expedient procedure, because it is often difficult to prove a criminal offense under the circumstances described above. Recourse must therefore be made to a procedure which is not tied down by the rules applied in a criminal court. In such cases, the court must be satisfied by an application by a child welfare officer and sustaining evidence, that a particular minor is in need of the court's intervention. One is here confronted with the concept that, whether or not the minor himself has requested such an intervention, society is obligated to look after the welfare of minors who are either unable to do so for themselves or who are neglected by their parents and consequently may be maltreated and abused by other people as well.

Almost invariably, all of these girls—whatever the charge brought against them—are connected with a procurer, who lives off their earnings. The girls are usually under his strong supervision, and he is expected to protect them from undue abuse and unfair competition, to provide the bond of security for release in case of arrest, and to pay any fine imposed by the court. On these scores, however, many girls have experienced great disappointments, because procurers often do not keep their promises. On the other hand, the procurer takes great care to ensure that the girl delivers her earnings to him without keeping any of it for herself. The situation is, as it were, a game with open cards, in which all participants try to break some of the rules which they may have accepted explicitly or implicitly. It is astounding to see in what wretched conditions many of the girls, especially the younger ones, live. Their life style is in direct contradiction to their expectations. Often their procurer wastes their earnings, but even such humiliating situations usually do not alter their dependence on him.

A wide range of circumstances and motivations may account for sexual misbehavior among young girls. These include disorganization of the family, lack of parental control, problems ensuing from a broken home, constant quarrels at home, learning difficulties in school, instability at work, inability to integrate with peer groups, loss of self-respect, feelings of vengeance towards parents or other members of the family, weak self-control but a strong tendency to wayward behavior, and association with bad company. Experience has shown that in the majority of instances, several of these factors come into play in influencing the behavior pattern of the girls involved. My observations have taught me, however, that not only are these factors of unequal importance in determining a particular behavior pattern, but that the importance of one or another factor increases or declines in relation to the overall situation at a particular time.

Hundreds of young girls join the ranks of young prostitutes each year. Most of them drift into prostitution accidentally, and one can distinguish a process which leads ultimately to their being regarded as social outcasts. Often this process begins with truancy from school, frequent changing of jobs, increased tension with parents and other members of the family, instances of staying out until late at night or sleeping away from home, and eventually, running away from home for brief or extended periods. Often, the inability of parents or social agencies to take appropriate measures at the crucial stages in this process encourages further deterioration.

The girl who goes astray is seldom aware of the eventual consequences of her behavior. At first she enjoys truanting from school, freeing herself of parental control, and making independent decisions which may appear defiant to her family. Often, her behavior is directed by unconscious motives. Once she has begun to roam about the streets, however, she is invariably picked up by a procurer, who has an infallible sense for identifying girls on the brink of going astray. Sometimes, these procurers pretend that they want to help the girl to straighten out her difficulties with her parents, and they therefore offer temporary shelter. Others start right off with sex relations or even with rape. In all instances, the procurer pretends to be earnest about his promises to look after the girl and takes pains to conceal his real intentions. But once the girl is no longer a virgin, she loses her status within her family and can only seldom return there. Worse still, because she is no longer a virgin she lacks the motivation to reform, since she knows what the reaction of her family will be. When the girl has reached the stage of feeling that she is an outcast or an unworthy human being, she sees her condition as a matter of fate, and from that point on all inhibitions fall away and the procurer has won the battle. This is the situation which presents itself among practically all groups of Oriental origin.

Statistics indicate an increase in the number of young prostitutes during recent years. During 1966, 302 girls between the ages of fifteen and seventeen were reported; this figure rose to 380 in 1967 and to 462 in

1968. There was a decrease to 428 prostitutes among this age group in 1969, but the number increased to 699 in 1970.[1]

These figures record instances in which parents complained to the police that their daughters had run away from home. It should be emphasized, however, that there are many runaway girls aged fifteen to seventeen or younger whose parents do not report to the police, even when their absence is extended. Parents may refrain from complaining to the police because of shame, resentment, annoyance, revenge, or fear. Many find it difficult thus to admit their failure; others hope against hope that their daughters will eventually return home; some are afraid that a complaint to the police may force the girl to turn to a procurer or criminal, and that they may thus aggravate rather than improve the girl's perilous situation. A study made of runaway children in Israel revealed conclusively that a very high percentage of runaway girls eventually drift into associations with criminals, live on the periphery of society, and turn to prostitution.[2]

There is no panacea for this process, except the courage to face the issue at the beginning. When the first symptoms appear, it is important to look at once for some measure or method of treatment that will prevent a further deterioration of the situation. Serious and sustained efforts by parents to stop such behavior are interpreted by their daughters as indifference and weakness. I am continually amazed at the amount of disappointment and resentment girls voice towards their parents during court sessions. At the same time, one can almost invariably sense a distinct desire to be reaccepted within the family circle. Many girls have also admitted that they are equally disappointed by their own behavior.

Experience has taught us that the rehabilitation of girls who have gone astray sexually is very difficult indeed. Recently, the difficulty has been enhanced—in Israel, as elsewhere—by the fact that many of these girls also become drug addicts. But it is also true that many of these girls are in conflict with themselves because of their disorderly behavior. Such conflicts become manifest at the beginning of such a career, when girls become pregnant, or when they decide that they would like to marry. And opportunities for rehabilitation are often unexplored because of shortcomings of the social services, the lack of appropriate facilities, and, perhaps most important of all, the difficulty in recognizing when and to what extent a girl is in conflict with herself.

Unfortunately, Israel has made no headway in the treatment of these

[1] See *Yediot*, no. 2 (June 1971), p. 9 (published in Hebrew by the Israeli Ministry of Social Welfare, Jerusalem).

[2] *Runaway Children* (Jerusalem: Israeli Police Force, 1969). (In Hebrew.)

girls. In 1962, however, an important law was enacted to protect females who are victims of procurers and to impose heavier punishment for procurers.[3] For some time the general public had been disturbed that procurers received light sentences in court and that there was insufficient protection for the women who became their prey.

The most outstanding features of this 1962 law are the following:

1. There is more protection for girls under eighteen years.
2. No distinction is made between a male or female procurer.
3. Evidence of a woman against her husband and her parents is now admissible.
4. A brothel is more appropriately defined as a place occupied or frequented by two or more females for the purposes of prostitution.
5. Punishment for procuration has been made considerably more severe. Moreover, according to certain sections of this law, imprisonment is obligatory.

Paragraph 10 of this law is especially significant because it stipulates a mandatory, rather than a conditional, prison sentence for procurers. In this regard, a decision handed down by the Israeli Supreme Court is pertinent.[4] Although paragraph 10 of the 1962 law makes imprisonment mandatory if imprisonment is the court's sentence, the court may instead, according to this decision, place the offender on probation, under the 1944 Probation of Offenders Ordinance; in other words, the 1962 law does not abrogate the 1944 provision for probation but makes it much less a matter of routine. This decision has far-reaching consequences, especially for probation as a means of treatment. There can be no doubt that as a result of the decision probation has gained in status. It would, of course, be fallacious to regard this method as a panacea, yet if we supplement the Supreme Court decision with the legal provision making a written report by a probation officer mandatory in specific instances (see Chapter 9), the value of that decision is enhanced.

THE PROTECTION OF CHILDREN

Public feelings always run high when sex offenses, particularly those committed against children, are discovered. Usually, however, these feelings are focused on the offender, and on ways and means of punishing him. We, as members of society, may be satisfied when the offender is

---

[3] Penal Law Amendment (Prostitution Offenses) Law, 5722–1962, in *Laws of the State of Israel*, Vol. 16, p. 17.

[4] Supreme Court, Criminal Appeal 69/63, October 31, 1963.

apprehended and appropriate action is taken for his punishment. To let it rest at this, however, is not sufficient. The more important question of what is to happen to the *child* who became a victim and whose character formation may have been affected by the experience still remains. Furthermore, are we as members of society satisfied that the methods of investigation consider the needs of the child-victim, or should we look for more adequate methods of investigation?

We would all probably agree that a victim of a sex offense, especially a child of tender age, needs special consideration because of the dynamics involved in this type of offense. Of particular importance are the effect and consequences as far as character formation is concerned. A child who has been a victim of a sex offense may develop behavior difficulties, neurotic traits, delinquent tendencies, and in the case of girls, a tendency towards prostitution. In fact, of the girls brought before me in juvenile court for promiscuous behavior, an investigation often revealed that they had earlier been victims of a sex offense. It takes considerable time before these tendencies become apparent, and all too often they are related to these traumatic experiences of a tender age.

Obviously, children react in different ways when they are sexually assaulted, depending on their personality, on their age, on the atmosphere prevailing at home, and on the circumstances and character of the offense. There are children who do seem not disturbed at all, others pretend not to be disturbed, and still others have very strong guilt feelings. Some children are ashamed of what happened to them, but some have a tendency to show off and tell their friends of their experience. Half-innocent provocations on the part of children sometimes also play a role in causing the offense. Often children become involved in sexual play out of curiosity or are dragged into it accidentally. Some continue this play for long periods without disclosing it, fearing that discovery might expose them to punishment by parents or to abuse from friends and acquaintances; others stop after one experience. The salient feature, however, is that in all instances what is going on is highly charged with emotions.

Apprehending sex offenders is greatly hindered because the victims are often ashamed to lodge a complaint about this type of offense. Offenders also usually threaten children with vengeance if they disclose what happened. These threats are taken seriously by children, and they add to the secrecy which surrounds sex offenses. Furthermore, many parents, and particularly mothers, prefer to conceal the fact that their child has been a victim of a sex offense for fear that they themselves may be considered responsible, through neglect, for whatever happened to the child. Thus, we can see in many instances the interesting feature of a shared secrecy between the victim and the offender.

When the prosecuting authorities have sufficient material against a particular person, they naturally base their case first of all on information from the child who was the victim, or who was a witness. Here we are up against the severe handicap, from the point of view of mental hygiene, that children are called upon to relate to the police what happened to them, elaborating on as many details as possible. For many children this may mean reliving an experience that was a most unpleasant and traumatic affair. Often, children have difficulties in going through this experience again and "blocking," "forgetting," and "giving false descriptions" occur. Sometimes these reactions are also prompted by guilt feelings in the child. The guilt feelings may originate from the child himself, or they may be the result of outside intervention, mostly by members of the family. Under these circumstances, even the most benign methods of investigation by the police can contribute considerably to the emotional difficulties of the child.

On the other hand, it is obvious that, inherently, the focus of the police investigation is to gather material in order to bring about the detection and arrest of the offender and eventually his conviction. No particular attention is paid to the emotional upheavals of the child concerned; in fact, this is hardly appreciated as being part of the issue. Yet parents and sometimes teachers observe changes which take place in children either immediately after the offense or at a later date. There are children who react by vomiting, depression, vagrancy, truancy, nightmares, and other symptoms. Sometimes it is only these changes in behavior that lead to disclosure of what happened, because children are often ashamed or afraid to tell their parents about it, and they can do so only after being questioned.

There is an even greater risk for the child if his appearance is required in court. There, the child is confronted with the offender, and he may be subjected to cross-examination. This may turn out to be a more traumatic experience for the child than the offense itself. Sometimes only the court appearance and the cross-examination bring home to him that he was the victim of a sex offense. The importance attached to his stand in the witness box will often supply the child's fantasy with material which stands in no relation to the offense itself. In other words, in this type of offense, a court appearance as a witness for the prosecution may cause a reactive behavior pattern. There is nothing simpler than to involve a child in contradictions while he is in the witness box. As a result of this, he may further be harmed by the fact that the judge may not believe him. From this, behavior difficulties may evolve, because we are dealing here with a special dynamic situation.

For quite some time, there were no legal safeguards in Israel to protect child victims of sex offenses from the trauma that might result from police questioning and court appearance. In 1955, however, a law was passed to deal with this matter.[5] The law contains the following major points:

1. No child under fourteen years shall be investigated, examined, or heard as a witness in an offense against morality, save with the permission of a youth interrogator.
2. A statement by a child as to an offense against morality committed upon his person, or in his presence, or of which he is suspected, shall not be admitted as evidence, save with the permission of a youth interrogator.
3. For the purpose of the law, a youth interrogator shall be appointed after consultation with an appointment committee. This committee shall consist of a judge of the juvenile court, who will act as chairman, an expert in mental hygiene, an educator, an expert in child care, and a high-ranking police officer.
4. Evidence as to an offense against morality taken and recorded by a youth interrogator and any minutes or report of an examination as to such an offense prepared by a youth interrogator are admissible as evidence in court.
5. Where evidence as referred to above has been submitted to the court, the youth interrogator may be required to reexamine the child and ask him a particular question, but he may refuse to do so if he is of the opinion that further questioning is likely to cause emotional harm to the child.
6. A person shall not be convicted on evidence by a youth interrogator unless it is supported by other evidence.

As can be seen, there are two important innovations in this law. First, the investigation of the child victim is put into the hands of experts who are trained in interviewing techniques and mental hygiene. Secondly, a child victim under fourteen years does not give evidence in court unless the youth interrogator has decided that he may appear.

The appointment committee in its deliberations has followed the spirit of this law and has suggested for appointment as youth interrogators people who are trained and experienced in the dynamics of behavior

[5] Law of Evidence Revision (Protection of Children) Law, No. 33, 5715–1955, in *Laws of the State of Israel*, Vol. 9, p. 102.

problems. The most suitable candidates for this job are psychiatric social workers, clinical psychologists, child psychiatrists, probation officers, and child-care workers. It is felt that an appropriate expert approach at the initial stage of the investigation may diminish or even obliterate the trauma caused to a child who has become involved as victim or as witness in an offense against morality. The first contact with the child while he is relating the story of what happened and the way questions are asked are of the greatest importance.

Certain of the essential requirements of a youth interrogator are foreign to his initial professional training. Inherent in his task is the need to acquire some knowledge of legal procedure, particularly in regard to offenses against morality. It is necessary that he understand behavior in court and at cross-examinations especially. A proper and fearless stand in the witness box, straightforward answers and jargon-free explanations are essential requirements for the interrogator. Fortunately, all these can be acquired more or less easily by professional people trained in the disciplines mentioned above. It might be more difficult for people trained in legal concepts to acquire real feeling and an understanding of the dynamics of human behavior and of interviewing techniques. An adequately trained youth interrogator can thus make a real contribution to the legal profession, which in the area of sex offenses needs a new and a more challenging approach.

Frequently the child's statement is not sufficient, and there is need for a physical examination, for visiting the place where the offense has taken place, and for participation in an identification lineup. These activities, if necessary, are part and parcel of the task of the youth interrogator. For him, a conflict may sometimes arise if he has to decide whether or not the child should participate in these activities. We have found however, that the presence of the youth interrogator gives the child the necessary support and confidence in these situations to minimize, as far as possible, psychological harm.

The youth interrogator has to be aware constantly that the material he is collecting may be the most important evidence to support the story of the child in court. He must therefore beware of information based on rumors. The method of question and answer can be applied, naturally according to legal rules and procedures. This is particularly relevant in those instances where there seems to be a tendency to distort, to repress, or to forget important details in the story. These situations need careful attention, and close study and examination cannot always be avoided.

The youth interrogator also has to keep in mind that it is he who may be cross-examined about the information which he is obtaining from the child. Therefore, he must pay attention to and take notes on not only the factual material but also on gestures, mimicry, and other affective moments and details during the interrogation.

The child's initial statement is always taken in a neutral environment. Parents turning to the police with a complaint are told that a youth interrogator will contact them about it. He will then make the investigation at the child's home or at his office, but never at the police station, because this would be a charged environment. To question the child at the police station may mean to expose him to a punitive situation and arouse guilt feelings in him, which in turn may have detrimental effects on future behavior.

Our experience has shown that youth interrogators are capable of getting much more information from the victims than even the most experienced police interrogator. Contrary to the latter's approach, which is directed by his habitual manner of interrogating delinquents, the success of the youth interrogator's method depends on an approach of understanding and special attention. This professional, understanding manner may open the heart of the child and may thus make it possible, and even convenient, for him to talk. At the same time that the expert's contact with the victim results in diminishing the traumatic effects of the experience, important and relevant information is extracted.

The following case would best illustrate this point. A youth interrogator visited a nine-year-old girl whose parents had complained that a sex offense had been committed on her. At that point, the child was completely unable to talk. At the second interview, which took place the following day, she was still very timid, and the youth interrogator realized that the child would not be able to disclose the necessary information in a direct manner. So she asked the child what the dwelling of the man looked like. After some hesitation, the girl took a sheet of paper and a pencil, drew a room and a roof, and then, while still drawing, explained a bit more freely: "Here is a table with three chairs. Above it is a lampshade, and there, in the corner, is a bed. Here was the man, and I was standing there. Suddenly he drew me up to the bed, and I don't know what happened next."

After having recounted this, the girl looked anxious and waited silently, as if wondering what the youth interrogator's reaction would be. She was extremely relieved when the woman continued to talk to her in the same normal way as before, without, for instance, putting to her the question of why she had gone to the room in the first place. The girl, being reassured by the behavior of the youth interrogator, was then able to talk further and to reveal all the important details in this case. At the end of the interview she could even express the fear that she herself was to blame, because she agreed to go with the man to his room. It was evident that the talk with the youth interrogator relieved her of her guilt feelings and that she looked at her own doings in this matter differently. After the statement was taken, the youth interrogator talked to the girl for a while, explaining to her that there are men who take advantage of innocent girls. To have used the word "innocent" in this connection was of primary importance to this young child.

In 1962, an amendment to the 1955 law was passed.[6] According to this amendment, in instances in which a youth interrogator has permitted a child to give evidence himself in court, the court may order that such evidence be discontinued if the youth interrogator is of the opinion that continuance of the testimony may cause mental harm to the child. Experience has shown that while giving evidence in court, some children who were thought able to stand in the witness box became panicky, showed symptoms of bewilderment, and fell into the mental state that the law was intended to prevent. It is up to the youth interrogator to call the attention of the court to the state of the child. The decision to discontinue his testimony, however, rests with the court.

Some countries have made provisions, mainly through administrative regulations, that children giving evidence in court in matters of sex offenses should be heard via camera only. This is done in order to lessen the ordeal for the child. But this provision is absolutely inadequate as a safeguard so far as the children involved are concerned. The appearance in court, the feeling of uneasiness connected with it, and above all, the unconscious fear of punishment may have traumatic and detrimental effects on the child. These feelings are not lessened even if the children are accompanied by their parents or other relatives.[7]

A case in point was a girl of nine years who made friends with a man in a public garden where she used to play. One day, while talking to her, he forced her onto his lap and played with her genitals. She was so horrified that she could not even cry, let alone escape. Some time later she was found there by her mother in a very disturbed state. The parents informed the police and volunteered what information they could. There

---

[6] Law of Evidence Revision (Protection of Children) Law, 5722–1962, in *Laws of the State of Israel*, Vol. 17, p. 12.

[7] It should be mentioned at this point that in countries where tape recordings are admitted as evidence in court, the law has a stronger position in relation to hearsay evidence. If tape recordings were used in Israel, however, they might dissipate hesitations and objections which often exist lest the evidence recorded and taken down by a youth interrogator be regarded as hearsay and therefore inadmissable.

followed a further ordeal for the child, who had to make a detailed statement to the police of what she did and what the man did. After this she was given a medical examination, and although her mother was present, the girl was rather shocked. Soon afterwards she was asked to attend an identification lineup, because a suspect had been seen in the same garden.

Not long afterwards, the girl showed emotional disturbances, which prompted the parents to obtain psychological treatment for her. When, after six months, she was summoned to give evidence in court, the father of the child was appalled, because she had recovered her previous equilibrium, and he feared that a confrontation in court with the offender and a reliving of the traumatic experience might undo the progress which had been made. In his despair he said, "It seems to me that my child has had to pay too high a price. Perhaps it would have been better and more in the interest of my child if I had not turned to the police at all."

A defendant's right to prove his innocence and to rebut a charge has been recognized as one of the fundamental human rights. At times this can be achieved only when the defendant is confronted in court by the witness. But the defendant may also take advantage of a child's fear of telling the whole story in court in his presence, or he may cast doubts on the child's story by involving him in contradictions, thus bringing about his own acquittal. Thus it may happen that the child who was the victim of a sex offense is further victimized in court and regarded there as a liar because he becomes confused by the questions put before him, or because he does not know how to comply with legal procedure.

Our experience in Israel has proved that offenders often threaten children with revenge if they disclose any details, and that children take these threats very seriously. We have seen children between the ages of ten and thirteen who were allowed to appear in court on the strength of their calm, poised manner while relating their experience to the youth interrogator, but who in the presence of the offender in court, reacted quite differently. Some could not reply to questions, others forgot very relevant details, still others trembled or became panicky in one way or another. Needless to say, such reactions reduce considerably the value of their evidence.

In Israel, as in other countries where the English common law system is applied, a conviction in a sexual offense case is possible only if there is evidence corroborating that of the complainant. This principle serves as a safeguard against mischievous, false, imaginary, or revengeful accusations. The danger of vindictive feelings in a situation which is highly charged emotionally—whether those feelings are overt or concealed—cannot be overlooked. Much harm can be done by mere accusations, even when they are found baseless on close scrutiny. It is here that the section of the law requiring corroborating evidence is of the utmost importance. In these instances, as in other criminal offenses, the onus of proof rests with the prosecution, and proof must be without any reasonable doubt. Thus, the legal rights of defendants are guarded.

The youth interrogator can also be of assistance in the field of prevention. He has been trained to understand and evaluate mental and social conditions, and he can, accordingly, take immediate steps to transfer to the appropriate authorities those cases in need of special care. His intervention comes often just in time, both from the point of view of the child's mental health and from that of the interest of the community. Although the functions of the interrogator are clearly defined in the youth protection law, his alertness to the overall situation is a significant feature in the implementation of this law.

Two cases may well illustrate this point. One is the case of an eight-year-old girl who was a victim of an indecent assault. The youth interrogator paid three visits to this girl's home, all at different times of the day, but never found the parents there. The girl always said that her parents had just left. The home was extremely neglected, and so were the children. This little girl was with, and in charge of, two younger siblings, aged six and three. The interrogator found out that the offender, the family's neighbor, knew about this state of affairs and took advantage of the fact that the children were left alone for long hours by visiting them constantly when the parents were away. On his visits, he used to bring the children small gifts, so as to bribe them not to reveal anything.

After gathering all the information about the sex offense committed there, the youth interrogator informed the local social agency of the plight of these three children. Later, upon inquiry, she was told that the social agency was taking steps to bring the children to the juvenile court, as needing care and protection. Thus, in this case, not only was the girl who had already become the victim of a sex offense taken care of, but also her younger siblings, who were otherwise also liable to become victims of further incidents.

The second case is that of a thirteen-year-old girl with whom a young man had had sexual intercourse and whom he had induced to become a prostitute. She was a dull girl, and the man's promises of money, frequent visits to the movies, fashionable new dresses, and so on, fascinated her. Fortunately the affair was discovered at the very beginning of her "career." The youth interrogator to whom the case was referred realized that the girl was already beyond her parents' control, and that no improvement could be expected as long as she remained at home. The girl was therefore brought before the juvenile court, which sent her to an educational institution, with a view to her eventual correction. She has since adjusted well, and there are good prospects for her rehabilitation.

We have seen that the sexual offender often poses as a nice and friendly man. He talks kindly to the victim, is generous in promising presents and even in actually giving them. He takes the child for walks, and is prepared to show him interesting pictures. His simulated kindness may motivate a child to follow and get involved with him. Some children manifest a sort of passive acceptance and seem to be absorbed mainly by the promises made to them. A girl of eight years related how a man approached her and told her that she was a nice girl and that he was going to give her some money to buy a doll. Then he pulled down her knickers, but suddenly became nervous and went away. The girl added: "He promised me the money for the doll, but he didn't give it to me." The frequency of stories like this suggests that the kindness of the seducer is an important factor. More than likely, most of the victims are not accustomed to such kind treatment at home.

Another problem in dealing with juvenile sex victims is the attitude adopted by the adults to whom the child relates his story. In many instances, adults tend to see in such a complaint a mere fantasy, a child's boast, or just nonsense. We have observed that many a time, the policeman who requests a youth interrogator to investigate a certain case will volunteer his personal opinion that there is probably nothing to the child's story because the suspect is himself the father of small children. This argument is not valid. Children only very seldom make up this kind of story. It can be safely assumed that in instances of this kind, there is a process of displaced incest. The man may have inhibitions against committing the offense on his child, but these are ineffective concerning children who do not belong to his immediate family circle.

In cases where sexual consciousness has not yet developed—say, up to ten years or so—children usually turn to their parents when molested. With the onset of preadolescence, juvenile victims are more hesitant to confide in their parents, and by the time they reach puberty, their reluctance to do so is marked. At the same time, if the matter comes to the parents' notice indirectly, parents' reaction is likely to be more rejecting than otherwise, occasionally with far-reaching effects on the child. It is astonishing to what extent even small children sense their parents' attitudes and reactions and behave accordingly when they become victims of a sex offense.

Youth interrogators can be of great assistance in dealing with the attitudes of adults. An example may serve to illustrate this.

Two boys, aged nine and ten years old, agreed to a young man's suggestion that they go with him to a blind alley off the main road, and there he seduced them to play with his genitals. By chance, another man followed them there, and he notified the police. All of them were brought to the police station. The two boys were told that a youth interrogator would take their statements at their homes, and they were accordingly sent home. The following day the youth interrogator made a home visit and recorded the following:

I paid a visit at the home of child B in order to take down his statement of what had happened the day before. It soon transpired that B's parents had no knowledge at all of the incident. They were taken aback, and they were very indignant that their child had concealed the incident from them. The same occurred with the second boy, A, who is a neighbor of B.

While I was taking the statement of the boys, the parents insisted on being present, to which I agreed. I could feel, however, that the parents were unable to accept the fact that they had not been told by their children themselves of what happened. I therefore thought it necessary to explain to the parents that their children were motivated by shame and remorse rather than by distrust. I also added in passing that in fact nothing really happened and that children at this age are sometimes led astray by curiosity and innocence. My explanations had immediate results, and the attitude of the parents changed noticeably.

It was my impression that the fact that these explanations came from me, whom the parents regarded as an official and an authoritative person, had a calming effect on them

The figures in Table 5.3 give us an idea of the ages of juvenile sex victims from a sample of 1,097 children who were investigated by youth interrogators during a period of two and a half years. The table is concerned with children under the age of fourteen, i.e., those who were investigated by a youth interrogator according to the 1955 law. It can be observed that the percentage of boys who were the victims of a sex offense increased constantly from the lower age groups to the higher. In the oldest group, that of children aged twelve and thirteen, male victims constitute 44 percent. This can be explained by an increase in homosexual activities to which they became victim by having reached puberty. Growing sexual feelings and curiosity are another factor in this increase. With girls in this age group there is an opposite tendency. Sexual awareness among girls in the early stage of puberty and the sensitivity which is part of the commencement of menstruation operate to increase inhibitions and suspicions. In other words, boys become more aggressive at this age, whereas girls are more withdrawn.

TABLE 5.3
AGE OF INTERROGATED JUVENILE SEX VICTIMS

Age group	Both sexes		Male		Female	
	No.	%	No.	% of age group	No.	% of age group
Under 5 yrs.	130	12%	18	14%	112	86%
5–9 yrs.	641	58	170	27	471	73
10–11 yrs.	166	15	52	31	114	69
12–13 yrs.	160	15	71	44	89	56
All age groups	1,097	100	311	28	786	72

These figures are based upon a survey made by the author.

A survey of these 1,097 cases revealed that about one-third of the offenders were actually brought to trial, because there was sufficient prima facie material against them. Twenty-five percent of them pleaded guilty at the first hearing in court, and in these instances it was not necessary to hear further evidence. Sixty-five percent were found guilty by the courts, and 10 percent were acquitted because of insufficient evidence, or because proof was not beyond doubt. In those instances in which evidence was submitted to the courts, youth interrogators allowed 20 percent of the child-victims to give evidence in court themselves. Even in these cases, the youth interrogator was present at the court hearing, and it could be observed how important this was for the child concerned. Undoubtedly he derived moral support and security from the youth interrogator's presence.

In 46 percent of the 1,097 cases the sex offense was committed indoors; the other 54 percent were committed in some public place, such as a public garden or street. In this latter category belong those offenses which were committed in the vicinity of schools, but they accounted for only 5 percent. This small figure is encouraging, because it means either that children are brought to and taken from school by an adult, or that they have been warned by parents and teachers not to talk to strangers. Offenders may also regard the vicinity of a school as unfavorable because of the danger of being seen by others and subsequently being easily identified.

One fact that we have learned through the use of youth interrogators is that the offender is often a relative of the victim, a friend of his family, a neighbor, or an acquaintance. This may account in part for the offender's success in seducing the child: the child is not suspicious when first approached by the offender because he knows him. In the instances in which the offender was apprehended (although not necessarily brought to trial because of insufficient evidence), 59 percent of the offenders were known by the child.

As the figures in Table 5.3 indicate, 70 percent of the juvenile victims were under ten years of age. This may indicate that the perpetrators of certain types of sex offenses find their most convenient victims among children of tender age. The offenses committed against these children were almost without exception of the indecent act type, and not actual sex relations. As has already been mentioned, there were very few cases of rape. One must assume that these offenders were interested in some sort of sexual outlet short of sex relations proper.

Since the 1955 law has come into force in Israel, more people have reported such offenses to the authorities instead of trying to conceal them. This is encouraging, and we hope to develop this approach further, for the sake of the child, the family, and society at large.

III

The Juvenile Court

6

The
Juvenile Court
in Action

COMPETENCE OF THE JUVENILE COURT

The juvenile court in Israel has two functions: (1) to adjudicate juvenile offenders within those age groups prescribed by law; and (2) to adjudicate minors who are in need because of neglect. The latter group will not be dealt with in this book because their complex manifold problems deserve an independent and comprehensive analysis. Suffice it therefore to mention that by the Youth Care and Supervision Law of 1960 the juvenile court may intervene at the request of an especially appointed child welfare officer on behalf of minors under the age of eighteen who live under conditions regarded as detrimental to their upbringing.

Much has been said and written on the legal and social philosophy of the modern juvenile court in the adjudication of juvenile offenders. There seem to be no basic differences in the concept of the functions of the court. Yet, the application of these basic concepts varies rather widely.

There are differing legal definitions as to what constitutes delinquent behavior, as to the competence of the juvenile court to try all offenses or only those of a special nature, as to the age of criminal responsibility, and as to the ages which the juvenile court should be competent to adjudicate. These discrepancies in the application of generally accepted ideas and concepts is due mainly to the different backgrounds of the various countries and their differing traditions of crime and punishment.

The competence of the juvenile court in Israel is regulated according to three factors: criminal responsibility, the gravity of an offense, and age groups of juvenile offenders.

Section 9 of the Criminal Code Ordinance of 1936, which is still in force, states that "a person under the age of nine years is not criminally responsible for any act or omission. A person under the age of twelve years is not criminally responsible for any act or omission unless it is proved that at the time of the act or omission he had the capacity to know that he ought not to commit the act or make the omission." One has to divide this paragraph into sections, for the first part of it is a mandatory provision, whereas the second is liable to different interpretations. In these latter instances criminal responsibility will depend on whether or not the prosecuting authority is able to prove that the particular child knew how to distinguish between right and wrong, and this according to the type of a particular offense.

Even so, sometimes situations arise where the juvenile court undertakes to interfere before the trial begins despite the mandatory provision, and although the age is indicated as nine years on the charge sheets. From experience we know that many children from Oriental communities who were born outside Israel have no birth certificate, which is not issued as a matter of course in the countries from which they have come. As a result, the age given by parents upon entering Israel is often an approximate age, figured out in relation to various children who are alive, or in relation to special events which occurred within the family circle. For this reason the juvenile court judge takes great pains to ascertain whether or not the child had already reached the age of nine years at the time of the commission of the offense. If there is any doubt about this, the file will be closed by the court.

If a child of this age is brought to the juvenile court, it always means that he has committed a large number of offenses or that he is so unruly that his parents or the school authorities cannot control him. The court appearance is then regarded as an expedient means of placing the child in an authoritative setting by court order. In these instances, if the child is tried in the juvenile court, this is done according to criminal law and procedure, in spite of the ordeal and stigma which is often part of that procedure, as we shall see later.

The second part of Section 9 of the 1936 Criminal Code Ordinance is generally not strictly adhered to. Usually, the prosecuting authorities do not prove to the court that a juvenile offender between the age of nine and twelve years "had the capacity to know that he ought not to commit the act or make the omission." It is taken for granted that in this age group there exists full criminal responsibility, but it is obvious that the wording of this part of Section 9 should be construed to mean that proof must be specific according to the special nature of the act or the omission, and that an examination of general intelligence, for instance, is not applicable. This interpretation has been upheld by the appellate court in Haifa (file no. 107/59). In the case on which the decision was based, the parents did not accept the fact that their child was found guilty, nor did they accept the verdict, although no punishment was ordered, and they appealed to the district court. The appellate court concluded: "It appears, and there are no differences of opinion, that at the time of the commission of the offense, the offender, the child B.A.G., was under twelve years. According to Section 9 of the Criminal Code Ordinance he was not to be responsible for a criminal act unless it was proved that at the time of the commission of the act he had the capacity to know that he ought not to commit the act. Such proof was not forthcoming in the court. . . . Accordingly we accept the appeal and reverse the conviction and the verdict." In most instances, unfortunately, the parents of juvenile offenders are either indifferent to what happens to their child in court, or they do not know the possible consequences of a court conviction, even in instances in which there is no formal conviction. They may not have the financial means to appoint a defense counsel, or may not even be aware of the possibility of lodging an appeal to a higher court. These disadvantages are enhanced because there is no public control over decisions made in the juvenile court, as the public is usually excluded.

In regard to both age groups—those aged nine years and those under twelve years—a trial in a criminal court may have far-reaching consequences. Standing police regulations provide that it remains at the discretion of a police inspector whether or not fingerprints are taken. If they are, they remain on file and may be dug up after the juvenile offender has become an adult, after he has completely forgotten the delinquent episode of early childhood. In all too many instances, this record of a court appearance may become a serious hindrance in getting an appropriate job.

Of all juvenile offenders tried in a juvenile court, those aged nine, ten, and eleven were represented as follows: during 1960, they constituted 15.2 percent; during 1964, 17.2 percent; during 1966, 13.6 percent; during 1968, 12.3 percent; during 1969, 10.9 percent; and during 1970, 11.2 percent. These figures include first offenders and recidivists. Most of the offenses committed by these age groups were of a mild character. For that reason, approximately 50 percent of them, on the average, were dismissed by the court, which means that their files were practically closed.

It would appear, therefore, that the age of criminal responsibility could safely be raised to commence at the age of twelve. Those under this age who require court intervention could be taken care of by applying the Youth Law of 1960, specifically Section 2(3) of that law, which

states that a minor is in need and therefore qualified for court intervention if he has committed a criminal offense but is not brought to trial
for it. Court intervention under this law would have the advantage that
all the stigma of a criminal procedure would be avoided, but the needs
of the child would be taken care of.

Apart from the definition of criminal responsibility contained in
Section 9 of the Criminal Code Ordinance of 1936, the Juvenile Offenders
Ordinance of 1937 contained three definitions of the ages of juvenile
offenders over which juvenile court had jurisdiction. The ordinance
gave the court jurisdiction over male offenders under sixteen years and
female offenders under eighteen years. The new Youth Law of 1971
raises the upper age limit for males to eighteen years,[1] but for the time
being, the competence of the juvenile court remains the same as it was
before the new law was enforced. Implementation of raising the age to
eighteen was deferred for special proclamation by the ministers of
social welfare and of justice. The law stipulates, however, that this
should be no later than 1 April 1975, unless a two-year extension is
approved by the Committee of Social Affairs of the Knesset.

In replacing the Juvenile Offenders Ordinance of 1937, the Knesset
has taken a very conservative and rigid attitude about the age of juvenile
offenders. The age of criminal responsibility remains nine years, and male
juvenile offenders over sixteen and under eighteen years are for the
time being, for all intents and purposes regarded as full-fledged adults.
The reason for this attitude may be found in the opinion of the police
that raising the age of juvenile jurisdiction over males to eighteen
might have negative repercussions, because male offenders in the age
group of over sixteen and under eighteen constitute a major problem.
These offenders, they argue, should therefore not be dealt with by the
juvenile court, which, they believe, is not sufficiently punitive. The
ministry of social welfare, which is responsible for the rehabilitation
of juvenile offenders, is also hesitant to support raising the age to eighteen
years, because this would necessitate special educational establishments
for this age group.

These arguments are not justified in view of the fact that the methods
which are at the disposal of courts for adults are also at the disposal of
the juvenile court. If it seems advisable to the juvenile court, and if the
juvenile offender is above fourteen years, punitive action which may

[1] Youth Law (Trial, Punitive Methods, and Treatment Measures), 5731–1971, in
Laws of the State of Israel (n.p.).

include imprisonment can be taken. Moreover, the special privileges which the Youth Law of 1971 provides for juvenile offenders may prevent delinquent behavior rather than foster it. Take, for instance, the strict provisions of limited police arrest prior to and pending interrogation, separated lockups for adult and juvenile offenders, the closed court sessions and the ban on reporting names of those who are tried in the juvenile court, and the requirement of a written report by a probation officer. The fact that the juvenile court accords to offenders a more individualized approach than is the case in a court for adults is an advantage rather than a disadvantage.

The argument put forward by the police is also not valid. We are here concerned with only two age groups, those aged sixteen and seventeen years. Official statistics show that over the last fifteen years or so, there has been practically no increase in offenses by these two age groups, nor are the more serious offenses committed by them.

During 1960, of all adult offenders, 4.9 percent belonged to these groups; this figure rose to 6.8 percent in 1965, and increased to 9.5 percent during 1970. These figures include first offenders and recidivists. There has been a tendency toward an increase in recidivism, but this may be due, at least partly, to lack of appropriate treatment facilities. Moreover, at present there is discrimination, as it were, against male juvenile offenders between sixteen and eighteen years. All Israeli laws in which young people are involved stipulate that adulthood begins with the age of eighteen. There is no plausible reason why this should not also be the case with offenders.

In considering the competence of the juvenile court in regard to the seriousness of the offense which can be tried there, one has to remember that the juvenile court is on the same level as the magistrate's court, which has limited jurisdiction. This limitation is based on the seriousness of a particular offense. It is therefore of interest to note that a divergent attitude was adopted when the Juvenile Offenders Ordinance of 1937 was enforced. Section 8(3) of that ordinance stated:

When a child or young person or female juvenile adult is brought before a juvenile court for any offense punishable with more than five years' imprisonment, and the court becomes satisfied at any time during the hearing of the case that it is expedient to deal with it summarily, the court shall put to the child or young person or female juvenile adult the following or a similar question, telling him that he may consult his parent or guardian before replying: "Do you wish to be tried by this court or by a district court?" and the court shall explain to the child or young person or female juvenile adult the meaning of being so tried and the place where the trial would be held.

This provision shows a clear tendency to include all offenses which should be tried by a juvenile court. Only in instances in which the juvenile offender or his parents prefer that the trial be held in a district court and when the punishment is more than five years' imprisonment could the trial be referred to such a court. Over a period of thirty years, the trend in Israeli juvenile courts has been that juvenile offenders and their parents have always preferred that the trial be held in the juvenile court.

This practice was challenged in 1967 by a decision of one of the judges in the juvenile court, who held that the competence of the juvenile court should be limited just as it is in a magistrate's court. The issue was not brought to the court of appeals, and the Knesset therefore decided to take a stand on the matter. On 11 February 1970, an amendment to the Juvenile Offenders Ordinance of 1937 was passed; it states that the minister of justice is empowered to delegate to the juvenile court the competence to adjudicate felonies and that these offenses should be mentioned by special proclamation. This proclamation was published on 2 April 1970; according to it the competence of the juvenile court is made much larger than the competence of adult courts at the same level. In fact, at present the jurisdiction of the juvenile court is limited only in cases of murder, rape, robbery, and national security. The Youth Law of 1971 confirmed that procedure.

Indeed, if the juvenile court is the appropriate place to adjudicate juvenile offenders who have committed minor offenses, it is even more the place to adjudicate juvenile offenders who have committed serious offenses. The latter may be even more in need of the understanding and expert approach which is accorded to juvenile offenders in a juvenile court. It is not in line with the basic philosophy of the modern juvenile court that the seriousness of an offense, as laid down in criminal laws for adults, should deny jurisdiction to a juvenile court. The approach and outlook of a court for adults, particularly in regard to serious offenses, is geared towards the handling of criminals, whereas the commission of a felony by a juvenile often has no other meaning than the commission of a minor offense.

JUVENILE COURT JUDGES

Judges of the juvenile court are full-time judges who are appointed in accordance with the provisions of the Judges Law of 1953.[2] Judges of civil courts are appointed for life, and their term of office can be ter-

---

[2] Judges Law, 5731–1953, in *Laws of the State of Israel*, Vol. 17, p. 124.

minated only by resignation, retirement, death, or dismissal according to special rules, in which instance a complaint may be lodged with a disciplinary tribunal specially set up. The law also gives the qualifications for judges at the different levels; there is no specific legal provision, however, for the qualifications required for serving in the juvenile court.

Since the juvenile court is a court of first instance, and as such, is on the level of a magistrate's court, qualifications for appointment to that court are laid down in Section 4 of the Judges Law: "A person is qualified to be appointed as a judge of a magistrate's court if he is inscribed, or entitled to be inscribed, in the Roll of Advocates in Israel and if he has been engaged, continuously or intermittently, for not less than three years—including at least one year in this country—in one or several of the occupations enumerated in Section 2(2)." In that section the following qualifications are mentioned: "(a) the profession of an advocate; (b) a judicial or other legal function in the service of the State of Israel or another service, approved by the minister of justice, by regulations, for the purpose of this section; (c) the teaching of law at a university or law high school approved by the minister of justice, by regulations, for the purpose of this section."

By administrative arrangement, however, judges of the juvenile court are delegated to serve in the juvenile court alone, and there is no system of rotation whereby a number of judges, or those presiding in the criminal court, also preside in the juvenile court. In Israel, the idea that adjudication and treatment of juvenile offenders within the juvenile court setting cannot be done on the basis of common sense or by the letter of the law alone has been accepted and put into practice. We believe that, while the observation of law and procedure is the basic tenet, a juvenile court judge should also be able to understand and interpret the dynamics of human behavior and that he should therefore have at least some practical experience in the field of child welfare. Knowledge of interviewing techniques and experience in community leadership and activities are also great assets, because of their importance in this special setting. A judge in the juvenile court should also be well acquainted with existing community facilities for juvenile offenders.

It is natural that a juvenile court judge will be advised in these matters by people who work in these special fields. Yet, if a decision is made by a judge, it is his own responsibility whether or not his decision is the best available solution. Moreover, his alertness to the special needs of those who are tried in the juvenile court enables it, as a respected and perhaps also a powerful agency, to initiate and coordinate appropriate activities of other community agencies active in the same field.

DEFENSE COUNSEL

At this juncture the status of the defense counsel should be discussed. For many years, the right of juvenile offenders to be represented by a defense counsel in the juvenile court was wrongly interpreted. That interpretation, due to a clumsy formulation in the Juvenile Offenders Ordinance of 1937, was that the judge of the court had to consent to representation by a defense counsel. A different interpretation was given about ten years ago, and the matter was settled by law with the enforcement of the Youth Law of 1971. Section 18 of this law states that the juvenile court may appoint a defense counsel for a juvenile offender if the court is of the opinion that this will serve the interests of the offender. The law provides further that "where a defense counsel has been appointed by the court, the cost of the defense, including the expenses and fees of the defense counsel and the witnesses, shall be borne by the state as shall be prescribed by regulations." And a further section states: "A defense counsel appointed by the court shall not receive from the accused or any other person any renumeration, compensation, gift, or any other benefit. Whosoever contravenes this provision shall be liable to imprisonment for three months."

The significance of these provisions lies in the fact that the judge, at his own discretion and on his own initiative, may appoint a defense counsel. This will most probably be done in instances in which the offense is of a serious type. But a defense counsel may also be appointed during the actual trial when evidence is being heard and it appears to the court that the juvenile offender should be properly represented.

These provisions do not exclude the privilege of a juvenile offender or his parents to appoint a defense counsel on their own initiative. In such instances, however, the cost of the defense will not be borne by the state. Furthermore, any defense counsel has to comply with Section 11 of the Criminal Procedure Law, 5725–1965, which says: "No person shall act as defense counsel unless he is duly qualified therefor and the accused has, in writing, desired to be represented by him or has empowered him in that behalf or the court has appointed him in that behalf under the provisions of Section 13."[3] Defending a juvenile offender apparently has special attraction for some people, for time and again one encounters people who request the court to be allowed to defend the juvenile offender in his trial. Such an applicant may be a friend of the offender's family, a neighbor, or some other well-meaning person. But he may also be some-

---

[3] *Laws of the State of Israel*, Vol. 19, p. 158.

body who is seeking some advantage from such a situation. The common denominator of all of them is usually the presumption that they are competent to come to the "rescue" of the juvenile offender concerned.

In order to meet the needs of different situations which might arise in a juvenile court, the new Youth Law of 1971 provides for two more resources which may assist a juvenile offender in his defense. In the first place, parents may now cross-examine witnesses, and they may also advance arguments, either instead of their child or together with him. This is a novel procedure, the importance of which goes beyond the mere legal issue. It can be assumed that the average parent is not an expert on legal issues, and from that point of view, he will not be of great help. His taking a stand in court on behalf of his child, however, has psychological and educational importance. The second resource is the judge himself. The new law states that if the juvenile offender has no defense counsel, the court should then help him in cross-examining the witnesses. Although Anglo-Saxon legal tradition prevails to a large extent in Israel, and the judge is not supposed to interfere in the trial except in unusual instances, the Knesset has taken a different view with regard to juvenile offenders.

Nevertheless, these two resources are often limited in providing an appropriate defense in its real meaning. By the nature of their status, the parents and the judge are able to examine only those matters and points which are brought to the notice of the court at the trial itself. They are not supposed to scrutinize the police file, nor are they in a position to interrogate prospective witnesses. In reality, safeguarding civil rights of juvenile offenders may begin by inspecting the police file in order to get to know all the material pertaining to a particular case. Such material would normally not come to the notice of the court, but it may very well sway the issue as to the guilt or innocence of the suspect.

A defense counsel who is interested in the general well-being of the juvenile offender will most probably not limit his interference to legal aspects alone but will concern himself with the offender's needs and general welfare as well. Although he is not an expert in these matters, his status as a defense counsel may give his suggestions special authority. On the other hand, it has been my experience that a defense counsel does not always take pains to become acquainted with the laws and procedures which apply to the juvenile court; his yardstick as to the needs of the juvenile offender are instead stereotyped to offenders in general. As for the juvenile offender, if a defense counsel is in charge of his case, he can conveniently sit back, as it were, and adopt the position of a spectator. The circumstances enable him to remove himself from the reality of the situation, because somebody is present to put things right for him. Invariably, both the juvenile offender and his parents adopt the attitude that, whatever the case may be, the defense counsel will settle the matter in their favor. If, however, the juvenile offender is eventually found guilty, he will be deeply disappointed because his defense counsel has failed him. This may lead to negative repercussions, which may result in the correctional and treatment methods used by the court being ineffective.

Needless to say, such situations are in contrast to endeavors of the juvenile court judge, who is naturally interested in involving the juvenile offender in what is going on in the court and in forcing him to face the reality of the situation. Experience has shown that time and again juvenile offenders make use of various manipulations in order to rid themselves of the impact of the court situation. To yield to such attempts can seldom be helpful to the juvenile concerned, for just to be nice to a person who is in need of real intervention hardly does him any good in the long run.

COURT PROCEDURE

Juvenile court proceedings in Israel are based, as it were, on two different structures which complement one another. There is the external frame of laws and rules of procedure which determines the legal aspect, and on the other hand, there is the internal aspect, the application and implementation of these laws and rules of procedure. This latter aspect is usually the more crucial one with regard to a juvenile court. Sometimes it is important to adopt a lenient attitude and to be very permissive, whereas at other times a stern attitude seems to be the appropriate approach. No rules exist in this matter, nor does it depend necessarily on whether or not the offense was serious. This would be only one aspect of others which would determine the attitude to be adopted.

A case in point is that of the girl Orah, aged fifteen years, who was brought to the juvenile court for having stolen genuine pearls worth more than U.S. $350. The girl had stolen the pearls from an open window on the spur of the moment. She was unaware that by definition of criminal law, such a theft is a felony, nor was she aware that the pearls were genuine. The circumstances were that she was on her way to a party, and she wanted to have something to be able to show off. After she and her father had indicated their preference that the matter be dealt with in the juvenile court by summary jurisdiction, the seriousness of the case came to light—not because of the section of the law with which she was charged, but rather, because of the very strained relations which she had with her parents. These strained relations could be observed upon her first appearance in court, for her father refused to release her on bail pending the commencement of the trial. I had to persuade him to sign the bond of recognizance used in such instances.

During our conversation in court, which lasted for quite some time, tension between Orah and her parents mounted, and while I was trying to soften the aggressive outbreaks on both sides, Orah said: "You can see how my parents behave and how they react. It is their fault that I am here in court. They think that a girl who does not always stay at home is leading a loose life. They don't want to get used to habits in this country. Life here is different from what it was in Egypt. They refuse to accept this, and they lock themselves in their home and want me to do the same."

The father replied: "We give her all that we have, and she doesn't need to go to work. She meets all sorts of people whom we don't know, and we also don't know their parents. She is in the company of people strange to us, and this is a big shame on the honor of our family. We tell her that she has to keep to the traditions in our family, but she won't listen to us. We can't understand the behavior of children in this country. This cannot be good for Israel."

Here, I was confronted with a real crisis, which had been going on for some time, but which came to a head in court, the social institution which people regard as punitive. The girl and her father both expressed the intrafamily conflict as it was reflected by their respective positions. Both turned to the judge as an arbiter who should decide the issue. But the situation also indicated that the girl said what she said out of fear of punishment and that her father expected the court to punish the girl, after he had failed in his endeavors to change her behavior.

I have made the observation that the attitude which the court takes on a particular issue can be of great importance. If the court can be tolerant toward the misdeeds of children, many parents can then also "afford" to be tolerant. The negative impact which the court appearance might have had on parents is thus diminished, and this may, in turn, lead to a better intrafamily communication. In the instance just mentioned, I found it advisable to adjourn the case in order to ascertain whether or not a change in the behavior pattern of both parties could take place. I was quite convinced that this could be brought about—if at all—only by using the court setting as a mediating influence. I therefore introduced at this point the probation officer, asking him to keep in touch with this family to iron out existing conflicts. I adjourned the case three more times, each time having a full conversation in court with all parties concerned. I made use of this technique because time and again it has been my experience that the mere fact that the case is still undecided may induce the juvenile offender and his family to mobilize potential forces which will eventually change intrafamily conflicts and delinquent behavior patterns. Orah was put on probation so that the situation which was established in the court setting could be effectively continued outside it.

In Israel, great importance is attached to establishing in the juvenile court a rapport between the judge and the juvenile offender. In order to be able to do this, the court excludes the public from its sessions, and even excludes professionals who work in the field but have no knowledge of or relation to a certain case under consideration. In other words, probation officers, defense counsels, or social workers who are not concerned with a particular juvenile offender are not allowed to be present at his trial. The fewer people there are in the courtroom, the more likelihood there is of making direct contact with the offender, and consequently, making an impression on him.

This procedure conforms with the theory, also accepted in many other countries, that hearings in a juvenile court should be private and attendance permitted only to those who are immediately concerned with the case under consideration. An exception is made for representatives of the press, but they are strictly forbidden to publish anything which is likely to lead to the identification of a juvenile offender, and sanctions are provided against a person who acts in contravention of this provision. As the public is not allowed to attend sessions of the juvenile court and the press is practically conspicuous by it absence, a special responsibility rests with the judge, a moral obligation towards the individual concerned and society alike. We are very alert to the potential dangers of court hearings without the presence of the public, and we are therefore geared to safeguard elementary civil rights of juvenile offenders and their parents. To mention only a few of these safeguards, a parent is advised by the judge of the procedure for appeal; a probation officer or other qualified person is sometimes requested by the court to help the parent in filing the appeal; if the proof brought forward to sustain a charge against a juvenile offender is insufficient, he will always be acquitted; if it transpires during the trial that a juvenile offender or his parents have grudges against the behavior of a policeman who was involved in the case under consideration, the judge will make an appropriate decision in order to find out what the real facts were; and so on.

Thus, usually not more than four or five people are present during a hearing, the prosecuting officer (who, incidentally, does not appear in uniform), one or two probation officers, and the juvenile offender with his parents or other relative. An endeavor is made to rid the courtroom atmosphere of forensic severity, while at the same time maintaining a formal environment. The offender always stands up when he addresses the court, and the same applies to parents and probation officers. Otherwise, the offender sits on a bench in front of the judge, his parents sitting behind him. The distance between the judge and the juvenile offender is not more than thirteen to sixteen feet. This proximity is an important factor, because it is one of many aspects which enables the judge to make direct contact with the offender.

The juvenile offender is often tense and anxious, although he may show an indifferent or nonchalant attitude. Such an attitude can quite easily be penetrated by the use of interviewing techniques, for basically the juvenile offender is afraid of the punishment a judge can levy on him. It would be inappropriate, however, were the judge to make use of his impressions before knowing details of the background of the juvenile. This information is supplied by the probation officer, who submits his report in writing after the plea of guilt.

Another important procedure is our practice that the judge himself commences the proceedings in court by explaining to the juvenile offender, in simple words, what the charge sheet contains. In doing this it is not so important to mention the relevant paragraph as to explain the meaning of the paragraph. Usually, the juvenile offender or his parents have no knowledge of or interest in a particular paragraph of a law. But when that paragraph is translated into simple language which he can understand, the offense then takes on a different meaning. In other words, the procedure whereby the prosecuting officer or the clerk of the court read out what the charge sheet contains has been abolished, because it had no real meaning for the juvenile offender who could not comprehend its contents, and because it interfered from the beginning with the establishment of an appropriate atmosphere in the courtroom.

The juvenile offender is encouraged to tell his own version of what happened and why he has been brought to trial. In this way he is given to understand that the court is not prejudiced against him and is not told from the outset that "you have done such and such." The great majority of juvenile offenders in Israel give an accurate account of the circumstances involved, often relating their story in great detail. Approximately 90 percent of all juvenile offenders who were charged in the juvenile court in Israel over the last twenty years admitted that they had committed the offense which was held against them. This includes those instances in which the charge was altered to a lighter one in view of what the juvenile offender said. In most cases the prosecuting officer agreed to such a change. If he does not, then evidence will be heard.

At this point, we must consider the matter of self-incrimination. This is certainly of real importance if looked at from a purely legal point of view. But here we come across one of the differences between a juvenile court and a court for adults. If the judge in the juvenile court is alert to the possibility of self-incrimination, no harm can ensue from the offender's giving hos own account. One must recognize and appreciate a basic factor, namely, that many a juvenile has a *need* to tell the court of what he has done. This can be considered a part of the need for reparation, which one can observe with many juvenile offenders. It would be absolutely out of order not to yield to such a desire, which is not a technical matter so far as the juvenile is concerned.

It is for this very reason that many juvenile offenders not only tell the police freely about the offenses of which they have been suspected, but also add those offenses for which they are not being questioned and of which the police have no knowledge, because no complaint was lodged. Often, the police make inquiries, as a result of the information supplied by the juvenile offender, as to whether or not such an offense was indeed committed, and in our experience, the police have very seldom been led astray. This is why police figures on discovering offenses and stolen goods among juveniles are considerably higher than those among adults.

These are the circumstances which prevail if a juvenile offender tells in court what happened in regard to the offense he has committed. To prevent a juvenile offender from giving freely his account is inconceivable and is certainly not in the interest of the offender himself. Nevertheless, if the judge has the impression that self-incrimination might be involved, it is his duty to ensure that the prosecution has to put forward evidence; if such is not forthcoming, the juvenile offender has to be acquitted.

The Knesset made the following provisions for testimony and statements by defendants in Section 145 of the new Criminal Procedure Law of 1965:

(a) The accused may
   1) testify as a witness for the defense, in which case he may be cross-examined; or
   2) make a statement, in which case he shall not be examined; or
   3) refrain both from testifying and making a statement.
(b) An accused person who elects to testify or to make a statement shall do so at the commencement of the evidence of the defense, provided that the

court may, on his application, permit him to do so at another stage of the case for the defense.[4]

This section applies to juvenile as well as to adult offenders and is an important safeguard against any misuse of basic civil rights. Last but not least, the protection of civil rights, which has recently been a matter of considerable concern, is again dependent on the qualifications of a judge who is serving in a juvenile court.

While the juvenile offender is relating his story, I make a point of not interrupting him, even if he is digressing and not telling directly about the offense. For many a juvenile offender it is a relieving experience of no little importance to be allowed to tell his own version in court in his own way. A fourteen-year-old boy, relating to me that he was tempted to steal at a swimming pool, finished his story by saying: "When I came home my father felt that something was wrong with me, but he just looked at me and said nothing. I was ashamed and told my father what I had done. After that we went together to the synagogue, and we prayed all day." A girl aged sixteen said, while recounting how she had stolen from a girl friend: "When I received notice to come to court, I had been fasting all day, but I was ashamed to tell my parents the reason for it." Such announcements indicate genuine repentance and a wish to make good. It can safely be assumed that in these and similar instances the court appearance made an important impact on the offender. In these two cases, punishment no longer seemed necessary.

Only at the conclusion of the juvenile offender's account is the prosecuting officer requested to add any facts or circumstances which seem relevant to the understanding of the case or which the offender omitted on purpose. When the juvenile offender denies the charge against him, or if the court decides that there is some doubt whether the juvenile offender has committed the offense, procedure commences in accordance with existing laws and rules pertaining to matters of evidence. As in any other criminal court, the onus of proof rests on the prosecuting authorities, and any doubt as to such proof will automatically lead to an acquittal.

The rule of Israeli law that the judge must record in writing the reasons for his judgment and sentence applies to the juvenile judge as well. He must therefore record whether the juvenile offender has admitted or denied the charge brought against him. In cases of denial, he must record whether, after having heard the evidence, he is convinced that insufficient

---

[4] Ibid., p. 176.

proof has been adduced to support the charge and his reasons for such a finding, or whether he is convinced that the offense was committed by the accused, and, if so, what his reasons were for such a finding. He must also record in the file the reasons for the sentence or disposal he imposes. The statement of his reasons for having chosen a particular way need not be a lengthy one.

CONCLUSION

Every society vests an enormous amount of power in its juvenile courts (or in its substitutes in the Scandinavian countries), but no society has made legal provisions for specialized training for those in charge of these courts. Juvenile courts are given the power to make such binding decisions as limiting parents' exercise of coercion over their own children, sending children and young people away from their homes, or imposing various conditions on parents and children, whether within their own home or removed to another place by court order. Sometimes such power is vested in order to protect children; sometimes it is done in order to protect a parent; at other times it may be necessary to restrain children and young people who are in need of care and protection, or who break the law and may become dangerous to society. The arbitrary use of power exists particularly in a juvenile court for two major reasons. In the first place, the juvenile court or its substitute is usually not open to the public, and only in rare instances is a defending counsel present. The press is also infrequently represented. In other words, there is no public control over decisions made there. Secondly, lack of professional knowledge among those in charge in juvenile courts enhances the danger of arbitrary use of power. In many instances, decisions are based mainly on impressions, on preconceived ideas of what is right or wrong, and on prejudice.

This legal investment of power is not fundamentally different whether young people are brought before a juvenile court for protection or whether they are charged with a criminal offense. It is also not important what name we give to such an agency. Some would prefer to call the juvenile court a family court, or a domestic relations court, or a child welfare board, in the belief that if one alters the name of such an agency, one has also altered its nature. Obviously, this is not the case. On the contrary, to change the name of an agency without changing its basic conceptions and requirements profoundly may have a detrimental effect. It is unfortunately a fact that presently there is no legislation in any country requiring special training for a judge prior to his appointment in a juvenile court or in its substitute. To my great regret, this applies to Israel as well.

The twentieth century, which is often also labeled the child's century, has witnessed a deepening understanding of the behavioral problems of children and young people. Because of the gains in understanding by child psychiatrists, child psychologists, and child therapists, many young people can be helped, which, in turn, is of advantage to society at large. It is my contention that adjudication of juveniles must not be confined to an appropriate application of law. There is no valid reason why a judge in a juvenile court should not be given special training to qualify him to serve in such a setting. For that purpose such a judge should be professionally trained in jurisdiction and in social sciences, particularly in those social sciences concerned with understanding the dynamics of human behavior and with the application of interviewing techniques. This should be part of university training. Indeed, a combination of various disciplines is essential for such training. The juvenile court will then be in a position to make a more vital contribution to curing as well as to prevention.

THE PARENT AND THE COURT

Why is it a sine qua non that parents be present in court when their child is being tried? The answer to this question may be quite different from place to place, but one can distinguish three major schools of thought. Some believe that parents are to be held responsible if their child goes astray and if the court levies some sort of punishment on them they will henceforth act more responsibly towards their children. This approach also implies that parents deserve to be punished because their child has become a delinquent. Others place the emphasis not so much on punishing the parents as on the more formal consideration that a minor should not be tried without his parents being present. This outlook is more concerned with the parent's understanding that his very presence in court places the responsibility for his child on him, even without the implementation of punitive sanctions. The court is able to explain its attitude on the matter directly to the parent and can hear the parent's views on his child and the offense. A third view holds that the presence of the parent is important mainly for the sake of the child. When the child is confronted in court with the powerful machinery of the state, he may derive some security from the mere presence of his parents, even in instances where relations between child and parents are strained. In fact, it may well be that in such cases the parents' presence is especially meaningful to the child, for in spite of the differences between them, he is not being abandoned in an hour of need and while being confronted with what he believes is a punitive agency par excellence.

Whatever viewpoint one may adopt, there can be no doubt that the presence of parents in court is of major importance and entails many complicated aspects worth discussing and analyzing in great detail. Such an analysis cannot be undertaken in the context of this book. Suffice it to say that once one has penetrated the shell initially displayed by children and parents alike many aspects of the relationship between them begin to come to the surface in the courtroom.

In a society like Israel's, where changes in the functions of family members are constantly taking place, the authoritative setting of the juvenile court may be of particular importance. It is therefore my contention that the juvenile court in Israel must pay great attention to bridging disrupted parent-child relationships. A punitive attitude towards parents would in most instances be out of place. Most parents of juvenile offenders are deeply ashamed that they must appear in court because of their children's misdeeds. These parents are in need of advice and often in need of actual help in their endeavors to raise their children properly. Stressing punitive action or adopting a moralizing attitude cannot be of real assistance to them.

The following case may illustrate a situation which frequently arises in the juvenile court in Israel. Two boys aged twelve were charged with having stolen some scrap iron. Both appeared in court with their fathers and denied having committed the offense. While I was explaining to the boys that I would have to adjourn the case so that the prosecuting officer could bring evidence on the matter, one of the fathers interjected that the case might just as well be closed there and then, because his son had nothing to do with the whole matter. From a talk with the boys, however, I gained the impression that the charge did have some basis and that only the presence of their parents had prompted them to deny it.

Experience has taught me that in such cases it is always advisable to have evidence put before the court so that the facts can be known to all present. After an adjournment of two weeks, to summon the witnesses, the boys were again accompanied to court by their fathers. After two of the witnesses had given evidence, one of the boys volunteered to make a statement and admitted to the offense. Then I announced that we would hear two more witnesses in order to shed light on the role of the second boy. Upon hearing this, the youth became restless, lowered his head, and there followed a long period of complete silence. Then his father, who had previously insisted that the case be dropped, suddenly said, "I don't know what is going on here! It is impossible that my son is a thief." I suggested to the father that his son may just have been going along with other boys and was dragged into the affair by accident, without even being aware that he was an accomplice to a delinquent act. I added that under such circumstances I would not necessarily regard him as a thief either. The father approached me and said in a whisper, "You must understand I was a teacher to Jewish children in Persia for over thirty years. I taught them to lead an honest life and obey the commandments. And now, how is it possible that here in Israel my own son should become a thief? I cannot admit this. I keep an eye on him all day long; I don't allow him to play in the streets because I think it is no good for his upbringing. If he should really have committed this crime, I could not tolerate the shame he would bring upon my whole family."

The focus of the court session was now centered on the father, and his boy drifted into the background. I had to explain that I regarded the affair as a less serious matter than he did. The father found this difficult to comprehend. Only after he had regained his composure and the atmosphere in the courtroom was again relaxed, could the boy relate his own version of the offense, to his great relief. Yet he avoided looking at his father while telling the court how he had become involved in the matter.

It became imperative to help the boy regain acceptance within his family and to assist his father in accepting the reality of the situation. This seemed a suitable case for a probation officer to handle. It seemed necessary to meet the parents' needs, to allay existing anxieties, and to soften rigid attitudes, while helping the boy reorient himself. Therefore I placed the boy on probation; had it not been for the situation that had developed before me in court, I would not have found this necessary.

A somewhat paradoxical situation often develops when parents keep rigidly to traditional behavior patterns which are out of place in Israel. They may refuse to adopt new methods of education, lest their children go astray; but it is often just this rigid attitude which brings about maladjustment in their children and may lead to delinquency. Antisocial behavior is the child's way of acting out his social maladjustments and is often the only way to demonstrate his dissatisfaction and "punish" his parents.

This conflict between the traditional mores of the parents and the contemporary behavior patterns of Israel to which their children are exposed is frequently seen in cases of girls with sexual problems. An example is the case of Rachel.

Rachel was over sixteen when she was charged in court with infanticide. She confessed to the charge and told the probation officer how it happened. She had been under great stress for quite some time, fearing that her parents would discover that she was pregnant. She knew that if her state became known to her family, she would be killed by her father or her older brother.[5] She therefore made great efforts to remain at her factory job and used all sorts of tricks to conceal her growing abdomen. One day when no one was at home she felt severe pains and went to the bathroom. Suddenly she realized that she was giving birth. Confused and frightened she frantically began to help by pulling. The newborn infant fell to the floor, bumping his head and severing the umbilical cord. Rachel left the bathroom bewildered, and when she returned after half an hour, she discovered thet her child was dead. Her older sister, who came home at this point, informed the police.

Rachel was now confronted with two difficult situations. She was aware that there would be a court action; but more serious still, she was afraid of being killed by her father or brother. When the police came to arrest her, Rachel was relieved, for she was now certain of her life.

The child's father, a young laborer with whom Rachel worked, had been dating her for some time and had promised to marry her. He belonged to the same ethnic group as Rachel, and both knew that within this group it was not customary for boys and girls to meet socially. They therefore took great pain to meet secretly, and nobody knew of their relationship. But when Rachel became pregnant, he withdrew his promise to her. Rachel's parents now confronted the boy's family with the ultimatum that he marry her immediately, thus obliterating the shame brought on both families. Both families realized the urgency of the marriage to forestall the threat of murder.

But the boy refused to marry Rachel, and his family claimed that they were unable to exercise any influence upon him because he had already abandoned their traditional way of life and paid no heed to their attempts at persuasion.

Rachel's father now turned to the police and argued that, since the boy refused to marry his daughter, it was the duty of the authorities to force him. He reasoned that "the government is very powerful, and he would not dare to refuse, because he would then be regarded an outcast." All explanations that the "government" had no say in this matter were met with disbelief. In his despair, Rachel's father declared, "What happened to our family is a tragedy. It is worse than if one of us parents had died."

---

[5] The custom in such instances is that the girl is killed, not the man, because it is she who has dishonored the name of the family and of the entire clan. The social status of the family is reestablished by removing the offending member, as if she never existed. In certain circles, the father, brother, or other male member of the family who kills a girl who became pregnant out of wedlock gains in social prestige.

Neither the father nor any other member of the family mentioned a word of sympathy for Rachel. They did not visit her during the time she was detained awaiting trial. The family's thoughts were concentrated on one aspect alone: how the honor of the family could be reestablished.

The court ordered Rachel to an educational establishment for a period of three years. Her behavior there was very satisfactory, for she was neither wayward nor disturbed. But she could not reconcile herself to the fact that she had been ordered to an institution where the great majority of girls were sexual delinquents. She was maltreated by the other girls, perhaps because she made a point of stressing that she was different from them. Worse still, the fact that her family continued to reject her worried her greatly.

In Rachel's case it took more than a year and a half of continuous efforts on the part of the staff of the educational establishment to change her family's attitude. They very slowly accepted the reality of the situation and agreed to visit Rachel occasionally, and finally, to accept her home again. A follow-up visit after three years revealed that Rachel had married, but relations with her parents remained strained, although they did not reject Rachel when she visited them.

Rachel's father took an approach that is characteristic in similar instances. When he realized his inability to convince the young man to marry his daughter, he turned to the government as the agency of last resort. He viewed the government as being omnipotent, and therefore possessing the means to force marriage upon the young man. His expression of deep disappointment upon realizing that this was not the case included a revelation of a major upheaval in his social environment: "This is a new world, but parents have no influence on their children. In the village where we were brought up, such a thing could never have happened."

Herein lies the source of the conflict. Almost all Oriental Jewish families in Israel originated in Moslem countries, where for centuries taboos concerning social contact between the sexes have been strictly implemented, and there has not been much opportunity for relations between the sexes, social or otherwise. Temptations are therefore easy to control.

For people accustomed to this way of life, however, difficulties arise when social contact between the sexes is permitted as something quite natural, as is the case in Israel. Under such circumstances, not only are temptations more difficult to control, but there is a tendency to believe that they should not be controlled at all. Many believe that biological needs seeking an outlet should not be suppressed by traditional habits and customs. Among Oriental (and strictly religious non-Oriental) Jews, pre- and extramarital sexual relations invariably lead to a disruption of family harmony because they challenge deep-rooted conceptions and values. Such a situation is highly charged with emotion and therefore not open to rational discussion.

The custom of child marriage most probably has its roots in this atmosphere. In many places the world over, it is customary to marry off children at a young age, even before the onset of puberty; with the first signs of puberty these children begin to lead a family life regulated by existing traditions and customs. Child marriage was frequently found among both Jews and non-Jews of this region. In court, mothers often cite the decline of child marriage as an explanation for their inability to exercise proper control over their daughters.

The case of Varda is another instance of the parent-child conflicts resulting from the breakdown of traditional sexual mores. Varda was fourteen years old when she was charged in juvenile court with soliciting. She confessed to the charge and related that for some time she had been meeting with friends outside her family circle. As time passed, Varda returned home later and later, until one night she found the door locked to her. Her mother refused to let her in. All the family members were astounded by the mother's reaction because she was especially permissive towards Varda.

The probation officer in charge of Varda was unable to reconcile her parents with her. The mother threatened to murder Varda should she dare return home. All the efforts made by the probation officer to help Varda were in vain, and neither a lenient nor a firm approach by the court proved to be of help.

Until the age of thirteen, Varda had behaved in an exemplary manner, and her parents loved her. What happened to change this pattern and cause her to become a prostitute at the age of fourteen? All attempts to find an explanation were of no avail. Psychological examinations revealed neither traumatic experiences nor a low level of intelligence nor indifference. On the contrary, Varda had a rather high I.Q., and during our conversation in the juvenile court she verbalized the negative aspects of her present condition and what the future held in store for her. There was, however, one very stormy session in the juvenile court, in which Varda's parents attacked the prevailing modes of behavior in their new environment and the impotence of its institutions. Her father told me that as far as he was concerned, he had done everything in his power to deal with the situation. As an example of his efforts he cited the following move. When Varda began to misbehave, he shaved off her hair so that she would be ashamed to go out and would therefore break off with her undesirable contacts. In fact, this is a rather common mode of reaction among Oriental Jews. One or more of the following reasons account for the belief in the success of this method. If a girl's hair is shaved off, her attractiveness will disappear; she will stay at home out of shame of being seen in public; a shock reaction may ensue, and then her behavior will begin to improve; it is a warning that murder may follow if the girl's behavior does not improve; during the time the girl stays at home, parents and other members of the family will demonstrate a liberal amount of permissiveness, and at the same time reject outbursts and threats; isolation for a few weeks, and sometimes for a few months, may result in breaking up undesirable contacts. When I told Varda's father that I had known many fathers who reacted in the same way but not in one instance with the result hoped for, he was visibly upset and left the courtroom without saying a word.

In another instance, the conflict of a girl aged fifteen and a half came to my notice when she mentioned the following during a long conversation between us in court: "My mother knows about my state of affairs, and by now she has also recognized the fact that I am pregnant. But I take great pains to hide my condition from my father because it would shame him. He was always kind to me, and I couldn't bear to do this to him." I have frequently observed that parents had some inkling about their daughters' disorderly behavior, but they do not know how to react or how to cope with the problem. They often fear that if they react as they would like to, the girl will simply disappear. There is always some irrational hope that the disorderly behavior will simply stop of its own accord. There are also many parents who are ashamed to turn to a social welfare agency for help, sometimes because of the possible negative reflection upon themselves. It is only when neighbors begin to talk freely about the problem that they find the courage to seek professional help. By then, however, it is very often too late to help their child.

Often parents with problem girls will agree to marry off their daughters, even knowing that marriage would be to her disadvantage, or that she will continue to lead a disorderly life, after marriage. The marriage, however, restores the social status of the family. Furthermore, the parents are relieved of their responsibility for her behavior, for it is now her husband's duty to look after her. By the mere fact of the girl's being married and having children of her own, they are certain that she will settle down. This is frequently mere wishful thinking, but parents nonetheless cling to this notion as a last resort.

The juvenile court as an institution can play a certain role in allaying anxieties and fears, and it can thus make a contribution to both the cure and prevention of juvenile delinquency. In court I try to involve parents in the courtroom activities and thereby establish a triangular relationship. The setting often provides an opportunity to hold a kind of public interview. I have, for instance, observed that when the court displayed tolerance toward the delinquent acts of a juvenile offender, parents found it possible to do the same, resulting in the improvement in the parent-child relationship. In a parent's view, if the court, which is the punitive authority, can be tolerant toward the misdeeds of his child, he can also afford to be so. The court's stance also implies that he was neglectful in his duties. The development of this attitude is often an unconscious process which begins in the courtroom and continues beyond it. One must recognize that the appearance in court may have a number of effects on both parent and child which are not directly measurable in their subsequent behavior. A judge in a juvenile court must be especially sensitive to the various expressions of family problems that become exposed in court, evaluate them, and deal with them accordingly in seeking the proper road to rehabilitation. In cases in which parents promise, on their behalf and on behalf of their child, that no further delinquent activity will take place, the court can afford to be lenient. This may be more than just a meaningless promise. In some cases a parent may claim that he has already punished his child for his offense, implying that there is no need for further punishment from the court. Although such announcements are often made because of the situation of stress or crisis in the courtroom, the very fact that such statements are made may be meaningful for child and parent alike.

In the juvenile court, apart from such general problems, one sometimes encounters misgivings on the part of parents because language difficulties prevent their following the proceedings or taking an active part in the conversation between the judge, the prosecutor, and the offender. When this is the case, the parent becomes an important onlooker, whereas in fact we are interested in his being an active participant so that he may fulfill his responsibilities as a parent. Apart from this, a parent may feel that he is not given adequate opportunity to voice his own opinions as to what has happened to his child. He may have something to say on why his child became involved in the offense that brought him before the juvenile court, regardless of whether or not the child is guilty.

A case in point was Tamar, a girl of fourteen. Tamar had stolen something from a classmate, and as a result, was put on probation for a period of two years. After six months had elapsed, the probation officer asked me to reconsider the case because of difficulties which had arisen between the girl and her mother and because the girl refused to continue attending school. The officer added that the mother was uncooperative, and asked me to try to secure her cooperation.

While I was discussing her problems with Tamar, I observed that the mother was following our talk, but with an air of aloofness. I tried several times to involve her in our conversation, but apart from single-word responses, not much was forthcoming. From the probation officer's report I knew that the family had come from Algeria, and I suddenly turned to the mother and asked her in French what suggestions she could make concerning her daughter. She immediately became alert and explained her point of view on the matter. It was obvious that it meant a great deal to her to be able to talk with me in her native language. Following our conversation and the mother's outpouring of fears and anxieties, it was possible to plan the rehabilitation of Tamar with more cooperation from her mother.

Parents often request to talk to me alone and ask me to remove their children from the courtroom for a while. This always takes place before sentence is passed—that is, after the probation officer has submitted his report. Only in rare instances do I agree to such a request, for I believe it imperative that a child be present when his parent talks to the judge about him. If the parent wants to cite the child's positive characteristics, but thinks he should not be present lest he become spoiled, I believe it is just as well that the child witness his parents' standing up for him and asking for a lenient attitude. I seriously doubt that this will have a damaging effect on him. On the other hand, if the parent wishes to relate the child's negative aspects to the court, the child's presence is equally imperative. I would assume that these negative aspects have previously been discussed in front of the child with relatives, friends, and neighbors. Such discussions were meant to impress the child and motivate him to change his behavior for the better. In court, however, the child cannot remain indifferent. And were these matters to be discussed in his absence, he might feel that they had swayed the judge's decision on his punishment. He would then completely identify the rejecting parent and the judge as two forces that had joined to punish him, and it can safely be assumed that in such a situation a juvenile offender would pay no heed to the court's warnings or be impressed by the fairness of the punishment decided upon. On the contrary, he might be prompted to commit further offenses.

In the triangular relationship between judge, parent, and offender, matters concerning and intended for the offender are sometimes addressed to the parent. In a way, this indirect approach often produces better results than the direct one. I have observed that the juvenile offender is often preoccupied and absentminded in court. This may be due to a wish to appear defiant, fear of punishment, feelings of revenge, or shame and remorse. The judge may therefore feel it necessary to use a very direct technique, employing language as simple and penetrating as possible. But my experience shows that, in the punitive setting which the court symbolizes, an outspokenly moralizing or paternalistic attitude towards the juvenile offender usually fails to achieve the desired effect. The offender has usually had his fill of such an approach outside the court and if a judge employs the same or a similar method, he will be ignored because of tone.

I therefore often make use of a different technique, namely, informing the parent of the various situations which may arise for his child should delinquent behavior continue. In most cases parents are responsive to such an approach and take the matter very seriously. Moreover, I have observed that the juvenile offender becomes very attentive to the discussion taking place in his presence between the judge and his parent. In many instances, such an approach has a greater impact on the juvenile offender, because the issue is of genuine concern to him and is not another instance of the moralizing with which he has become bored. One is not always able to judge the ultimate effect of such an approach. It may, for example, be very important for the juvenile offender to recognize that the judge is taking pains to discuss with his parents problems that may trouble him as well. It may also be important for him to realize that the judge is listening very carefully to his parents' grievances.

Sometimes I am confronted by aggressive parents who cite instances of injustice perpetrated against themselves—whether by an employer, a landlord, the police, city officials, etc.—and who seem to imply that these wrongs are really to blame for the fact that the child became delinquent. Others indicate that, since they have been the victims of such unfairness and injustice, they are not concerned that their child has trespassed against the law. Listening attentively to what parents have to say in court and trying to involve them in what is going on there also meets their personal need to relate their difficulties and problems to an authoritative agency and frequently results in a more relaxed attitude and a greater amount of cooperation from them.

Another facet of parent-child relationships can be observed in a different area. Some parents demand that their child be placed in an educational establishment because they are unable to control his behavior. Others do not initiate this move but accept it quite gladly because they feel it is the lesser evil. Still others fervently object to such an order.

Although they agree that their child is beyond their control, they express anxiety about the consequences for their own social status. The attitude of parents to the replacement order per se, and more specifically to a particular educational establishment, often affects their child's adjustment there. Children have an infallible sense about their parents' attitudes in such situations. Accordingly, some will repeatedly escape from the institution or write home and promise good behavior, or make their parents visit them often, and so forth. They find numerous ways to manipulate their parents and demonstrate the seriousness of their repentance and desire to be home again. For many children being sent away from home is a most important lesson, and afterward some of them are better able to adjust. On the other hand, it is astonishing how often parents forget what it was like when their child lived at home. Overt or concealed guilt feelings prompt them to yield to their child's manipulations. A situation comes into being whereby the child develops an unrealistic image of his home once he has been moved to an educational establishment, and the parents overlook their child's difficulties once he is no longer at home. It is no paradox that it is this very combination that may often ultimately lead to a better, healthier parent-child relationship.

Until very recently, there was scant provision for the presence of parents during the trial of their child. Section 10 of the Juvenile Offenders Ordinance of 1937 stated: "When a child or young person is charged with any offense, the court may, at its discretion, require the attendance of his parent or guardian and may make such orders as are necessary for the purpose." Although this ordinance was deleted as of 23 August 1971, the section in the new law dealing with the presence of parents in court remained practically the same, namely, the requirement of their presence is left at the discretion of the court.[6] This new law prescribes that a parent has to be informed by the court when the trial is to commence and that he must be informed of the contents of the charge against his child, but there is no legal provision making it mandatory for a parent or guardian to be present in court. Only when a parent or guardian does not respond to a court summons to be present at the trial may an order of arrest be issued, and it is only in this way that a parent can be compelled to be present at his child's trial.

There is, however, another provision in the Youth Law of 1971, which is innovative. Section 11 states that the police should inform the parent

[6] Youth Law (Trial, Punitive Methods, and Treatment Measures), 5731–1971, in *Laws of the State of Israel* (n.p.).

of a child, or another close person, that he has been apprehended. If there is reason to believe that informing the parent or guardian may have detrimental results for the child concerned, a probation officer should be informed instead. The intent is to safeguard the welfare of the child, who may come to harm by the spontaneous reaction of a parent. Yet there is no legal provision that a parent should be present when his child's statement is taken down at the police station. The taking of the child's statement may be of far-reaching consequences to him, and at this crucial stage he should at least have his parent, guardian, or other relative present. This is not merely a technicality, but rather, a matter of safeguarding the basic civil rights of children and juveniles. Such rights must be laid down in the law proper.

There is a widespread opinion that parents encourage their children not to tell the truth to the police or the court, and that it is therefore advisable to have them remain in the background when the police are taking the statement of the child concerning the offense. Those who hold this view would agree, however, that after the statement has been taken, a parent or guardian should be allowed to be present. Others maintain that juveniles will most probably be afraid to tell the truth in the presence of their parents, and that it is therefore in the child's interest that parents should not be fully informed about the circumstances of the offense. Obviously, there is a certain amount of truth in these views. But I believe that the proficiency of the police interrogator and his attitude toward parents whose children have broken the law is more influential in these cases than a parent's willful intention that his child withhold the truth.

It is also my impression that in their work with juvenile offenders, the police are hampered by their own preconceptions and rigid attitudes. Their behavior and attitudes toward criminals are severely stereotyped, and practically no distinction is made between a juvenile offender and a criminal. Such an approach is no doubt expedient for the police; yet the absence of an individualized approach toward juveniles is to be regretted. It is my firm belief that much can be accomplished by more flexible police techniques without endangering efficiency or security.

If one is genuinely trying to achieve justice it is most important to enlist the cooperation of parents and other relatives. Parental cooperation is also of vital importance if a genuine effort is to be made to rehabilitate juvenile offenders. All too often, only lip-service is paid to these ideas. But they are a challenge for fresh thinking and for the development of a more dynamic approach which, in the end, will benefit children, parents, and society.

7

Therapeutic
Use of the
Court Setting

In a juvenile court one is repeatedly confronted with the difficult question of what to do with a juvenile offender, that is, what kind of measure or treatment one should apply. In most instances this is the most crucial question with which the juvenile court is faced and is a matter of paramount importance, because it may have far-reaching consequences for juvenile offenders and their parents alike.

In countries such as Israel where the English common law system is applied, the procedure in the juvenile criminal court is regulated according to the principles applied in a criminal court. In any criminal procedure, including that of a juvenile court, three major objectives are regarded as basic requirements: a court has to ascertain the facts of each case; following this, the law has to be applied in accordance with these facts; and the court has to determine the method of treatment in each instance. Although the first two objectives are of a purely judicial nature, in which law and procedure must be strictly adhered to, the third objective —what to do in each individual case—is not confined to rigid rules. Whereas the first two objectives are statutory, the third one needs a flexible approach toward individual offenders. Naturally, this has to be done within the legal framework of any given society. The important point to remember, however, is that the third objective is the most difficult task in the work of any juvenile court. Accordingly, the court is empowered with rather a great amount of leeway in deciding which measure seems indicated as a general deterrent to juvenile delinquency or which seems desirable for the treatment and rehabilitation of individual juvenile offenders. It is perhaps for this reason that the juvenile court is regarded as being more "offender-minded" than "offense-minded."

The juvenile court is in an exposed position while dealing with juvenile offenders. It has to deal with minors who have committed an offense against a law, and it is therefore the duty of that court to take action to ensure that further offenses by the same juvenile will not be committed again. At the same time the court is also concerned to ensure that other minors do not commit offenses. Here, one must consider whether or not a particular sentence is apt to function as a deterrent. As one is dealing in these instances with persons who are still in the process of growing—both mentally and physically—and who have not yet reached maturity, the juvenile court, more so than any other court, is obliged to consider and to take into account many aspects related primarily to the offender rather than to the offense.

The juvenile offender is not an entity by himself because of the mere fact that he is a child or young person dependent on others and is likely to be easily influenced. One has to consider parents, siblings, friends, school, jobs, and conditions of environment and neighborhood. These may give us some clue to understanding the motivation behind the offense. Furthermore, when we come to consider what to do with the juvenile offender, we again have to take into account some or all of these factors, because since the juvenile offender is not an entity in himself, there can seldom be a process of readaptation or rehabilitation if these factors are disregarded. Whatever the reason determining the behavior of the juvenile offender, whether the result of environmental or of emotional factors, or both, the juvenile court cannot but pay attention to them in its endeavor to do justice—both to the individual concerned and to society at large.

THE JUVENILE AND THE COURT

Most juvenile courts today employ procedures established soon after the First World War which have not changed significantly in the last forty years or so; nevertheless, we continue to congratulate ourselves on our progressive approach in the treatment of young delinquents. This applies both to countries where Anglo-Saxon laws and procedures prevail and to the Scandinavian countries, whose approach is very different. Yet close inspection may suggest that the juvenile court has reached a blind alley and is failing to develop its potential contribution to the treatment of juvenile delinquents. The juvenile court has for the most part remained aloof from recent advances in the understanding of behavior difficulties and problems in interpersonal relations, and has thus failed to profit by them. The authoritative character of the court makes it naturally less elastic than other social agencies in introducing and applying new and improved techniques.

Even those who deny that the juvenile court is properly to be regarded as a child welfare agency should consider whether the treatment of young offenders could not be made more effective in the light of recent discoveries of the dynamics involved in the treatment of behavior disorders.

I myself regard the juvenile court as a child welfare agency with its own special nature and limitations. Yet the function is the rehabilitation and social care of juvenile offenders and of children who are in need of care and supervision, that is, cases of neglect. In my opinion the personal appearance of a young offender before a juvenile court may have considerable value. The court is a social institution of strictly limited scope and purpose, which must as a rule make its impact on the offender in the course of two brief contacts, at hearing and at disposal. The technical problem, therefore, is to make the maximum use of the potentialities and limitations of this institution for the purpose of promoting or initiating change in delinquent attitudes and behavior patterns. The situation, in which the offender is compelled to give an account of himself and his actions to a court as the representative of the community, has a powerful influence for good or ill, according to the skill with which it is managed. In my view, this skill is of a professional order and requires specialized study and training.

In passing, it should be mentioned that we must beware of using such words as "liberal" or "progressive" in this connection. There is too sentimental an attitude in this area. But in sentimentality there is repressed or unconscious resentment, and this may turn out to be unhealthy. There can be no doubt that lawlessness and crime produce strong public reactions and feeling, usually of the *lex talionis* kind. The court is the channel through which these public feelings are directed and from which some kind of gratification is expected. This factor fulfills unconsciously or even consciously a definite function and public need. Thus the juvenile court is expected to individualize in helping the offender in his rehabilitation, and simultaneously, to satisfy a public need for punishment because of his acting unlawfully. These two aspects are not always compatible, and on this issue many conflicts may arise. Our discussion, however, is not centered on severe or less severe punitive actions taken by a court. It is taken for granted that those empowered with jurisdiction over juvenile delinquents have the rehabilitation of the young offenders at heart and do not think in terms of corporal punishment or other disciplinary measures as the best—or most lasting— solution. We should, of course, not underestimate the strong sentiment in regard to juvenile offenders, which may bring feelings of revenge into the open in disguised forms. This explains why there is, from time to time, something like a public outcry demanding the introduction of more severe disciplinary measures in the treatment of juvenile offenders.

It is important for the judge to be aware of the irrational and unconscious pressures in the community which are directed toward him. Such elements exist on both sides of the perennial controversy concerning rehabilitation versus retribution. The liberal or progressive camp often presents a sentimental picture of the delinquent as being purely the victim of society, or of his parents, which expresses underlying attitudes of identification with him, of protective paternalism, and of rescue and championship against an unjust world. On the other hand, lawlessness and crime provoke in a large sector of the community a strong demand for retribution, which is basically desired for the relief of the community's emotional tension, irrespective of its efficacy in reforming the offender. If these sentiments are allowed to play too strong a role in legal reforms, violent swings of the pendulum are likely to occur. It is necessary for the judge to withstand all these pressures, and to conduct his interviews in court and make his disposals as purely as possible with regard to the rehabilitation of the offender.

The offender also has his guilt feelings and his expectations of punishment as the appropriate solution, and will bring to his trial a good deal of anxiety. Even many recidivists and hardened offenders have much more anxiety than they are prepared to reveal. The progressive school of thought holds that everything should be done to reduce the offender's guilt feelings, which are likely to be detrimental to him, and that the judge should adopt a mild and permissive attitude such as may be appropriate in psychotherapy. Further reflection upon and knowledge of the psychology of delinquency suggests, however, that for a judge to attend to the delinquent's troubles and needs and to overlook the fact that he has committed an offense is likely not only to enrage considerable sections of the public, but also to increase rather than diminish the delinquent's guilt and anxiety. Kindness alone will not help the delinquent; sympathy and understanding must be mingled with a serious regard for truth, a concern for right and wrong, and an attempt to increase the offender's insight into himself.

A case in point is Shimon, a tall, well-built lad of sixteen who appeared before me on a charge of housebreaking. He had done well on intelligence tests and was well read and knowledgeable; he was also pleasant in appearance, though somewhat nonchalant in manner. Some months previously he had joined a youth group undergoing agricultural training in a kibbutz. He had obtained leave of absence for his court appearance, but without divulging the reason. He admitted the housebreaking, but said he had stolen only part of the articles mentioned in the charge sheet. He explained that he had demanded a raise of salary which was, to his mind, due to him. When he was refused the increase, he decided to steal some of the tools of the workshop where he was employed. He could see nothing wrong in it. He told his story in a very self-assured manner and appeared to be entirely free from anxiety and unconcerned with having committed an offense. It seemed that he was probably counting on receiving lenient treatment because of his membership in the kibbutz training group.

For about twenty minutes, I was unable to penetrate his indifference. He tried to justify or excuse his breaking into the workshop and made little attempt to convince me that such a thing would not happen again. Eventually, I asked him whether he remembered having appeared before the same court on a serious charge two years previously. He was taken aback and reluctantly admitted it, adding that he had been much younger then. I remarked that he was older now; he hung his head for a moment, but quickly recovered. He seemed unable to recall what had been decided on that occasion, but under pressure he recalled that he had been put on probation. He had completely "forgotten" his signing of a probation order and the discussion with me which had preceded this. He announced triumphantly that he had successfully completed his probation long ago, but I reminded him that the order was still valid for another two months, and here he was in court again. He seemed quite surprised at my insistence and showed a great deal of resentment at this revival of long-forgotten things. He now realized, however, that he was not going to "get away with it" and became rather uneasy. I again explained the seriousness of the charge, for which one possible punishment was a prison sentence. He then came to life and pleaded to be allowed to remain with his training group. I made him struggle for this and made no final disposal, adjourning the case until a later date and leaving him meanwhile with his group. His attitude on leaving the court was considerably more serious than on arrival; he realized that amendment and not excuses were required if he were not to lose something he valued.

In this case I considered it necessary to arouse anxiety in the boy, in order to induce him to take responsibility for his actions. Until this point he had always been able to evade the issue, and probation had not altered this attitude. He was well aware of his charm and accustomed to exploiting it. This appeared to be the first time he had been forced to give an account of his deeds, and he was surprised to find the judge firmer and less sympathetic than on his first appearance (though not condemning nor moralizing). By providing this new experience, I found it possible to penetrate to some extent his defenses.

It is regarded as a sine qua non that court procedure should be efficient. There should not be a long span of time between the apprehension of the offender and his hearing in court. Once guilt is established, sentence should be pronounced without delay. All this is in the interest of justice. I have my doubts, however, whether in the juvenile court this should always be the case once the point of sentencing has been reached. In relation to juvenile offenders, it may be in the interest of the offender's rehabilitation to delay pronouncement of the sentence. Sometimes, when a case is thus adjourned, a process of change may start in the juvenile offender, initiated by the court and continued outside it, with remarkable results. It is also frequently necessary to map out a plan for rehabilitation, in which case, time is needed for implementation and consolidation.

Frequently, one is confronted with an offender who has been a truant from school or who is loitering about doing nothing. When charged in court with having committed an offense, the offender will usually maintain that he has returned to school or has started to work. Such statements are always made to imply that those problems which may have existed are now under control and that the court can therefore be lenient. To accept such statements on face value would in many instances amount to fostering delinquent behavior patterns. Yet the mere fact that the offender found it necessary to act before coming to his trial may be indicative of a genuine desire to make good. In order that we may find out whether this is manipulative behavior or a genuine intention, an adjournment may be a helpful measure. The mere fact that the trial is still undecided may force the offender, even against his previous intention, to continue in the manner which he explained to the judge. He is, as it were, rallying potential forces which should save him from punishment. A juvenile court cannot but take such a situation into account and make appropriate use of it. When the Juvenile Offenders Ordinance of 1937 was enforced, it allowed for such a procedure.

Section 8(7) of the ordinance made provision for an adjournment, stating, in part,

Before deciding how to deal with [the juvenile offender], the court shall obtain such information as to his or her general conduct, home surroundings, school record, and medical history as may enable it to deal with the case in the best interests of the offender, and may put to him or her any question arising out of such information. For the purpose of obtaining such information or for special medical examination or observation, the court may from time to time remand the offender on bail or to a place of detention.

The major point in this section, in terms of my argument here, is that it is not at all necessary to bring the offender to a place of detention, nor is it essential to bring the trial to an end then and there, but it is legally possible to remand the offender on bail, so that the court can obtain information "as may enable it to deal with the case in the best interests of the offender." There can be no doubt that this provision of the law is meant to enable the judge to use his discretion.

The new Youth Law of 1971 does not mention specifically that the court may adjourn a case from time to time. Regrettably, there is also no mention that the court may do so if this should be in the best interest of the juvenile offender. Yet it is apparently still possible to adjourn a case at the court's discretion, provided that the juvenile offender is put temporarily under the supervision of a probation officer, pending final disposition by the court (Section 20 [a][2]).

In recent years, our Supreme Court has followed a similar line when an appeal is lodged by a juvenile offender on the ground that he was given too heavy a prison sentence. These are instances in which the juvenile offender had previously been sent to an educational establishment, but had absconded constantly and committed further offenses—hence, the prison sentence. Because of the serious delinquent behavior in these cases, the Supreme Court is often hesitant to interfere in the decisions of the lower courts. An interim decision is therefore often made, according to which the juvenile offender is provisionally released from the youth prison for a period of two, three, or six months, and again ordered to stay in one of the educational establishments. The Supreme Court usually stipulates that after this period the case will be reviewed again and a final decision will then be made on the appeal. The idea behind this procedure is that after the juvenile offender has experienced prison life, he may be motivated to fight his temptations regarding absconding and may also endeavor to cease committing further offenses. He is well aware that if he does not keep his promise this time, he may forfeit his freedom again. This approach is still rather new, and its effectiveness is not known so far. One would need a follow-up study made over several years before drawing any conclusions. But this approach by the Supreme Court is a significant contribution in promoting treatment endeavors.

It would of course be futile to put too many or too heavy demands on the juvenile during such a testing period, because that would defeat its purpose. To impose conditions with which the offender is, because of his circumstances, simply unable to comply is to doom him to failure again. It must be recognized that such imposition is not a technical matter, but one of vital importance in the process of rehabilitation. If a juvenile court judge uses mainly a moral yardstick, disregarding the actual potentialities of a juvenile offender at a specific time during his personal development, failure is almost certain—resulting, in turn, in a more severe sentence by the court, because the offender has forfeited the "chance" given him.

An authoritarian institution such as the court may have a therapeutic effect. We must come to recognize and appreciate the double-track relationship in a court situation. Often, the effect of the courtroom experience results from those intangible matters which are going on in the courtroom and which cannot always be immediately assessed. I cannot stress sufficiently, for instance, that merely being nice to a person in trouble is hardly of any help to the individual concerned. But if the occasion and circumstances warrant it, if the person in trouble is helped to gain some insight into himself, it can become a meaningful experience. It may enable him to make a better adjustment and to see the positive and negative aspects in human relationships. The court is in a position to be instrumental to this end—and from here rehabilitation can begin.

The following case may illustrate what I have in mind. A girl fifteen years old was charged in juvenile court with having stolen money from the room of a hotel in which she was staying overnight. When she came to court for the first time, she related that her mother had died some years before and that she refused to stay with her stepmother. She had run away from home, gone to different towns, and tried to make a living by working at different places. She said that she stole the money from a girl with whom she shared a room in the hotel because she had been unemployed for some time.

The girl's behavior in court and her story indicated that she left as many things unspoken as she actually revealed. Since the girl's residence was in a different city from that in which she had stolen the money, I referred her back to her original residence and ordered her to report to the probation officer there so that a report could be submitted to the court before disposal. The case was adjourned for a month, and at the date fixed by the court, the girl reappeared as required. The probation officer, however, announced that his report was not ready because the girl came to see him only once and then disappeared. It transpired that the probation officer had suggested to her that she be examined by a woman psychiatrist, but she refused. She also would not agree to be examined by a general practitioner. The probation officer had been trying to have such an examination made, as requested by the court, because during her court appearance she had displayed certain characteristics which made one suspect that she was pregnant.

Yet, the girl reappeared in court; in fact, she travelled from a different city to be there, to the great astonishment of the probation officer and the court alike. It would have been very easy for her to disappear entirely and not to come to court at all. I assumed therefore that her appearance in court expressed her need for help. Indeed, by this time, I had no doubt that the girl was pregnant. It was also clear to me that she did not want this to be known and that this may have been a major reason for her running away and her refusal to be examined. I could not rid myself of the feeling that this girl was in imminent danger.

I explained to the girl that the court could make no decision unless a report by the probation officer was presented first. I expressed my regret that she did not go to the probation officer as we had arranged. She complained about this procedure and about the fact that because she had made one mistake, she had to come to court so often and report to the probation officer so often. She promised to behave correctly in the future, expressed repentance for her deed and asked to be discharged. After all, it was only half a pound, she said. This was the tenor of her argument, which she repeated time and again, from whatever angle I tried to approach the matter.

By then I was quite convinced that a further adjournment would yield no results and that she would not report to the probation officer any more. It also became quite clear to me that if I wanted to pull her out of her shell, I had to do something more drastic and aggressive. I therefore told her that I realized that she was in trouble and that I would like to help her. I mentioned that at the moment I was not so much concerned with the offense as I was with her condition. I said that I could see she was pregnant, and I wondered what I could do for her.

The girl was taken aback, but she did not react at all to what I said. She ignored entirely my remark about her pregnancy and only asked again to be discharged. I stated again that at the moment I was not going to discuss the matter of the offense, but that I was interested in helping her in her present state. I said that I wondered whether she had been to see a doctor and started to discuss some of the hygienic aspects of pregnancy. This immediately put the girl into a different state of mind, and she said that her pregnancy was still a secret from those who knew her. She thought that she was in her seventh month of pregnancy, and started to talk about herself, her difficulties in finding a job in her present condition, and related freely how it all happened.

It was easy to observe how relieved the girl was once she could accept her pregnancy by telling about it in court. She could do this because she felt that the court did not have a moralizing, patronizing, or punitive attitude towards her. If the court could accept her with this dreadful sin of hers, perhaps she might not be an outcast after all. That she could discuss her secret freely with the court had great meaning for her, and it changed her whole behavior from then on. She went straight from court with the probation officer to see a doctor, and she kept her appointments with him. She gave birth to a son who was given to an adoption agency. A follow-up study, five years after probation terminated, revealed that the girl was happily married and that she had adjusted fairly satisfactorily.

I believe it is not sufficient simply to impress the juvenile offender with the solemnity of court procedures; it is also necessary for the judge to gain some insight into the processes of the offender's mind. The tension created by the court setting is of great value, for it can be used therapeutically. The court can also elicit the desire to make reparation which is undoubtedly present in many young offenders. There is, however, a school of thought which holds that a juvenile court should not concern itself at all with such matters, but confine itself to adjudication and expounding the law in relation to the offense and to the age of the offender. This view ignores that the primary issue is the psychology and causation of behavior problems, an understanding of which is essential to any effort at either prevention or cure.

Here again, situations sometimes occur in which the alertness of the court may be of help to the juvenile. The case of Carmella is an example. Both her parents were very concerned about Carmella's behavior. She began to truant from school at the age of twelve and thereafter never returned to school life. They tried to place her at different jobs without favorable results. By the time she was sixteen, her parents had despaired of rehabilitating her, though they had never turned her away from home.

Carmella was charged in juvenile court with theft, although there was suspicion that she was also connected with girls who were known to be prostitutes. She pleaded not guilty, but was found guilty after the evidence was heard. During the proceedings, she displayed great hostility toward both her parents and the judge, insulted the witnesses, and behaved in a vulgar and provocative manner. I explained to her why I believed the witnesses, making it clear that the court knew nothing of her and had no prejudice against her, but was judging the case according to the facts. After this explanation she became less defiant, though she remained suspicious.

During the next eight months, Carmella appeared six times on charges of theft and soliciting. Her last appearance was together with a girl a year older than herself who was known to be a prostitute. They pleaded guilty to a charge of having knowingly received stolen goods. Their story was confirmed by the prosecution. Carmella talked a great deal at the court session. She had left home some weeks before and had been leading a rather loose life. She now proposed to return to her parents and take a seasonal job. I adjourned the case for two months so that the probation officer could see whether Carmella kept her appointments with him and prepare a plan for her rehabilitation.

On the appointed day Carmella appeared without her companion. She said she did not know why her friend had not come. I noticed that she was wearing a wedding ring and asked whether she was married. She said she was neither married nor, in answer to a further question, engaged. But she was obviously taken aback. I said I had noticed her wedding ring and wondered what it meant. She said with a laugh that she had borrowed it from her mother and would give no further explanation when pressed; it was just an impulse. I suggested that she might be interested in getting married, but she denied this with a smile, saying that she was still too young and no one would want her. I wondered aloud who it was she had in mind. Carmella was amazed and turned away without replying. After a pause, I pursued the same question. Carmella hesitated and then said that she had become friendly with a boy from a neighboring village who visited her twice a week and took her out. When asked whether she would like to marry him, she said they had never discussed the matter and she did not know his intentions. Asked again whether she would like to marry him, she admitted that she did, but again said she did not know his wishes. I pointed out that much might depend on her behavior. If he were a decent fellow, he would probably not be inclined to marry a girl who was leading a loose life; but if she could make a clean break with the past, it might make all the difference. Carmella now tried to convince me that she was determined to make a fresh start, assuring me that if she succeeded, she would confess her past to the boy, as she would not want him to hear about it from others. She thought he would believe her. There was no doubt that Carmella was in earnest, and at times she seemed to be talking to herself, as if persuading herself to make a fresh start.

This incident was only one of many factors, including the relationship with the probation officer, which might determine Carmella's future progress. By interpreting the wearing of a wedding ring as a sign that she wanted to marry, and perhaps felt ready to do so, I felt it important to help her verbalize her innermost feelings. She was able to speak, albeit with a natural reluctance, because throughout her court appearance she had never encountered a moralizing attitude, although she knew that I disapproved of her way of life. My attitude was free of righteous indignation or condemnation; in fact, I accorded her respect in spite of herself. I doubt whether her wish to marry was fully conscious before this interview, but I felt that our discussion had helped her to harness it as a motivation for reform.

It is my contention that most juvenile offenders, when appearing before the juvenile court, are somewhat tense and anxious to know what the court is going to decide. Generally they have some guilt feelings, which may express themselves in overt or disguised forms. A defiant attitude is frequently nothing else but fear, insecurity, and sometimes even remorse. We have to learn to interpret what is really behind the overt behavior of juveniles in court. In the courtroom we have a situation in which anxiety can be used therapeutically. In order to help the offender in his endeavor to make good, we always put at his disposal a probation officer. His probation is a sort of testing period, during which he is put under pressure by the court, but during which he is also given all the help necessary to bring about a change in his behavior. In other words, potential forces are manipulated, often to the surprise of the offender himself.

The following case may illustrate what I have in mind. Aaron, a boy of fourteen, came to the juvenile court charged with stealing. His mother had complained several times to the police that he stole things from home and that he was roaming about. Yet, whenever he reappeared at home, she never informed the police about it. Nothing was known about his father, the mother and son having arrived in this country in 1951. Then at last he was caught red-handed while attempting to steal in a store and brought to court after having spent two days in jail for interrogation. When Aaron entered the courtroom, he showed his defiance openly. His head was fixed downward, his hands in his pockets, showing off a "don't care" attitude. When I asked him a few personal questions—age, address, name—he let me repeat each question twice as if he didn't understand it the first time. His replies were factual and very brief. This went on for a few minutes, and then I said, "You are annoyed at me that you were brought to court." He looked up at once, rather astonished, and said, "I don't want this woman to be here," nodding over his shoulder to the bench behind him. I replied that this woman was his mother. Aaron said, "Yes, but I don't want her to be present in court. If she stays on, I won't talk." I told him that I was in charge in court and that I was also responsible for deciding whether his mother stayed or not. I added firmly, without going into details, that I wanted his mother to be present. I went on in the usual way to discuss with him the charge against him. Aaron apparently accepted gladly my decision regarding his mother. His defiance toward me subsided a bit, although he remained very suspicious and on guard. By the end of this session he exchanged a few words with his mother on his way out of the courtroom.

This first session in the courtroom indicated a few salient points I had to take into account during future meetings with Aaron: (1) there seemed great emotional tension and resistance toward his mother, apparently ambivalent because he was glad that she stayed on; (2) he had displayed a marked tendency to identify the judge with a parent figure and to react negatively toward him; (3) he had made a noted attempt to determine court procedure by demanding removal of his mother. This demand also served to test the judge and the new situation he was in.

According to the suggestion made by the probation officer, Aaron was sent to the remand home for observation and psychiatric examination. He at once told me that he would abscond from there and implied that all my endeavors in this respect were in vain. He kept his promise and within a brief period disappeared from the home several times. While at large he continued to commit offenses and was often brought to court during this time. His behavior was always very provoking at the beginning, but it subsided when there was no retaliation on my part. Mine was a permissive attitude. By then I was under the impression that Aaron was a neurotic boy and that it would lead me nowhere were I to yield to his provocations. I was also not sure how to handle this situation.

After two serious but unheeded warnings that further disappearances would land him in jail, he was sent there for three weeks to await trial on a charge of housebreaking. He was very annoyed at me for this, though he behaved in a much less aggressive manner than at previous sessions. I had the feeling that this was partly due to his need for real punishment, but also to the fact that during his frequent visits to court, some relationship which Aaron seemed to like had been established between us.

A short while after this, I sent him to one of the educational institutions, from which he again escaped. When apprehended and brought to court, he complained that nobody was really interested in him: the probation officer had not come to court, nor had his favorite instructor from the remand home. I explained that they could not know that he would be apprehended by the police, and he replied, "You aren't interested in me either." I answered, "If you are always running away and never stay in one place, how can anyone help you?" He replied stubbornly, "I'll continue to do it." I asked him where he was always going, and he replied to Tel Aviv, to his friends. I commented that he was probably also going to his mother. He became very silent, and after some hesitation, confirmed this. There was a pause, during which he seemed rather nervous, and I let the pause continue for a while. Then I said, "You go to your mother because you want to disturb her. You don't want her to have a boyfriend." Aaron, astounded, looked straight into my face, and with much emotion, burst out, "I'll disturb her! I'll go to the wife of her boyfriend, and I'll tell her all about their relations. You think that I can't do this? You'll see what I can do! Every time I'll run away to her, and I'll make trouble for her and disturb her." After this explosion, he seemed exhausted. I interjected that it was difficult for me to understand why, on the one hand, he was running away from his mother, and on the other, was running to her. There was again a pause, and then he said with emotion, "What do you think— I want to marry her?"

By saying this, Aaron gave vent to the problem which had occupied his mind all the time and had been largely the cause of his restlessness. Until then, he had been unable to talk about it to anybody. This had been made impossible by his constant running away and his distrust of other people. These, in turn, had been prompted by his fear of establishing meaningful emotional ties with others, which was probably based on disappointments in early childhood. Part of his revenge toward society was in disappointing all those who tried to help him. He became an expert in manipulating them to do all sorts of things for him and to suggest all sorts of plans on how to treat him—only to change them again as soon as they were accepted. He had tried this in juvenile court as well. When he found out in court that he would have to take responsibility for his deeds or else pay for his irresponsibility by being limited in his freedom, he started to change. There could be no doubt that his experiences in the juvenile court had special meaning for him. They enabled him to begin a sort of reorientation with regard to his own problems and his relationship with others. After the court session just mentioned, Aaron continued to abscond, but each time he stayed in the educational institution for a longer time. Moreover, he ceased running to his mother entirely.

Though Aaron is still in a rather precarious situation, he has no doubt made real progress. His approach to the people around him has changed. He can now even "afford" to build up relationships with them. At the time of this writing, he has not run away for many months nor committed any new offenses. Moreover, he has finally accepted our advice to enter psychotherapy, which has increased his chances of rehabilitation.

The authoritative setting of the juvenile court, and the impact it can have upon juvenile offenders, allows it to utilize approaches not available to other agencies. When deemed appropriate, the court can be permissive —even to the extreme. On the other hand, it can be punitive, or both. It depends largely on the qualifications of the judges and their interpretation of the function of juvenile courts. Juvenile delinquents have an infallible sense of what the basic attitude of people towards them is. In administering its function, the juvenile court must become alert and sensitive to the needs of each offender. This is probably also how it will become more effective.

Each juvenile court cherishes a belief in the effectiveness of its handling of juvenile offenders. The mere paraphernalia before and during court appearance, as well as the court setting as such, are all tuned to making an impression on offenders. But most people would agree that one cannot rely on them alone. In order to bring about even the slightest change in the juvenile offender, something more needs to be done. Consequently, we have to think differently of court procedures as they exist today and to try to evaluate anew the part they can play in the treatment process. There seems to be general agreement that the juvenile court, dealing with intricate problems in the personality of individuals and their relationship to society, should possess or acquire the necessary qualifications for handling such problems. This is unfortunately too often merely an assumption not put into practice.

The juvenile court, without abrogating its very function, has to enable the offender to feel accepted and respected with all his faults, and indeed, in spite of them. This, if genuinely done without a moralizing, patronizing, punitive, or rejecting attitude, can become a most valuable instrument. Such an attitude by no means excludes the imposition of punishment. Nor does it shrink back from stressing the stern attitude the court must take because of the delinquent behavior of the offender. In fact, this latter can become important in his personal and social reorientation.

In summary, although the juvenile court belongs to the judicial system, it is, to all intents and purposes, a social agency concerned with the rehabilitation of juvenile offenders. The judge should therefore have professional knowledge in two disciplines—jurisdiction and social casework: he should have the highest available qualifications as regards both the law and knowledge of behavior and interviewing techniques in order to perform his function with optimal efficiency. Historically, these two disciplines have not been combined in one person, but there is no reason why this should not be done in the future and every reason why it should in view of the complexity of modern behavior problems.

If handled on the basis of legal knowledge and casework technique, the court situation can be of therapeutic value, but it is certainly not a complete therapy in itself. Proper handling by the judge will have little effect unless integrated with the work of other professions. Often he can only give a lead, or he may be called in at some crucial point in the process of treatment, as when the offender is found not to be responding to probation, or when curtailment of a probation order is advisable. In both instances, the reappearance of the juvenile offender before the court can be of therapeutic value; on many occasions the intervention of the court has resulted in a radical change in the relationship between offender and probation officer. The judge is thus a member of a team, his function being limited but well defined; his work will be effective only if coordinated with that of probation officers and the instructors and headmasters of approved schools, whose contact with the offender is lengthier and more sustained in character.

8

Detention and Examinations

This chapter offers a brief account of detention policies. Special emphasis is laid upon the hazards arising from an order of temporary detention, which is apt to be an important factor in producing and in developing delinquent behavior patterns in the future.

One can distinguish two major and different types of detention: police detention, which is mainly done to secure a statement from the suspect about the alleged offense, and sometimes to keep the delinquent in custody until trial begins; and detention to secure psychological or psychiatric examinations—this is done by court order, after the trial has started.

DETENTION BY THE POLICE

The Juvenile Offenders Ordinance of 1937 made provision for arrest and release on bail by the police as well as by the court. Several provisions vary according to the age of the juvenile offender concerned, although the legal procedure for dealing with them in the juvenile court is uniform.

1. If a person under eighteen years is apprehended by the police and cannot be brought forthwith before a court, he shall be released on bail, with or without sureties, unless the charge is a grave one, or if it is in the interest of the offender to remove him from his environment (sections 4 and 5).
2. Arrangements should be made so that persons under sixteen years do not associate with an adult while in a place of detention (section 6).
3. A person under eighteen who is not released on bail pending trial can be committed to custody in a place of detention instead of in a prison; if, however, the court certifies that his depravity makes this inexpedient, he may, if over fourteen years, be sent to prison (section 7).

4. If it is proved to the court that a boy under sixteen (under eighteen in the case of a girl) had committed an offense, the court may remand the offender for the purpose of obtaining information about him, for a medical examination, or for observation (sections 8 [7], 8 [8]).

The police have generally had power to keep a suspect in custody for investigation for 48 hours; if they decide that a further period is required, they must apply to the court for a detention order. There are usually two different stages at which such a request may be made: first, to complete investigation of the offense and perhaps also to secure the goods stolen; secondly, until final disposition of the case takes place. In the first instance, the court is sometimes put into a difficult position. On the face of it, it would seem unreasonable to object, because the facts about the offense are known only to the police, and one cannot at this stage expect that all details will be revealed. Close questioning at this point, however, may reveal that the period demanded is too long, and there are other important motives for the request.

The police may, for instance, be of the opinion, with cause, that the suspect may regard release from detention as giving him the upper hand in his fight against the police; or that he will continue to commit offenses after release; or that his release will encourage his friends to commit offenses. These arguments are often based on preconceptions and prejudice, but cannot be discarded as being unrealistic. But this view is the usual police view, and the court, in issuing a detention order, must decide each individual case on merit, and cannot be swayed by blanket opinions. After all, detention by court order is finally the responsibility of the judge. Before issuing such an order one has to be satisfied that this step is essential. In my experience, the requested period of detention could often be greatly curtailed if the court took the trouble to probe deeply the validity of the demand.

The Youth Law of August, 1971, introduced more stringent provisions governing custody.[1] It states that a minor above the age of fourteen shall not be kept in custody for investigation for more than 24 hours, unless an order of custody has been signed by the judge. Only when a minor cannot, for some special reason, be brought before a judge during this 24 hours, can a police officer of the rank of police station commander extend such custody for another 24 hours. There is a proviso, however, that the police officer has to put down in writing the reasons for extending custody. These reasons must be brought to the attention of the judge.

[1] Youth Law (Trial, Punitive Methods, and Treatment Measures), in *Laws of the State of Israel* (n.p.).

If a minor under the age of fourteen is involved, the law is still stricter. The period of custody is curtailed to twelve hours only, and if the responsible police officer finds it necessary to extend the custody for another 12 hours, he can do so only if this is essential for public security, or for the minor's own safety, to remove him from the company of undesirable associates, or if there is reason to believe that he has committed a felony for which the law prescribes seven years' imprisonment or more, and his release might conceal relevant evidence. Again, the police officer must put down in writing the reasons for extending custody, and they have to be brought to the attention of the judge. Furthermore, in those cases where a judge may sign an order of custody for 15 or for 30 days, such custody has to be restricted to 10 or to 20 days respectively when a minor is concerned. It is evident that these legal provisions recognize the importance which the Knesset attaches to police custody. Such custody is not merely a formal matter.

It is important to bear in mind that, for a court, the apprehended person is a *suspect,* whereas the police regard him as a person who has committed a particular offense. This is the basic approach to an apprehended person, although this is not openly stated. By their very nature, the police are concerned with a mass phenomenon, while a court has to approach this mass phenomenon on an individual basis. Police detention is not merely a technical matter, but may have far-reaching consequences for the juvenile concerned.

There is one factor of paramount importance. Although we are concerned here with temporary detention, the physical and spiritual conditions of police detention are very seldom satisfactory, and are often even demoralizing. It may be that for adults the judge need not be concerned with these conditions. But a juvenile court judge cannot but take them into account when issuing a detention order. One need not dwell on details to prove that there is a great risk of further delinquent behavior if temporary police detention is inadequate.

It seems obvious, if release on a recognizance can be made with or without sureties, and if the signature of the offender himself is sufficient, that expediency indicates such release. In Israel, this is indeed the prevailing practice: more than 95 percent of all juvenile offenders are released on bail pending trial in the juvenile court. After the police have taken a statement from the juvenile suspect, a parent or some other responsible adult related to the juvenile or known to him signs a bond of surety that the juvenile will be brought to court when summoned for trial. The police usually have no difficulty in securing such a bond, and only in exceptional cases, when a suitable adult cannot be found or if there is refusal to vouch for the suspect, is the juvenile court requested to make a decision regarding release.

Only very seldom is detention until final disposition of the case ordered. The section covering detention can of course be interpreted rigidly, and then an additional responsibility rests on the shoulders of the judge. Two arguments are sometimes advanced for continued detention: that if an offender is on bail pending trial, he will most probably continue to commit offenses, or that he may disappear until the trial begins and thus cause inconvenience and delay of justice. Experience in Israel and elsewhere has clearly shown that neither argument is watertight. There is no evidence that juvenile offenders who are on bail awaiting trial continue to commit offenses or disappear before trial.

It is always a small group which is troublesome and which requires special measures. In Tel Aviv, a city of 700,000 inhabitants, a small number of boys committed a large percentage of all offenses. The figures registered by the police unit for juvenile offenders speak for themselves: during 1966, 47 boys—all recidivists—were responsible for 64 percent of the housebreaking that was committed by juvenile offenders. During 1967, 39 boys—also recidivists—were responsible for 61 percent of housebreaking. And during 1968, 60 boys committed 36 percent of all the housebreaking committed by juvenile offenders.

No general conclusions should therefore be drawn without analyzing in detail the circumstances involved. The drop in housebreaking crimes in 1968 was due to the fact that a number of recidivists were sent to the Borstal which began to function at this time.

DETENTION FOR EXAMINATION

In Israel, a detention order for psychological or psychiatric examination is usually requested by a probation officer after the determination of guilt, when the court must consider how best to dispose of the case. On the face of it, it seems justifiable to detain a juvenile offender for examination, and one is therefore inclined to overlook some factors that should nevertheless be scrutinized.

Previously the legal provision for a detention order for the purpose of examination was rather scanty. Section 8(7) of the Juvenile Offenders Ordinance of 1937 made general provision for the court to obtain information about the background of the juvenile offender. Judges in the juvenile court in Israel usually made an order for six to eight weeks, during which time, it was assumed, appropriate examinations and observation could be completed. It should be stressed in passing that in many instances professional "observation" is often as important as the examinations themselves. From the wording of section 8(7) it transpired, however, that to obtain this information no detention order is necessarily required. In other words, "special medical examination" is possible without detaining the juvenile offender. According to the new Youth Law of 1971, detention for observation is limited to 90 days. On application, another 30 days is possible.

Removal from home by court order includes various types of placement, but the salient feature is the fact of removal from home. A distinction has to be made, however, between removal on a placement order, which is generally for a comparatively long period, and removal for a short period, as by a detention order for the purpose of examination. This latter measure does not lack its perils for the juvenile offender concerned, and each case should therefore be dealt with rather carefully on its merits. In Israel we refrain from detaining juvenile offenders even for a brief period, unless this is absolutely essential, believing that detention may have far-reaching negative repercussions. Juvenile offenders in Israel who are in need of a psychological or psychiatric examination are ordinarily examined on an out-patient basis, at one of the existing child guidance clinics, in a hospital out-patient department, or even in private by an expert, on a fee basis. The probation officer who deals with a particular case may decide on the necessity of such expert examination while preparing his report for the court, or he may be requested by the court to arrange it. It is to my mind an important feature in this arrangement that it is the probation officer who deals with these matters. It can be assumed that he is known to the offender and his family, and that some kind of relationship has been established between them during preparation of the report. This fact is apt to prepare the juvenile offender and his parents emotionally for the psychological or psychiatric examination, which may arouse anxiety. I am convinced that these examinations, if carried out while the juvenile offender remains in his natural environment, are not only less expensive but also more reliable than those carried out in a detention center or remand home.

It is a rather universal custom to detain a juvenile offender for psychological examinations. It must first be pointed out that such detention is, legally, equivalent to an arrest. Conditions in a detention home are therefore rather strict, and severe security measures are usual to ensure that the juvenile offender is brought to court at the time fixed by the judge. In many quarters this procedure is followed with juveniles of a tender age, and with first offenders. For these two groups, a popular saying has it, a few weeks in detention will "teach the offender a lesson."

There is no evidence that such an experience of hardship and deprivation makes him think twice before committing another offense; and there is no proof that detention for examination has no bearing on further delinquent behavior patterns.

Detention has detrimental effects which should be borne in mind:

1. A detention home cannot prevent unwarranted association between the casual offender and the more experienced delinquent. In detention an attitude of defiance may be strengthened resulting in commitment to a delinquent career.
2. In a detention home, anxiety about what is going to happen and fear of punishment may foster, rather than prevent, delinquent behavior patterns.
3. If detention is ordered where not absolutely essential, annoyance with parents, police, court, and society at large is apt to thwart rehabilitation.
4. Detention creates a classic situation of crisis that requires a professional attention which is usually not forthcoming in a remand home. Instead, emphasis is laid on regimentation, leading to further resentment and to aggressive behavior.

It can safely be said that in a detention or a remand home a vicious circle is established, which leads in many instances directly to more delinquent behavior. For many this is the lesson they learn there. Or, to put it differently, detention promotes, not prevents, delinquent behavior.[2]

Before making such a decision, the court must consider whether a psychological or psychiatric examination is necessary before finally disposing of a case, and if such examination can be done ambulatorily. It can be categorically stated that each step which is aimed at sparing the juvenile offender, particularly the inexperienced one, emotional upheavals, is in fact contributing to prevention of delinquency. Obviously, there are juvenile offenders who have to be temporarily removed from home for examination, but indiscriminate use of detention is hazardous. Temporary detention, for whatever purpose, should be used much more selectively, in view of the risk of furthering delinquent careers.

There is a fundamental and important difference between a psychiatric examination which is requested in a court for adults and that which is requested in a juvenile court. Such examinations of adults is required, in most instances, to find out whether the defendant can be held respon-

[2] Sherwood Norman, *Think Twice* (National Council on Crime and Delinquency, 1968), p. 7.

sible for committing the offense, in such matters as murder, manslaughter, rape, robbery—that is, offenses for which the law dictates severe punishment. In the juvenile court, an entirely different outlook in most instances motivates such an examination, for instance: What are the motivations for the delinquent behavior pattern? To what extent does a behavior disorder exist? To what extent can delinquent behavior be attributed to reactions to home, school, friends, etc.? What should be done to reeducate and rehabilitate the juvenile offender? Among adults, then, the issue is the narrow one of responsibility and punishment, whereas among juveniles it is causes and rehabilitation.

Juveniles are held at the detention home, Mitzpah Yam, run by the Ministry of Social Welfare—as are all other educational establishments for juvenile offenders. The home is run on the lines of an open camp, with a security wing. The general atmosphere is rather permissive. At the home a psychiatrist examines boys after preliminary psychological examination. In our experience, an adequate psychological examination, together with an observation report by the boy's teachers and instructors, can convey quite a complete picture of the personality of a particular offender. The psychiatrist, who is employed with a government hospital, can, where necessary, admit offenders to that hospital for close examination and observation—an arrangement that has proved to be of great value.

If the juvenile offender and his parents or guardian agree to such admission, it is superfluous to issue a special court order, because this admission occurs by their consent, and falls within the realm of the order remanding for observation and examination. If they do not agree to admission to a hospital, the remand home will turn to the court, which then proceeds as prescribed by law, i.e., to issue an admission order which is based on a medical certificate, either for an indefinite period, if there is a psychotic breakdown, or for examination.

Many years of experience have shown that psychotherapeutic treatment was not available for juvenile offenders where examination revealed the need. This applies equally to those who are in one of the educational establishments, on probation, or under some other care. It is one thing to enlist psychological and psychiatric services for diagnostic purposes, and quite another matter if treatment proper is required. This deplorable state of affairs leads necessarily to some sort of resentment and helplessness, particularly if such treatment is recommended by the expert himself.

The circumstances under which a detention order may be necessary can be summarized in the following way:

1. Juvenile offenders who constantly run away from home and wander from one place to another. They do not in the beginning necessarily commit many or serious offenses, but because of their waywardness they are apt to become real delinquents. They seldom report to the probation officer, and no report can therefore be prepared for the juvenile court.

2. There are some offenders who live at home and who do not cooperate with the probation officer while he is trying to prepare the report. Their attitude is one of concealed or overt defiance to any kind of authority, including their parents. Both this group and the previous one will manipulate people and circumstances to thwart endeavors to change their behavior. They can be made to cooperate, if at all, only by compulsion of a court order.

3. There are other cases in which the juvenile court would like to have a more complete picture of the motivation and behavior patterns of the juvenile offender. The material so far gathered may indicate that a placement order is advisable, but further observations and appropriate examinations might be helpful in deciding what kind of placement seems desirable.

4. There are those with definite emotional problems, for whom observation—rather than examinations which are usually already available—can better determine the proper kind of placement.

TABLE 8.1
DETENTION ORDERS IN
JUVENILE COURTS, 1964–69

Year	Total no. of convictions	Detention orders	
		No.	% of total convictions
1964	5,391	91	1.6
1965	5,616	96	1.7
1966	5,740	97	1.7
1967[a]	3,864	85	2.2
1968	4,623	171	3.7
1969	5,125	176	3.4

Source: Israel, Central Bureau of Statistics,
No. 370, Table 1, p. 5.
[a] During this year the amnesty caused a decline in convictions but an increase in detention orders.

TABLE 8.2

FREQUENCY OF DELINQUENT BEHAVIOR AMONG JUVENILES DETAINED FOR EXAMINATIONS, 1964–68

Year	Offenders by no. of offenses								Total
	1–5	6–10	11–15	16–20	21–30	31–50	51 +	Unknown	
1964	35 (27.3%)	34 (26.5%)	16 (12.5%)	10 (8.0%)	14 (10.8%)	10 (8.0%)	7 (5.4%)	2 (1.5%)	128 (100%)
1965	51 (37.4%)	26 (18.9%)	15 (11.0%)	13 (9.6%)	11 (8.0%)	10 (7.0%)	4 (3.0%)	7 (5.1%)	137 (100%)
1966	58 (35.5%)	35 (21.4%)	19 (11.6%)	10 (6.1%)	17 (10.3%)	17 (10.3%)	4 (2.4%)	4 (2.4%)	164 (100%)
1967	32 (15.6%)	44 (21.5%)	27 (13.0%)	19 (9.3%)	35 (17.1%)	22 (10.8%)	16 (7.8%)	10 (4.9%)	205 (100%)
1968	97 (26.8%)	82 (22.7%)	59 (16.3%)	37 (10.2%)	36 (10.0%)	31 (8.6%)	13 (3.7%)	6 (1.7%)	361 (100%)

Source: David Reifen and Salman Rosenzweig, *Juvenile Offenders: Background and Mode of Life* (Jerusalem: Ministry of Social Welfare, 1971), Table 5, p. 30. (In Hebrew.)

Note: This table includes juveniles who were referred for examination by educational establishments.

A few figures may illustrate the frequency with which detention orders for examination and classification have been made. As will be seen from Table 8.1, there was an increase in detention orders after 1967, owing in a considerable degree to a change of policy concerning placement orders.

Table 8.2 illustrates one component among those detained that can be considered seriously delinquent. (The word "serious" refers to delinquent behavior patterns, and to the personality of a particular offender, not necessarily to the seriousness of the offense. To my mind the decisive feature is the repetitiveness of the delinquent pattern.)

The seriousness of the delinquent behavior pattern can also be assessed by noting the age at which delinquency was first registered by the police (Table 8.3). Registration does not necessarily imply that there was also a court procedure. It can be assumed that in many instances, court intervention was not automatically enforced, and that it was only when repeated offenses occurred that previous police registration became of interest to the remand home. Incidentally, the court is supplied with such information only when guilt has been determined.

The conspicuous feature in Table 8.3 is the high representation of the younger age groups, i.e., those aged nine to twelve years. The lowest representation was in 1966—45.7 percent of a total of 164—the highest in 1968 with 71.0 percent of a total of 361; during the other three years the figures were 53.9 percent (of 128) in 1964, 59.2 percent (of 137) in 1965, and 65.0 percent (of 205) in 1967. Such a high representation of the very young is a clear indication of behavioral difficulties and perhaps disorders which find expression in a delinquent pattern. But it also clearly points to the inadequacy of community facilities for dealing with the special needs of the younger age groups. It is unfortunate that juvenile courts had no alternative for disposal but to send them to a remand home, despite the hazards involved. It would, however, be erroneous to maintain that such high figures for the very young constitute a decisive reason for keeping the age of criminal responsibility at nine years. It must be remembered, incidentally, that these are cases that were exceptional enough to be sent for examination and classification to the remand home.

At this point it is of interest to find out what the remand home recommended, and to what extent the actual court decision concurred. Table 8.4 counts only those juvenile offenders who were detained at the remand home for examinations and classification. The average period of detention was six weeks. After this the offenders were brought again to court for final disposal. These recommendations by the remand home are the result of special deliberations, in which all those who had contact with

TABLE 8.3
AGE OF COMMENCEMENT OF DELINQUENT ACTIVITIES AMONG
DETAINED JUVENILES, 1964–68

Year	Offenders by age group					
	9–10[a] yrs.	11–12 yrs.	13–14 yrs.	15–16 yrs.	Un-known	Total
1964	34 (26.6%)	35 (27.3%)	35 (27.3%)	22 (17.2%)	2 (1.6%)	128 (100%)
1965	41 (30.0%)	40 (29.2%)	33 (24.1%)	16 (11.7%)	7 (5.1%)	137 (100%)
1966	34 (20.7%)	41 (25.0%)	57 (34.8%)	28 (17.1%)	4 (2.4%)	164 (100%)
1967	62 (30.3%)	71 (34.7%)	44 (21.4%)	19 (9.2%)	9 (4.4%)	205 (100%)
1968	141 (40.0%)	112 (31.0%)	76 (21.0%)	26 (7.0%)	6 (1.0%)	361 (100%)

Source: David Reifen and Salman Rosenzweig, *Juvenile Offenders: Background and Mode of Life* (Jerusalem: Ministry of Social Welfare, 1971), Table 3, p. 28.

[a] Criminal responsibility in law begins at 9 years.

Note: This table includes juveniles who were referred for examination by educational establishments.

the juvenile offender, often including his parents and the offender himself, but not a judge, participate.

Table 8.4 reveals a high correlation between the recommendation of the detention home and actual court decisions. It will be noted that the court more often imposed a prison term than the home recommended; when the home made no recommendation, the court had of course to decide. The discrepancy that exists is due to the fact that final responsibility for the decision rests on the court, which must take into account public as well as individual interests.

	Total no. of cases	No. of offenders by			
		Educational estab-lishment	Proba-tion	Probation with residence	Probation for trial period
1964	92				
–Recommendation		28	14	12	19
–Decision		31	11	7	29
1965	101				
–Recommendation		32	18	18	21
–Decision		35	13	17	25
1966	100				
–Recommendation		23	10	20	34
–Decision		24	18	18	34
1967	129				
–Recommendation		58	14	20	22
–Decision		50	15	20	25
1968	249				
–Recommendation		119	30	39	41
–Decision		109	40	33	44
All years	671				
–Recommendation		260 (38.8%)	86 (12.8%)	109 (16.3%)	137 (20.5%)
–Decision		249 (37.1%)	97 (14.5%)	95 (14.2%)	157 (23.4%)

Source: David Reifen and Salman Rosenzweig, *Juvenile Offenders: Background and Mode of Life* (Jerusalem: Ministry of Social Welfare, 1971), Table 11, p. 45.

Note: This table includes juveniles who were referred by court order for examination.

8.4
DETENTION HOME AND COURT DECISIONS, 1964–68

method of treatment

Imprison-ment	Hospital-ization	Home for defectives	Tentative recommen-dation	No recom-mendation	Trial further postponed
4	4	1	2	6	2
6	2	0	5	0	1
0	1	0	3	6	2
5	1	0	4	0	1
0	1	0	0	10	2
1	1	0	2	0	2
3	0	0	1	1	10
4	1	0	3	0	11
0	4	7	2	1	6
0	4	0	6	0	13
7	10	8	8	24	22
(1.0%)	(1.4%)	(1.1%)	(1.1%)	(3.6%)	(3.3%)
15	9	0	20	0	28
(2.3%)	(1.3%)	(0)	(2.9%)	(0)	(4.2%)

IV
Specialized
Community
Services

9

The
Protection of
Children in
Israel:
Basic Legislation

Israel, as a new and independent state, is in a unique position. There has been on the one hand, a distinct tendency to renew old Jewish laws that existed in this country thousands of years ago. These laws have been kept alive among Jews the world over, and have been continually reexamined and reinterpreted by Jewish scholars. They have become one of the most important binding forces among Jews during the dispersion. For centuries these laws have regulated the way of life and modes of behavior of Jewish communities. They are still adhered to by many, and have special significance for them in Israel, where they were first established, and where they have taken shape.

On the other hand, there is a strong desire to keep pace with contemporary developments, and to enforce laws that are based on new conceptions, those which prevail in modern society in the second half of the twentieth century. Although there is no overt conflict, the issue came to the fore after 1948. With the establishment of Israel as an independent state with a majority of people adhering to the Jewish faith, many expected a return to the ancient laws of the old country. Obviously, a compromise between these two tendencies has to be found. It is commonplace that legislation in matters of crime and punishment and in matters of child welfare is based on the historical and cultural conditions and traditions of a particular country. It is a somewhat different matter for those countries which have become independent during the last few decades, and which have not yet worked out their own legal system. Many of them continue to administer laws, procedures, and treatment methods

145

which were introduced by the former governing administration, although great changes may have taken place in the conditions obtaining in such countries since they have become independent.

Israel is a case in point. One can safely say that there exists, on the whole, a large amount of agreement concerning child welfare and criminal law and procedure. Legislation, however, is a different matter. The laws, procedures, and treatment methods in existence in this country, called Palestine until 15 May 1948, have been as heterogeneous and conglomerate as the population itself. During Turkish rule, until 1917, jurisdiction was regulated according to Ottoman law, and after the British military rule ended and the British civil administration took over as a mandatory government on behalf of the League of Nations, jurisdiction followed laws and procedures obtaining in Great Britain. For instance, matters of personal status were regulated by the British mandatory government in 1922, and marriage, divorce, alimony, maintenance, etc., became dependent upon the laws and customs of one of the then recognized religious communities. Yet not only did Ottoman law continue to be administered in many respects during the period of the British mandate over Palestine, but many of these laws and also laws and procedures introduced by the British mandatory government, have continued to be applied in Israel to this day. Thus the Criminal Code Ordinance of 1936, which provided a general penal code for Palestine, is still in great part in force. Section 2 of that ordinance states: "From and after the commencement of this Code the Ottoman Penal Code shall cease to be in force in Palestine. Any reference to any provision in the Ottoman Penal Code in any Ordinance in force at the time of such commencement shall, so far as is consistent with its context, be deemed to be a reference to the corresponding provision in this Code." Further, section 4 states: "This Code shall be interpreted in accordance with the principles of legal interpretation obtaining in England and expressions used in it shall be presumed, so far as is consistent with their context and except as may otherwise be expressly provided, to be used with the meaning attaching to them in English law and shall be construed in accordance therewith."

When Israel came into being, an immediate concern was the maintenance of law and order. On 19 May 1948, the Provisional Government of Israel decided that: "The law which existed in Palestine on the 5th Iyar 5708 (14 May 1948) shall remain in force, insofar as there is nothing repugnant to this Ordinance as to the other laws which may be enacted by or on behalf of the Provisional Council of the State, and subject to such modifications as may result from the establishment of the State and its authorities."[1] The Provisional Council of State was replaced, through free elections, by the first Knesset (Parliament of Israel) nine months later. Since then, a growing number of original Israeli laws have been enacted and, in due course, original Israeli laws will replace the remnants of foreign legislations.

Israel is in the advantageous position that in enforcing new laws it can make use of new trends and ventures, the result of modern thought, since its circumstances enable it to start afresh. There is an additional advantage in the fact that practically all agencies concerned with the implementation and administration of laws are centralized and their procedure is uniform over the whole country. This is an important feature when matters of training, appointments and the implementation of regulations and general policy are considered. The agencies in question supervise the courts, the police force, the probation service, the prison administration, the youth authority for juvenile offenders, the after-care service, etc.

Before discussing specialized community services it is useful to gain a general understanding of Israeli laws which have bearing, direct or indirect, on juvenile delinquency and which complement the picture in Chapters 10–13.

EDUCATION

Until the establishment of the State of Israel in 1948, there was no compulsory elementary education in this country. It was therefore natural that the Knesset was most eager to introduce a law to this effect as soon as possible. By the Compulsory Education Law, 5709–1949 any "child"—those in the age group of five to thirteen years inclusive—is obliged to attend a recognized school, and by doing so he is entitled to education free of charge, first, from five to six years old, at a recognized kindergarten, and after, for eight years at an elementary school.[2] A "young person," aged fourteen to seventeen years inclusive, who for some reason or another has not finished all grades of elementary school must fulfill the prescribed eight grades in special schools for young persons—in most instances evening schools.

A most important amendment on 2 July 1969, raised the age of compulsory school education to fifteen years, over a five-year period.

---

[1] Section 11 of Law and Administration Ordinance, No. 1, 5708–1948, in *Laws of the State of Israel*, Vol. 1, p. 9.
[2] Compulsory Education Law, 5709–1949, in *Laws of the State of Israel*, Vol. 3, 1949, p. 125.

Furthermore, the whole system of elementary and secondary education has been remodeled along new lines, with three separate age groups, two of them receiving free, compulsory education, the third, comprising those aged sixteen to seventeen years, being given the opportunity to continue their schooling. At this level education is neither compulsory nor free, and is geared to further studies; there are, however, scholarships for gifted pupils. It is hoped that this new system will more effectively reconcile the needs of the child and the demands of a technological society.

Although elementary education is firmly established by now, there are still many children who do not finish the grades prescribed by law. Two basic aspects of this are intertwined and have to be looked at as an entity. There are in Israel many children who encounter difficulties during the process of systematic learning, and there are schools which do not develop teaching methods appropriate to the special needs of these children. The problem therefore is twofold: first, *children* who do not keep pace with the ordinary school curriculum, and who eventually drop out without finishing compulsory elementary school education; second, a *school system* which is not necessarily geared towards preventing those children from leaving school prematurely. In a heterogeneous society like that of Israel this problem is of paramount importance: technological development requires an increasingly wide general knowledge and there is a growing demand for specific knowledge in particular. Even jobs of a simple or semi-skilled nature now require at least ten years of school education. Raising the compulsory school leaving age will not, per se, provide those who encounter, for one reason or another, difficulties, with an incentive to attend school. Special methods must be designed to stimulate and to foster school attendance. A genuine implementation of compulsory school education has to pay special attention to the lower grades of the elementary school system, otherwise it may widen rather than narrow the educational gap.

MARRIAGE

It was customary among certain sections of the local population, particularly among those originating from Moslem countries—Jews and Arabs alike—to marry off girls at a tender age. Not infrequently one encountered young women and mothers, as young as fourteen or fifteen years old, who were attending to their household and to their children, instead of attending elementary or secondary school. This custom developed over the centuries as an important barrier to immorality and was concerned with strong taboos against social intercourse between young males and females outside the family circle; girls were thereby protected from temptation, as it were, and the social status of the family was not imperiled. In the juvenile court, mothers would sometimes explain their inability to take proper care of their children, on the ground that they were children themselves when they were married. This fact has been a source of great grievance for many, although this became conscious only in Israel, where they met with quite different customs.

I encountered such a situation recently in the juvenile court in Tel Aviv. The mother of a boy aged fifteen years who was charged with several serious offenses said that she was unable to control her boy. It was evident that she had taken no interest in him, nor in her other two children. It was also evident that she was very much afraid of him. The report which was submitted by the probation officer mentioned that this mother was born in Persia, where she was married off at the age of twelve years to a man ten years older than she. He had been married before, but had no children. When she was fourteen years old, he divorced the mother because she did not become pregnant. The mother remarried at the age of twenty. She has no affection for her three children of this marriage, and all of them have come to need special care.

Child marriage was so frequent that one of the first laws in Israel in the field of child welfare abolished it. The Marriage Age Law, enforced in 1950, allowed no girl under seventeen years to marry.[3] The law provides sanctions for a person who marries a girl under this age, for the parent or guardian who gives his consent to such a marriage, and for the person who performs the marriage ceremony. By special application, however, a district court judge may give consent to marry at an earlier age, if reasons are given. If a marriage ceremony is performed below the age prescribed by this law, such a marriage can be nullified if application is made to the court while the girl concerned is still under nineteen years. This covers instances in which the marriage was performed outside Israel. This law is now generally accepted, although at first it encountered objections in various quarters.

LABOR

Just as child marriage was a custom in this part of the world, so was child labor—indeed, it was even more widespread. It can be assumed that this fact prompted the British mandatory government to introduce, in 1945, legislation to regulate, to a certain extent, the employment of

---

[3] Marriage Age Law, 5710–1950, in *Laws of the State of Israel*, Vol. 4, 1949/50, p. 158.

children. The Employment of Children and Young Persons Ordinance, was, however, of short duration. The Knesset replaced it with two laws which are to a certain extent complementary: the Youth Labor Law and the Apprenticeship Law. It is no accident that these two laws were discussed and passed by the Knesset at practically the same time. The Youth Labor Law, 5713–1953, defines a "child" as a person below sixteen years, and an "adolescent" to be a person of sixteen to seventeen years inclusive.[4] According to this law a "child" who has not attained the age of fourteen years shall not be employed in any kind of work, save for itinerant trading if he has a special permit. Children below the age of sixteen years may not work in places such as hotels, dance halls, treatment centers for the mentally ill, etc.—that is, places which may have a detrimental effect on their well-being.

The law provides for appropriate medical examinations, for regulation of working hours, for vocational guidance, rest hours, yearly vacations, etc., and sets penalties for contravention. The Youth Labor Law has gained wide recognition, and practically all factories and organized workshops adhere to it, but it is less observed in small workshops run by one or two persons. There is a host of young children who drop out of elementary school, and who look for employment in just such small places and small workshops, hoping not to be caught there by the law. Theirs is usually not regular work: they float from one job to another, and their salary is naturally not in accordance with regulations. This group includes a rather large number of errand boys, who are also usually of tender age.

This area will become more problematic and complicated because the raising of the school leaving age has been accompanied by a raising of the working age.

The Apprenticeship Law, 5713–1953, defines a "juvenile" to be a person who has not yet reached the age of eighteen years, and an "apprentice" as a juvenile who works in order to acquire a trade by guided practical work and by attending approved trade lessons within the meaning of the law.[5] The law makes provision for the length of time and the curriculum of the apprenticeship period, for wages, examinations, vacations, number of apprentices who may be employed at a certain place, and the qualifications and duties of employers. There is a legal provision for the appointment of a trade apprenticeship board with an elaboration of its duties, and provision for supervisors and inspectors.

---

[4] Youth Labor Law, 5713–1953, in *Laws of the State of Israel*, Vol. 7, 1952/53, p. 94.
[5] Apprenticeship Law, 5713–1953, *ibid.*, p. 86.

The law carries penalties and has proved effective for the welfare of those young people who come under its purview.

CHILDREN IN NEED

The procedures and treatments involved in the trial of juvenile offenders are necessarily a matter of controversy. The sociocultural background of a society, traditional methods of treating offenders in general and juvenile offenders in particular, the age of criminal responsibility, type of offense, existence of gangs, drug addiction, etc., all affect opinions. There is less controversy about children who come to the juvenile court from socially inadequate homes, as wards of society. Sometimes this group is called predelinquent, the implication being that their home conditions are bound to lead them to delinquency.

Yet it is still important to differentiate between these two groups, for court intervention stems from diagonally opposite motives. Of primary importance is age. There is a minimum age limit for juvenile offenders, that is, an age of criminal responsibility, whereas in the case of children who are in need of care and protection there is no minimum age limit, as home conditions sometimes compel social agencies to apply for court intervention on behalf of a child soon after birth, or at a tender age. In Israel, for instance, approximately 70 percent of children brought to the juvenile court because they are in need of care and protection are below the age of ten years. Sometimes—and in this respect the situation differs from that of juvenile offenders—all children of a particular family have to be taken care of by society, because that family endangers the raising of these children. Unfortunately, reeducation and readaptation measures may be similar or even the same for both groups, although their needs may be quite different. Although this is due in many instances to inadequate facilities and placement difficulties, more attention should be paid to the different basic requirements.

The Juvenile Offenders Ordinance of 1937 contained a special section dealing with children who are in need of care and protection. This was replaced by a new law, which came into force on 7 July 1960.[6] We consider that matters of care and protection should not be part of a criminal law and of criminal procedure.

Under this new law, a child welfare officer may make application to the juvenile court on behalf of any minor under eighteen years. The law

[6] Youth (Care and Supervision) Law, 5720–1960, in *Laws of the State of Israel*, Vol. 14, p. 44.

enables the officer, for instance, to enter private houses, to place minors in cases of emergency even without a court order, for a period of up to seven days, during which time the case must be brought to court. Enforcement of court orders, except for special cases, and supervision of children placed under court order is also the duty of the welfare officer. Any court order under this law can be made for a period of not more than three years. If a request is made for a renewal of the order, the court has to be satisfied that the conditions under which the original order was made still exist. Decisions by the court can be altered, amended, or rescinded at the request of the welfare officer, the minor, or his parents or the person responsible for him. Application must be made in writing, and the court makes the decision at a hearing of all parties concerned.

Application to the court to decide whether or not a minor is in need of care can be made on the following grounds:

1. There is no responsible person to take care of the minor.
2. The person responsible for the minor is unable to take proper care of him or to supervise him, or he neglects to do so.
3. The minor has committed an act which is a criminal offense, but he has not been brought to trial for this offense.
4. The minor is vagrant, begging alms or hawking goods at an age when this is an offense according to the Youth Labor Law.
5. The minor is under bad influences or lives in a place which is permanently used for some criminal purpose.
6. The minor's physical or spiritual well-being is affected or likely to be affected, for any other reason whatsoever.

As can be seen, there exists a wide variety of grounds for court intervention, if deemed necessary. Most cases so far have come to the juvenile court under paragraphs 2, 5, 6. It is particularly the last paragraph which affords a wide scope for intervention.

The child welfare officer's application must be supported by evidence. There are no rules, however, regarding the amount of evidence required. In a case of appeal which came before the Supreme Court, that court supported a juvenile court decision to the effect that in these instances a court is not bound by criminal procedure or by the law of evidence. The juvenile court judge has of course to give his reasons in writing, as any decision by courts has to be made in writing.

It is an interesting reflection on the problems involved in these cases that 90 percent of minors who were thus brought to court according to this law had to be placed away from their parents, either in an educational establishment, with foster parents, or in infant or baby homes.

GUARDIANSHIP

Another relevant law enforced in 1962 deals with the rights and duties of persons below the age of eighteen, as well as the rights and duties of parents and guardians toward them.[7] The Knesset defined the term "minor" in section 3 in the abovementioned law as follows: "A person who has not reached the age of eighteen is a minor. A person who has reached the age of eighteen is of full age." The law makes provisions for parents' responsibility towards their children, and the duties of children towards their parents. There are actions which have to be approved by court, and the court's determination is binding on the parties, if there is no agreement by parents. The court decides also about guardianship and the duties and functions of guardians. Many sections regulate the numerous aspects of this law.

NEGLECT AND DESERTION

An amendment to the Criminal Code Ordinance of 1936 that has repercussions for child welfare was enacted in 1965.[8] The amendment makes neglect and desertion of children by parents a criminal offense; if the parent of a child under the age of fourteen years does not provide such child with food, clothing, bedding, and other essentials to the extent required to provide well-being and health, he shall be liable to imprisonment for three years, unless he can prove that he tried but is unable to supply those essentials.

It is not known to what extent these sections will in fact be implemented. One can safely assume that, in most instances, proceedings in court will be commenced on behalf of a particular child according to the Youth (Treatment and Supervision) Law of 1960. For the central concern is the welfare of a child, and although it is appropriate that there is a legal provision to proceed with a criminal action against parents, the primary issue still remains the welfare of the child. Even if criminal proceedings are begun against parents, the child must still be cared for. And proceedings against parents in such instances do not, per se, change their attitude towards their children for the better.

---

[7] Capacity and Guardianship Law, 5722–1962, in *Laws of the State of Israel*, Vol. 16, p. 106.

[8] Criminal Code Ordinance (Amendment No. 24) Law, in *Laws of the State of Israel,* Vol. 19, 5727–1965, p. 49.

10

The
Probation
Service

Probation was introduced into this country in the Young Offenders Ordinance of 1922. At that time, however, it was very seldom used, and practically no facilities were available for its implementation. Whenever a court concluded that a young offender under twenty years should be placed on probation, it requested a voluntary worker to take over care. It was customary to call on some member of the particular religious community concerned —Jewish, Christian, Moslem—with experience in education or social welfare, to act as probation officer on a voluntary basis. No presentence report was required, and in most instances not much was known about the personality and background of the young offender. Consideration of an offender for probation was usually based on age, the type of offense, and whether or not it was a first offense. Probation officers were called in by the court haphazardly, when a judge happened to know of the method of probation, and when his general impression in a particular case was that probation would be expedient.

A proper Probation Service was established by the Juvenile Offenders Ordinance of 1937.[1] Section 9, dealing with the various aspects of probation, was then applicable only to those who came within the purview of the juvenile court, i.e., those under sixteen years, and could no longer be used in courts for adults for those under twenty years. From 1937 on, full-time probation officers have been appointed, with the functions, first, of obtaining information for the court before it makes any final disposition of the case; and secondly, of supervising those juvenile offenders who were put on probation by the court. The most important innovations of the Juvenile Offenders Ordinance were:

[1] Juvenile Offenders Ordinance No. 2 of 1937 (enforced on September 22, 1938).

154

1. A probation order could be made for a period of up to three years.
2. A probation order could be made whether or not the court proceeded to a conviction.
3. The juvenile court, as a special court to deal with juvenile offenders, was mentioned for the first time.
4. It was made customary for probation officers to attend all sessions of a court sitting as a juvenile court.
5. It became customary for probation officers to submit a written report before sentence, although this was not obligatory.

The Ordinance of 1937 provided (section 8[7]) that before deciding how to deal with the offenders the court should obtain information about general conduct, home surroundings, school record, and medical history, to enable it to deal with the case in the best interests of the offender. The section did not stipulate that this information should be obtained from probation officers alone, but left the sources to the discretion of the court: probation officers, the local social welfare agency, a headmaster, teacher. Since that time, however, the probation officer in Israel has become a much more recognized and established official figure in the juvenile court than was the case before. The new Youth Law of 1971 conferred on the probation officer a number of important functions that were not his province hitherto.[2]

The law lays down, for instance, that a probation officer is provided with executive powers in instances in which he was informed by the police that a minor is suspected of having committed an offense. By the Welfare Law of 1955, certain powers had been bestowed upon welfare officers: "Where a welfare officer has been ordered as specified ... he may, for the purpose of preparing his report, enter any place where the minor or the mentally sick person is or is likely to be, and examine any person who in his opinion possesses information relating to the minor or the mentally sick person, and the person examined is bound to give the welfare officer correct and complete answers; provided he shall not be bound to do so if the answer would tend to incriminate him" (section 3).[3] This section was incorporated in the Youth Law of 1971. Whereas a welfare officer can act in accordance with section 3 only if empowered to do so by a court order, a probation officer can perform such a function even without a court order.

---

[2] Youth Law (Trial, Punitive Methods, and Treatment Measures) 5731–1971, in *Laws of the State of Israel* (n.p.).

[3] Welfare (Procedure in Matters of Minors, Mentally Sick Persons, and Absent Persons) Law, 5715–1955, in *Laws of State of Israel*, Vol. 9, p. 139.

Legally speaking, a probation officer was, before the law of 1971, supposed to begin only after the court had found the offender guilty. In many instances such procedure led to delay and proved to be cumbersome. In practice, the probation officer used to begin his investigations soon after the juvenile offender was referred to him by the police, i.e., before court appearance, although the report itself would not be submitted until guilt was established. The Youth Law of 1971 provided legal authority for this procedure.

Since the Ordinance of 1937, it has been the established policy of the juvenile court that a probation officer is always present at court sessions, whereas adult probation officers prepare a report or are present in court only when requested to do so by the court. By this very fact, the juvenile probation officer obtains a special status within the juvenile court setting, and has access to all information which emerges during the trial. A probation officer is not only expected to suggest in his report methods of treatment (as of 1961; see p. 160, fn. 5), but under the Youth Law of 1971 can later request the court to change a particular treatment measure that has been decided upon, provided that measure is still in force at the time when the change is requested.

The written report is now mandatory and it is the probation officer's duty to submit to the court not only the official report but any further examinations requested by the court as well. Generally, the report should include information on the past behavior of the offender, his upbringing and home conditions, his parents and siblings, his medical history and that of other members of his family. Since the court is concerned with children and young persons, minors who are still dependent on their parents, relatives, or other adults, the investigation must extend to these adults also, whether or not they are in fact guiding or supervising the minor concerned. Here again we see the different approach made to juvenile as contrasted with adult offenders.

It is generally agreed that the recognized aim of the juvenile court is the resocialization of juvenile offenders through authoritative intervention. But a judge of the juvenile court is in no position—either by his qualifications or by his commission—to investigate personally the living conditions of juvenile offenders, or to make arrangements for placement and rehabilitation, and must work through specialized community services toward these ends. So the process of resocialization, a legal function initiated by court order, is executed by auxiliary services, either government or voluntary agencies. In this field, the welfare worker is by his vocation the most qualified person to perform the complicated task of, on the one hand, carrying out the directions of the court, and, on the other hand, ensuring the participation of the individual.

There is a unique relationship between the juvenile court and the welfare worker, one which needs to be examined in some detail; I will here confine myself to this aspect, leaving aside other joints at issue in the duties of a welfare worker. Modern developments in the field of social work call for a reconsideration of the contribution which a welfare worker can make while serving a court. Previously, the major contribution one expected was an objective picture of the economic conditions and family background of the juvenile offender. Nowadays much more emphasis is laid on the psychology of interpersonal relationships within a particular family, on emotional upheavals and experiences accumulated in the process of growing up, on known or mostly unknown motivations and behavior patterns, and on the sociological aspects of life in the community at large. The profession of welfare worker now requires both academic knowledge and intensive practical training, common sense and a sensitive approach to the individual and to general sociological phenomena. A welfare worker is no longer concerned only with alleviating material distress, but with the more difficult and more socially meaningful job of helping the individual adapt to the rapidly changing conditions of the world in which we live. In dealing with juvenile offenders, the application of an individual approach to a mass phenomenon is of considerable significance.

There are three categories of welfare workers who may be in the service of a juvenile court. Probation officers work only with a court; their clientele is determined by court order. Welfare workers who are trained social workers serve a court when called upon to prepare a report. Welfare workers who lack training but are drawn to this kind of work for different reasons may also work with a court, either permanently or provisionally.

THE PROBATION OFFICER

Without wanting to minimize the usefulness of all three categories available to a court, it cannot but be recognized that the probation officer has a special position. The probation officer is actively engaged in the fight against juvenile delinquency, and he shares therefore a considerable amount of the responsibility which the court must carry. The probation officer is working in the frontline, as it were. More than any other welfare worker, he is geared towards a deeper understanding of criminology, psychogenesis, and penology because of his training and function within the court setting. It is therefore quite natural that a court can rely more heavily on the investigations of a probation officer than on those of any other welfare worker. The same holds true to an even larger extent in the supervision of those who are put on probation by court order.

It is my profound belief that any juvenile court must have professionally trained workers if it is to make a real contribution to treatment and prevention. The magnitude and multiplicity of the problems with which a juvenile court is confronted in an increasingly complex society and the heavy responsibilities which rest on the shoulders of a juvenile court judge demand the use of trained personnel, if the court's effectiveness is not to be severely hampered.

In Israel, the majority of probation officers hold degrees or diplomas in social welfare. Others hold qualifications in education. Training in social welfare gives the highest professional qualifications for this kind of work, particularly if one considers the wide range of social and personal problems involved in the treatment of juvenile offenders. There are a number of questions which confront all those who work in some way or another with the juvenile court. This would naturally include those who are concerned with formulations concerning the legal structure of the juvenile court. Some of the following questions are therefore concerned with law and procedure, whilst others are more a matter of administrative agreement and arrangements.

The most pertinent problems are the following:

1. Is an investigation mandatory, or is it undertaken without legal provision?
2. Is an investigation ordered in serious cases only?
3. Is the yardstick for a "serious" case the type of offense or is it the condition of an offender, or is it both?
4. Is the investigation undertaken at the prehearing or presentence level?
5. Does the law prescribe the content and nature of the investigation, or is this left to the discretion of the investigator?
6. Is special training required for those who undertake an investigation on behalf of the juvenile court?
7. What is the legal status of those who undertake an investigation on behalf of the juvenile court?
8. Is the report which is submitted by the investigator to the court regarded as part of evidence?
9. Is the investigation carried out by the police, especially if there is a juvenile police unit in existence?

SUPPLEMENTATION OF PROBATION

The Probation of Offenders Ordinance of 1944 and later amendments laid it down that the probation service is part of the Ministry of Social Welfare. The departments for juveniles and adults are separated. The adult probation service was established in 1951, and only very slowly did it come to be regarded by the judiciary as a partner in law enforcement. The judiciary and public opinion alike previously held the preconception that probation can contribute to the rehabilitation of juvenile, but not adult, offenders. Even today, one finds considerable reluctance to believe in its effectiveness for adults.

The ordinance of 1944 reiterated the principle laid down earlier that the court may make a probation order without proceeding to a conviction, or may make such an order while proceeding to a conviction, for both adults and juveniles alike. A probation order is made for a period of not less than one year (amended to six months in March, 1971) and not more than three years. There are provisions for residence or other conditions for securing good conduct, and a clause covering possible payment of compensation or costs. There are procedures governing offenses committed while on probation, failure to comply with the probation order, amendment of a probation order, and the like.

In 1953 important innovations in the 1944 ordinance had a considerable impact on implementation of the order for probation.[4]

(a) Probation, listed in the Criminal Code Ordinance of 1936 as a punishment, was deleted as such from that code. Thus the law established that a probation order could no longer be regarded as a means of punishment. This was a logical consequence of the provision in the Probation of Offenders Ordinance of 1944, by which a probation order may be issued without proceeding to a conviction (which may, however, be inserted if for some reason or another the probation order is nullified, and some other means of disposal is ordered instead).

(b) A probation order may be made only after a written report by a probation officer has been submitted to a court. If probation is to be regarded as an important method of treatment within the community, there must be some selection of those who are put on probation. If there is no report by a probation officer, the test for selection

---

[4] Probation of Offenders Ordinance (Amendment) Law, 5714–1953, in *Laws of the State of Israel*, Vol. 8, p. 44–45.

remains the type of offense, the impression the offender makes on the court, whether or not the offense is the first offense, the age of the offender, or some combination of these. This is by no means a sufficient guide to the court, being based to a large extent on impressions; no treatment method should be chosen by such means. If, on the other hand, an appropriate investigation is carried out, the chance of error and haphazard decision is considerably lessened.

(c) By the original provision of the 1944 ordinance it was mandatory that a woman or girl should be under the supervision of a female probation officer (Probation of Offenders Ordinance, 1944, section 14[2]). Experience has shown, however, that it is sometimes expedient for a male probation officer to be in charge of a female probationer, and vice versa. A probation order should not be hampered by legal provisions which may imperil its success as treatment. Probationers are therefore no longer dealt with by probation officers according to their respective sexes, but rather according to their personalities and needs.

(d) A probation order by which a person is released on probation without having been convicted shall not entail the consequences of a conviction in any respect, save where a contrary intention appears from the ordinance or any other law.

The Knesset went a step further in a law of 1954, implemented by special proclamation on 1 December 1961, which stated that a written report by a probation officer is mandatory on a court in instances in which a law provides for a prison sentence of six months or more.[5] The proclamation provided further that this provision is limited for offenders who are under the age of twenty-one years on the date of the commission of the offense.

In many countries a probation officer does not have the responsibility of making recommendations concerning punishment. But by this section the probation officer may include in his report a recommendation to the court as to the nature of the punishment which has, in his opinion, a chance of reforming the offender. This section provided for the first time by law that a probation officer is in fact required to submit to the court a recommendation as to the nature of a particular sentence. The law does not suggest, however, that recommendations by a probation officer should be binding on the court.

---

[5] Penal Law Revision (Modes of Punishment) Law, 5714–1954, in *Laws of the State of Israel*, Vol. 8, p. 206.

The importance of probation as a method of treatment was enhanced with the enforcement, in 1962, of a new amendment to section 18 of the law of 1954, introducing a conditional prison sentence.[6] The amendment arose from experience in the administration of section 18; it provided first, that: "where the court imposes conditional imprisonment, it may make a probation order for the whole or a part of the period of suspension, and the provisions of the Ordinance shall, subject to the provisions of this Law and mutatis mutandis, apply to the probation order." Secondly, it stated: "if a court has convicted an accused person of a further offense, but has not imposed imprisonment for the [second] offense, it may, notwithstanding what is said in another section of that law, order the extension of the [original] period of suspension for an additional period not exceeding two years, if it is satisfied that in the circumstances of the case it would not be just to implement the conditional imprisonment. Reasons for such extension must be recorded in the file." These two innovations mean in practice that the offender is not left on his own to make good when he is given a conditional prison sentence. It may be during just this period that he is vitally in need of assistance in staying out of trouble. He receives practical assistance if a probation order is attached to a conditional sentence. Furthermore, we have come to realize that a considerable percentage of offenders do not always realize the danger of imprisonment if given a conditional prison sentence, and their own immaturity or unwarranted associations may lead ultimately to the commission of a further offense. Thus the provision for another postponement of the conditional prison sentence may keep out of prison those offenders who try to make good. It is, as it were, an additional and final chance. These two provisions are an indication of a permissive approach to the shortcomings of those offenders who have not yet made a profession of crime.

Probation is not restricted to a certain kind of offense—except in case of a mandatory life imprisonment, when it can naturally not be used. Nor is it restricted to first offenders alone.

SUCCESS OF PROBATION

If probation is not as often used by courts in Israel as it is elsewhere, this may be due to the following factors.

---

[6] Penal Law Amendment (Modes of Punishment) (Amendment No. 5) Law, 5723–1963, in *Laws of the State of Israel*, Vol. 17, 1962/1963, p. 102.

1. Probation, particularly for adults, is still rather a new method in Israel, and many judges are perhaps not yet convinced of its efficacy.
2. Since only professionally trained people are nowadays accepted into this service, there are not sufficient candidates to fill existing vacancies. A court may legitimately consider whether or not to make a probation order if there is no certainty that the order will be implemented.
3. Higher salaries would attract more highly trained men, increasing the rate of success. This would have an impact on judges when they come to consider the different methods of disposal for a particular offender.

In Israel there is no adequate follow-up of the success of probation. The figures given in Table 10.1 are only an indication of the frequency with which this method was applied in Israel during 1960–70.

The figures as given in Table 10.1 need some explanation to put them into proper perspective. Figures are compiled according to the number of convictions which were made during a particular year. All probation orders issued during any given year are counted, even though several may be against the same person. Further, it is quite conceivable, where there is more than one offense, that a probation order was issued with a conditional prison sentence, or that a court decided to impose a short prison sentence as a deterrent or as punishment for one offense, and a probation order for another. It should be stressed, however, that for a particular offense a probation order can now be made in conjunction with a conditional prison sentence, or in conjunction with any other method of punishment or disposal. The amnesty of 1967 explains the decrease of convictions and the comparatively high percentage of probation convictions during that year.

The probation officer's mandatory written report has occasioned conflict with the judiciary. One does indeed encounter a certain reluctance to be guided by another discipline in matters which belong traditionally to the domain of the criminal court alone. For social and medical services focus their examinations on social, psychological, and criminologenic factors, matters of which the judiciary has usually no intimate knowledge, and for which judges may even have a certain distrust. Resistance is further enhanced by the frequency with which the court is compelled to adjourn a case for the sole purpose of receiving a report by a probation officer. Matters become even more complicated if the social investigation reveals personal aspects of the offender that may have had direct bearing on the commission of the offense. By introducing this new element a social investigation may cause judicial uneasiness and

TABLE 10.1

PROBATION ORDERS AND CONDITIONAL PRISON SENTENCES IN JUVENILE COURTS, 1960–70

Year	Total no. of disposals[a]	Total no. of probation orders	% of probation orders to disposals	No. of probation orders only	% of probation orders only to disposals	Total no. of probation orders and conditional prison sentences	% to total probation orders
1960	4,858	685	14.1%	669	13.8%	16	2.3%
1961	4,845	743	15.3	716	14.8	27	3.6
1964	5,391	895	16.6	834	15.5	61	6.8
1965	5,616	882	16.0	821	14.6	61	6.9
1966	5,740	994	17.3	916	16.0	78	7.8
1967	3,864	758	19.6	709	18.3	49	6.4
1968	4,623	990	21.4	926	20.0	64	6.4
1969	5,125	1,100	21.4	993	19.3	107	9.7
1970	5,697	1,114	17.8	1,008	17.6	106	9.5

Source: Israel, Central Bureau of Statistics, *Special Series*, No. 370, 408 Table 1, p. 5; Table 6, p. 9.

[a] Offenses counted are those which require the taking of fingerprints, i.e., against public order, against the person, against morality, against property, fraud, and forgery.

uncertainty at the point of sentencing, and there is bound to develop an undercurrent of resistance to social services, and to mandatory provisions to enlist professional advice. However, a serious concern with the causes and effects of delinquency must be based on full knowledge of the social and psychological aspects. It has a wider and sounder basis because of the social investigation. On the other hand, if the social investigation has led the judge to a reconsideration and to a revised view of the envisaged prison sentence, it has served the interest of justice.

Before deciding whether probation is successful, one needs clarification of "successful." Can this be gauged by an objective measurement, such as a repeated police record, or repeated court appearance? Can one rely on subjective evaluation such as improvement in delinquent behavior, although there still occur minor offenses, or steadiness at work instead of loitering? The yardstick for "success" or "failure" may depend largely on the attitude of an investigator to the general issue of crime and punishment. It seems to me that a purely formal and statistical approach can hardly do justice to probation as a method of disposal by criminal courts.

Two additional aspects have still to be briefly discussed, because they are of major importance for the practical implementation of the probation order. One belongs in the domain of adminstration, while the other is part of what might be called the treatment process.

PROBATION AND THE COURTS

The basic fact that a probation order is made according to a statutory provision establishes a triangular situation: the court—the offender—the probation officer. During the duration of probation this triangular situation is not necessarily static, because a salient feature of probation is that the case can be reopened in specific instances: failure to comply with the order; a request by the probation officer to insert new conditions —i.e., residence—; a request to terminate the probation order early or to prolong it. This last, however, can never be done for a period of more than three years altogether. We are dealing with a dynamic situation, and there exist potential resources which can be further developed.

To which administration or agency should a probation officer belong? In Israel the probation service, for adults and juveniles alike, is an integral part of the ministry of social welfare. Probation officers are, while executing their duties, under the direction of an administration different from that of the court administration, which is part of the ministry of justice. What legal power, therefore, has a judge who issued a probation order to request information from the probation officer about the actual process of probation in a particular case? Furthermore, can he interfere on his own initiative after he has issued a probation order, and can he request, on legal grounds, that a different course from that used by the probation officer be taken during the period of probation? Does such a situation perhaps lead to a double loyalty—to the court which issued the probation order, and which, as it were, reflects on the work of the probation officer part of the authority invested in a court order; or to the ministry of social welfare, where he is employed?

In Israel, probation officers are employees of the state, appointed by a government selection committee. They have the same rights and obligations as any other government employee, and their appointments are not dependent, for good or for ill, on individual judges. This system of appointment at the will of the judge, practised in some countries, seems to me utterly inappropriate. Such a procedure means that probation as a method of disposal following a statutory provision becomes a matter of personal relationship between an individual judge and a particular probation officer. After all, other correctional personnel such as instructors and head masters in educational institutions or in prisons are not appointed by individual judges, and their duties do not depend upon personal likes or dislikes. Why should this be different for a probation officer?

Nonetheless, I do believe that a probation service should belong to the court administration, while maintaining the same appointment procedure as is customary for all government employees. The mere fact that the probation service is part of the court administration should promote a better understanding and cooperation between two disciplines, leading ultimately to a more frequent use of probation because the judiciary will become better acquainted with it.

The triangular situation is very relevant. The confidentiality of the probation officer's report is obviously an issue of major importance. Among probation officers there is a widespread attitude that, if the report is not to be regarded as confidential, many details which might have been included for completeness should be left out; thus the value of the report is considerably minimized. If, on the other hand, the report is a confidential document, conveying detailed information on the background and social conditions of the offender, its value for the court is enhanced.

Although we are concerned with a presentence report, which has no bearing on the primary case of guilt or innocence, this report may sway the issue when punishment is considered. Here, confidentiality may have far-reaching consequences. In Israel, the issue of confidentiality of the probation officer's report was still not settled legally until recently. Only as from 15 January 1966, does a clear legal provision exist. Section 173 of the Criminal Procedure Law states that a copy of the report of a probation officer, in those instances where such a report is mandatory, and the results of any other examinations and investigations shall be delivered to the prosecutor and to the defense counsel, and that the court shall hear any argument as to anything contained therein. The court may also order that a copy be delivered to the accused. Most relevant, however, is the section which states that "on the reasoned proposal of the probation officer or on its own motion, [the court] may, for special reasons, order that the whole or part of the contents shall not be disclosed to the parties."[7] The section makes it clear that, as a rule, the report by the probation officer should be delivered "to the prosecutor and to the defense counsel." Furthermore, the court may also order that a copy of it be also delivered to the accused. The section which gives a probation officer legal status to voice his opinion on confidentiality is of great interest. It seems to me that this solution does justice to all concerned. On the one hand, it enables the parties to receive the necessary information which a report entails, on the other, it makes provision that this information be withheld if deemed desirable. Obviously, the onus of proof rests on the shoulders of the probation officer, who will have to put before the court good reasons why the contents of the report should not be disclosed. Confidentiality is of particular importance should a court decide to put an offender on probation. If material which the offender thought or was hoping would be regarded as confidential information is disclosed at the trial, such disclosure might imperil a successful period of probation. One has to remember that we are dealing with many intangible matters. A careful and tolerant attitude can foster rather than hinder the rehabilitation of an offender.

I have tried to convey that the basic object of judicial intervention in the juvenile court is to ensure the resocialization of those who are tried there, in different ways and directions. In all the underlying idea is to base sentencing on material which is prepared by persons who work in conjunction with the juvenile court so as to enable the judge to evaluate the conditions in which the child or the young person lives. Here again, therefore, we are dealing with a process of individual examination in a judicial setting designed to treat a mass phenomenon,

---

[7] Criminal Procedure Law, 5725–1965, in *Laws of the State of Israel*, Vol. 19, p. 158.

and must make use of complementary services. The juvenile court needs social services to achieve its objective and, interestingly enough, these social services often need court intervention in order to achieve their treatment objectives. Thus there exists a unique relationship between the juvenile court and the social services, particularly between the probation officer and the court. In matters of seriously delinquent behavior, no sentencing can or should be done without the collaboration of the probation officer who is in direct contact with the court.

11

Educational
Establishments

Juvenile courts have adopted the premise that a juvenile offender should be removed from his own home and environment only after careful investigation.[1] Sufficient is known by now to make it clear that removal from home may actually foster, rather than mitigate, delinquent behavior patterns. On the other hand, it cannot be overlooked that removal may sometimes be effective in the rehabilitation of juvenile offenders; sometimes a court has no alternative.

A case in point is T. S., twelve years old when he came to the juvenile court. The report submitted by the probation officer showed that when he was eight years old, he came to Israel with his parents from Iraq. There his father had been employed as a carpenter, but in Israel he failed to get a job in his trade: his proficiency was low, and he could not pass the required trade union examinations. He was therefore engaged for occasional jobs, but gradually he drifted into apathy, and after some time made no particular efforts to secure work. Instead, his wife became more and more the major breadwinner.

T. S., who had difficulty adapting to regular school attendance, soon realized that there was no control of this any more at home, and began to play truant. After four grades of elementary school, he was almost never present. The school report revealed that T. S. was of poor intelligence, that he had difficulty getting on with other children, and that sometimes he became rather aggressive.

T. S. was brought to the juvenile court for selling empty boxes stolen at the market place. It was clear that no serious offense had been committed, nor was any damage caused to the owner of the boxes, which

---

[1] The term "educational establishment" refers to places to which a juvenile offender is sent by court order. Some are set up by the government for the training and rehabilitation of juvenile offenders only.

were returned. There could be no doubt, however, that T. S. was badly in need of care. His parents had no control over him, he would not return to school, he was roaming about in streets and market places, and was friendly with a group of delinquent boys. A delinquent career could be anticipated for him.

The court had no choice, therefore, but to commit T. S. to an educational establishment, hoping that he would be able to adjust to conditions there. It turned out, however, that T. S. found it very difficult to stay at this place, and absconded frequently. This went on for several months; often he didn't go home either, but stayed with friends at hideouts. Fortunately, one of the instructors of the educational establishment succeeded in establishing a relationship—albeit loose—with T. S. It was he who always brought T. S. back, until he could finally settle down. In this instance it was feared that a formal approach, such as notifying the police, might lead him even more astray.

T. S. had been committed to the educational establishment for a period of three years. Here again, this long period stood in no relationship to the nature of the offense. Such a commital order indicates that a yardstick entirely different from that used with adults has to be applied to juvenile offenders. T. S. acquired during this period a considerable amount of emotional stability which was beneficial for him on his return home. By then, he had also matured to such an extent that he could keep a factory job, and was helping his mother to support the family.

In the juvenile court one is often confronted with the picture of a juvenile offender who is the victim of his home situation or of social facilities inadequate to his special needs. Such conditions may lead the court to an unconscious identification with and protective paternalism towards him. Often a judge cannot but be impressed by the hardship, the emotional and economic deprivation, which many juvenile offenders have endured from early childhood, and it is only natural that he is inclined toward a lenient attitude. The neurotic or the more experienced offender will sense such an underlying current with a particular judge, and will try to manipulate the issue in his own favor.

Although such situations do exist, much can be said in favor of the basic approach in Israel that the decision to send a juvenile offender to an educational establishment should be based mainly on the seriousness of his educational and general social condition, and not necessarily on the seriousness of the offense which he has committed. Sometimes, a minor offense reveals a serious behavior disorder, and in such instances a placement order may be indicated. On the other hand, one frequently encounters in the juvenile court situations in which a serious offense was committed, in law, but where the offender presents minor problems only. It would to my mind be inappropriate for us to be guided unduly by the character of the offense, because young people who are in the process of growth should be dealt with from an entirely different standpoint from that used with adults. If we regard the juvenile court as a place which can meet the basic needs of juvenile offenders—needs their home has not, and probably will not meet, then the yardstick for a particular offense must be different. Whereas a prison sentence for adult offenders indicates the seriousness of a particular offense, a placement order to an educational establishment indicates rather the seriousness of the condition, educational and social, of a particular juvenile offender. Obviously, there are certain prerequisites for a basically different judicial approach to juvenile offenders. They include the preparation of material by professionals before a placement order; careful selection of the cases suitable for placement; and intimate knowledge of community facilities and resources.

TYPES OF EDUCATIONAL ESTABLISHMENTS

In Israel, there are educational establishments catering solely for juvenile offenders, but there are others of a general nature that will accept juvenile offenders that fall within the range of the young people they cater for. On a smaller scale there are also some kibbutzim who will accept juvenile offenders within one of the youth groups who spend a training period in a kibbutz. Here again the educational standard and general behavior of the juvenile offender—not the fact that he has committed an offense—and whether or not he is on probation are relevant. Over the last few years approximately two-thirds of those who had to be placed away from home have gone to one of the schools established for juvenile offenders, whereas the other one-third has been placed elsewhere. Time and again, we have seen that the major behavioral difficulties that one encounters with many juvenile offenders make a placement order within a general educational establishment or a foster family almost an impossibility.

The following list gives a picture of the variety of available placements. Needless to say, these figures may change somewhat over the years, depending on the types of offender subject to juvenile court placement orders.

Placement Facilities for Juvenile Offenders

Government establishments specifically for juvenile offenders	61.6%
Private and public agencies	19.2%

Government and public establishments for the mentally retarded	9.3%
Probation with condition of residence	5.1%
Foster families	4.8%

In 1955 rules based on the Juvenile Offenders Ordinance of 1937 were published, establishing a youth authority within the ministry of social welfare. It is the duty of the youth authority to set up educational establishments for juvenile offenders; to select and to direct juvenile offenders to placements which seem appropriate to their special needs; to initiate and to supervise training programs for institution personnel, etc. It has been felt that all services for children who are in need should be taken care of within this ministry irrespective of whether or not they are based on a court decision. The mere fact that there exists a placement order issued by the juvenile court should not imply a punitive approach, although enforcement and implementation are sometimes facilitated and even stabilized by court intervention. For instance, if a juvenile offender absconds from an educational establishment to which he was committed by the youth authority on the basis of a court order, he will be brought back by the police if the establishment itself has failed to return him. The police need no special warrant for doing so, but intervene by reason of the order of placement which was initially issued by the juvenile court. Moreover, if it should transpire, for educational, administrative or other reasons, that a juvenile offender has to be removed to another establishment after the initial placement, this may be done by the youth authority without even notifying the juvenile court, which hears about it only when an offender absconds, or commits an offense for which he is brought to court.

In Israel, educational establishments for juvenile offenders are all, with one exception, of the open camp type, and the régime is permissive to a considerable degree. Many juvenile offenders have responded favorably to such an approach. Most of them have grown up in a rejecting environment, full of conflicts and temptations, in which they have been deprived of elementary material and emotional needs. In our schools they experience, perhaps for the first time in their lives, a personal approach. Their shortcomings are taken into account, and they are not rejected because of them—a new experience, with a beneficial effect. Although much is demanded, according to their potential abilities, there is no punishment for failure. The fostering and supporting conditions which prevail in the educational establishments enable many a juvenile offender to arrive at a different outlook on himself and on society in general.

A follow-up study on the results of different placement facilities—which should be further developed and which abandoned—would be of great help for further planning. Unfortunately, none exists. Yet generally speaking, it has been our experience that private and public agencies and foster families are often unable to cope with the various forms of behavior disturbances of children and their parents. Although the mere fact of their willingness to accept juvenile offenders can be regarded as an indication of great good-will towards children and understanding of their difficulties, there is less tolerance for the parents concerned. Parents, for their own reasons, sometimes thwart the progress made by their children—a frustrating experience for those who have tried to make good the earlier damage. While within public and private agencies the burden of dealing with children and their parents is divided among several people, the instructors in a particular school, a foster family is alone in facing difficulties. One can observe that initial tolerance decreases as difficulties accumulate. It is no coincidence that educational establishments set up specifically for juvenile offenders seem to be the most appropriate places for the more serious delinquent behavior patterns, because they are geared per se to cope with the difficult situations inherent in delinquency.

The following case may illustrate some of the difficulties one encounters, if parents, for their own reasons, hinder a smooth process of adaptation. The headmaster of an educational establishment wrote to the court about Allon, aged thirteen years, who had absconded from the school:

Allon has now been at our place for over a year. He is a nice boy and well liked by his companions, possibly because of his complaisant nature. Yet he has so far made no real contact with any one of the adults working in our establishment. His attitude towards them is one of great suspicion, and sometimes also of defiance. His reservation is conspicuous, and finds expression in his stories that "very soon" his parents are going to take him away from the establishment. Indeed, his parents started to bombard the authorities with letters about his release two months after he was committed by court order to an educational establishment for juvenile offenders. This has continued, and in the meantime Allon gives the impression that he is expecting "any minute" to be released, in his own words, "as my parents promised me." When the parents realized that their endeavors were in vain, they suggested that the boy be referred to another establishment where another son of theirs was educated. On investigation it transpired that Allon's parents had quarreled for many years, each one of them trying to bring Allon or another child on his own side, as a weapon.

During the deliberations of the staff, we have come to the conclusion that the aggressive attitude of the parents towards our establishment makes it practically impossible to keep Allon with us any longer. We suggest therefore that he be transferred to another school, where he will be able to settle down. We are all definitely of the opinion that it would be detrimental for him to be sent home to his parents.

The headmaster did not realize that he was really saying that the staff of the establishment had become tired of the situation, and that they could no longer stand the hostile and aggressive attitude of Allon's parents. What the staff overlooked was that this pattern would repeat itself in another establishment, and that not much could be gained from a removal.

There are other problems. Members of the staff of the educational establishments set up for dealing with juvenile offenders often give way to misgivings about their helpfulness. Any educational establishment can decide to return a difficult juvenile to the youth authority, but this cannot be done by the school set up by the government for this very purpose. There is a tendency for such staff members to leave the establishment entirely, as time passes and there is an accumulation of frustrating experiences.

LENGTH OF COMMITTAL

Table 11.1 gives the length of the various committal orders during the years 1964–1969. In this table one can observe several interesting features.

There has been a constant decrease in committal orders issued for a period of one year. The juvenile court has recently had to deal with the more serious type of offender, for whom a one-year sentence in an educational establishment does not seem adequate. Reeducation is a difficult process, and immediate results should not be expected.

On the opposite end of the scale we find that committal orders for four years have also decreased (orders for even larger periods ceased entirely as of 1966) although not so greatly. Judges in the juvenile court have come to realize that juvenile offenders reach a saturation point, and that a committal order for a long period may have a negative rather than a positive effect. Here again one can see the essential difference between a committal order to an educational establishment and a prison sentence. If a long committal order is made for punitive rather than educational reasons, we do not serve the interests of rehabilitating the juvenile offender. Although it is to my mind legitimate to take into account punishment, this has to be evaluated in an entirely different fashion than for adult offenders. Among the latter, the seriousness of

TABLE 11.1

LENGTH OF COMMITTAL OF JUVENILES TO EDUCATIONAL ESTABLISHMENTS, 1964–69

Year	Total no. of committals	No. of committals by length of time								
		1 yr.	1½ yrs.	2 yrs.	2½ yrs.	3 yrs.	3½ yrs.	4 yrs.	5 yrs.	6 yrs.
1964	542	69	50	158	51	150	10	46	6	2
1965	573	62	51	216	40	126	31	45	1	1
1966	406	48	25	148	21	113	27	24	0	0
1967[a]	271	23	26	115	20	74	0	13	0	0
1968	390	10	48	154	37	113	0	28	0	0
1969	337	5	49	141	38	89	0	15	0	0
All years	2,519 (100%)	217 (8.7%)	249 (9.9%)	932 (37.0%)	207 (8.3%)	665 (26.4%)	68 (2.7%)	171 (6.7%)	7 (0.2%)	3 (0.1%)

Source: Official figures from the youth authority, Ministry of Social Welfare.
[a] The decrease during this year was due to the amnesty.
Note: Only the first committal order has been counted in this table.

the committed offense may often make punishment the major issue. In these instances, rehabilitation and reeducation become matters of secondary importance. For juvenile offenders the issue of rehabilitation has always to be taken into account.

Most committal orders were given for two years (37.0 percent) and, taken with orders for two-and-one-half and three years, constitutes the majority of committal orders (71.7 percent). This is, in my opinion, a good indication of the overtly individual approach of the juvenile court, which takes into account the realities of the situation of the young people, without losing sight of the need for correction.

In Israel a court cannot dispose of a case by an indeterminate sentence, either for adults or for juveniles. This is fortunate for juveniles, for an indeterminate sentence can easily work to the detriment of rehabilitation. As a general rule, juvenile offenders, either at the beginning or later, dislike the idea of spending many years in an educational institution. If they do not even know how long they are supposed to stay there, it may discourage them from making an effort toward rehabilitation. With no specific goal, it is useless for well-meaning adults to explain that it is for their own good to stay in an educational institution for a long period.

The indeterminate sentence puts the decision about release on the shoulders of the authority responsible for rehabilitating the juvenile offender. An order of release is made according to the merits of each case, a point of no mean importance. In fact, the great majority are released within two to three years, as is true in the United States and Europe. After a certain point not much progress can be observed, and there is always the danger of getting too used to the school; this may hamper independent thinking and development, and thus thwart a process of real rehabilitation. Release rather than further detention becomes expedient in this case. Again the intangible factors involved in dealing with young people must be stressed. Experience has shown that juvenile offenders detained for long periods are more prone to maladjusted behavior than those who stay for brief periods only. It is sometimes maintained that if the period is fixed by the juvenile court it has a punitive meaning for the offender, whereas an indeterminate sentence is regarded differently. This is pure hypothesis. For the juvenile offender the punitive connotation is there whether the period is fixed by the court or by another authority.

On the other hand, a fixed period of time is something tangible a juvenile offender can hold on to. Even the youngest count the months and even the days still remaining. The fact that they know when their stay will end can be made use of therapeutically, and may also have some value for the staff itself. It seems therefore that this method is more positive and more suitable for juvenile offenders.

NUMBER OF COMMITTALS

Table 11.2 details the number of committal orders, and compares them with other methods of disposal used by juvenile courts. The constant decrease in committal orders is an encouraging feature, but the absolute figures make clear that there is no corresponding decrease in juvenile offenders. A major reason for this decrease is the different method of issuing committal orders initiated in 1966.

TABLE 11.2

COMMITTAL TO EDUCATIONAL
ESTABLISHMENTS COMPARED
WITH OTHER METHODS OF DISPOSAL, 1964–69

Year	No. of convicted juveniles	No. of committal orders	% of committals to total convictions
1964	5,391	542	10.1%
1965	5,616	573	10.2
1966	5,740	406	7.1
1967	3,864	271	7.0
1968	4,623	390	8.4
1969	5,125	337	6.4

Source: Official figures from the youth authority Ministry of Social Welfare.
Note: Only the first committal order has been counted in this table.

THE RELEASE BOARD

The need for a Release Board dealing specifically with juvenile offenders who have been placed in educational establishments by court order led to the clauses in the Juvenile Offenders Ordinance (Amendment) Law, 5717–1957, incorporated into the 1971 Youth Law, dealing, among other matters, with early release. The amendment established a release board consisting of five persons: a judge in the juvenile court as chairman, the director of the youth authority or his deputy, the principle probation officers for juveniles or his representative, and a physician and educator, both appointed by the minister of social welfare. The minister was given power to release a juvenile offender from any educational establishment upon the recommendation of the release board, provided the juvenile offender had been in the school for at least one year. In special circumstances the release board could recommend release before the year elapsed.

An early release can be made with or without conditions. If however, the release stipulates that the juvenile offender has to be under the supervision of the after-care service, such supervision is limited to three years. The release board may not recommend an early release unless the director of the establishment where the juvenile offender is residing, the probation officer, and the juvenile offender himself have been given an opportunity to express their opinion. An early release can be refused only after an opportunity has been given to the juvenile offender, his parents, and his defending counsel, if any, to put forward their opinions on the request.

The juvenile offender, one or both of his parents, and the director of the educational establishment are heard orally before the release board. Before the meeting, written reports by the director of the establishment, the probation officer who prepared the report to the juvenile court prior to placement, and the after-care service are distributed to each member of the release board. A sample of 384 applications considered by the release board over a number of years showed that 64.5 percent were submitted by parents; 29.7 percent by offenders themselves, and 5.8 percent by directors of educational establishments. In some cases neither the parents nor the juvenile offender concerned consulted the director about their intention to request an early release—a fact which would not prevent the director from supporting the application before the release board. But in only 34 percent of all applications which were made by parents or juveniles themselves did the director of the establishment think that there was sufficient ground for an early release. Such support was always underlined by the applicant in his initial request to the board. Incidentally, there is no application form, because we prefer to leave it to the applicant to address the board in his own way, and to elaborate the reasons for early release in his own language.

The mere fact that parents of the juvenile offenders concerned may apply to the release board without even consulting the director of the school means, first, that applications which have no chance at all of approval are sometimes submitted. This entails waste of time and, more important still, often results in a frustrating situation for both the juvenile and his parents. The juvenile offender is nearly always unrealistic about his chances of early release and, if his application is refused, his condition at the educational establishment may deteriorate. On the other hand, the opportunity to apply for an early release is a basic right of a person who is removed by court order from his natural environment. This basic right is nowadays accepted in many countries for adults who have been to prison, and there is no reason why it should not be granted for juvenile offenders as well. In fact, the triangular confrontation that evolves before the release board—offender, parent, director—has special meaning for all concerned, because the release board encourages a free exchange of views, and positive as well as negative aspects are rather fully discussed. Through this confrontation, indeed, we have become aware of many potential therapeutic aspects. The release board often for this reason postpones a decision to a later date, so as to enable further developments to take place. During this period the offender may be told to make a greater effort in specified fields, such as in his studies or at work, until further discussion of his request can take place. Furthermore, parents are often requested to make definite and better arrangements for the child before he can be returned home. Offenders and parents thus come to realize that it depends to a large extent on themselves whether or not an early release is granted. The emphasis is put on real attainments, and not on wishful thinking.

On the other hand, the release board is sometimes eager to make an immediate decision on release, so that supervision by the after-care service can be stipulated. At this time after-care is obligatory only if it is made a condition of the release board. In some instances, only two, three, or four months' detention remains. But the material submitted to the release board and the conversation with offender and parent at the board meeting may indicate that without the helping hand of the after-care officer, and without some formal commitment by the offender and the parent alike, there is not much chance for a genuine rehabilitation, and any progress made at the school will most likely be jeopardized.

The following table lists decisions made by the release board about 326 juvenile offenders.

	No.	%
Released at first meeting	130	39.8
Released at second meeting	92	28.2
Total released	222	68.0
Refused at first meeting	74	22.7
Refused at second meeting	30	9.1
Total refused	104	31.8

We made the interesting observation that the majority of applications by parents were based on the ground that their child had grown up sufficiently to bear his share in supporting the family. Another reason often given was that the child had learned his lesson and that no further delinquency was likely to occur. Experience has shown, however, that many juveniles do not acquire real working habits during their stay at the establishment, at least not to such an extent as to enable them to keep a job on a competitive basis. As a result they often drift from one job to another; this becomes an important contributing factor to further instability and to repeated delinquency. The situation is frustrating particularly in the case of those who had acquired a fairly good working record at the educational establishment, but who fail to compete for or to keep a job in town for any length of time. Those children who are still at compulsory elementary school age meet another difficulty. They may have made real progress at the educational establishment, but, even so, most of them are unable to keep pace with regular school requirements. After some effort on their part they will most probably drop out from school and roam about. It appears that in many instances the demands made by parents and society alike are too heavy for juvenile offenders to cope with. By ordinary standards, these demands are not more than average—even less than that. But quite a number of juvenile offenders need further and special care after their release, and if such care is not forthcoming they will drift back into delinquency.

To meet the special needs of those children and young people, we have developed in Israel "day-centers" for the sole purpose of catering to those who cannot keep pace at school or at work by ordinary standards.[2] These day-centers are organized on the basis of a half day of general schooling, and the other half day of instruction in one of the available trades. The curricula for these studies and trades are especially designed to strengthen potential abilities and to create an atmosphere of acceptance and on the other hand, of demands based on individual merit and ability. First, the day-centers enable a juvenile offender, or a wayward child, boy or girl, to be within a structured environment, with a definite educational and rehabilitational program, and motivate interest in these programs so as to strengthen self-assurance. Secondly, they enable these children and young people to remain within their own families, avoiding possible emotional upheavals and disadvantages of institutional life.

---

[2] The Youth Law of 1971 makes statutory provision that attendance at a day-center is one of the treatment measures at the disposal of the court.

If these day-centers are well organized, and if they provide for a sufficient number of trades, they can become of vital importance for those released from an educational establishment, as a stepping stone into city life again. They are sheltered places to ease the effect of confusing situations, and of failure and rejection. As structured places, they provide for a smooth integration into the ordinary standards and requirements of the community. Time and again in the experience of the release board such centers have proved to play a significant role in final rehabilitation.

12

The Juvenile Police and The Prison Service

THE POLICE FORCE

The police force in Israel is a national force, which was founded with the establishment of Israel. Its organization, internally and in relation to governmental agencies, dates back, however, to the Palestine mandatory police force, which acted until the establishment of the State of Israel. The legal framework now existing is still the Police Ordinance of 1926 (amended in 1971), and the Criminal Procedure (Arrest and Searches) Ordinance of 1924 (amended in 1971). Thus here again, the police force is guided in its directives which are still mainly those introduced in this country by the Palestine mandatory police force. It proved comparatively easy to establish the Israeli force, ranging from the rank and file up to high-ranking officers, and in many respects the British system in the administration of the police force was taken over. Recruiting sufficient manpower has, however, presented a great difficulty, particularly in face of mass immigration from many countries with different customs and traditions.

The minister of police is responsible to the government and the Knesset in all matters concerning the police force, whereas the implementation of the various duties of that force is put into the hands of the inspector general of police. The Police Ordinance of 1926 with the amendments introduced by the Knesset states that the function of the police force is: "The prevention, detection and prosecution of crime, the apprehension of offenders, the safe custody of those arrested, the maintenance of public order and the safety of persons and property."[1]

[1] H. E. Baker, *The Legal System of Israel* (Jerusalem: Israel Universities Press, 1968), p. 54.

The police force is ruled by special legislation. A policeman is considered, while in Israel, to be always on duty; he may be transferred from one part of the country to another, and he may not engage in any kind of employment save with special permission of the inspector general of police. The Police Ordinance provides for the establishment of courts of discipline for the trial of policemen of all ranks.

It belongs to the duties of the police force to prosecute offenders who are tried in the magistrates' courts, which include all juvenile courts. These prosecutors are specially selected and trained for this duty, and they are empowered to fulfill this function by special appointment.

In recent years the police force has also incorporated a special unit of policewomen, who are specifically employed in traffic duties, but are gradually being engaged also in patrol duties and the investigation of juvenile offenders.

The juvenile police unit began on a minor scale in 1956, and extended its activities nationwide as of 1960. The criminal investigation department of the police national headquarters now has attached to it a juvenile delinquency department, which deals with all matters related to juvenile offenders. The assumption is that a special unit, which is established to deal with juvenile offenders alone, will ultimately lead to a better understanding of their problems. The same understanding governs the establishment of the juvenile courts, their methods of investigation, interrogation, and prosecution.

In Israel, juvenile police units are housed in separate premises from other police units, and their personnel wear plain clothes. Almost every year there is a special in-service training course of about three weeks, which emphasizes the legal, social, and educational aspects of dealing with children and young people. There are three conspicuous problems which need full discussion in the matter of this juvenile police unit.

1. What is the yardstick for selection, and, on the other hand, what motivates people to volunteer for such a unit?
2. What can be done to avoid frequent changes in this special personnel? Such frequent change might undo the whole system, and it may also make the in-service training scheme superfluous.
3. What system can be established to foster personal advancement within a juvenile police unit, which has, per se, limited possibilities?

As could have been expected, there has been a considerable rise in the numbers of juvenile offenders since the special police unit began to function. These policemen are engaged on a full-time basis in the fight against juvenile delinquency, and it is only natural that they detect more offenses, they become aware of more hideouts, and they also become fairly well acquainted with delinquent and predelinquent behavior patterns of individuals and of groups. By virtue of their being exclusively engaged with juvenile misbehavior, they develop a sort of follow-up over time, which in turn may be felt in the field of prevention as well as of cure.

It has been our experience in Israel that policemen belonging to the juvenile police unit are able to get more information from suspects than was previously the case. Their approach is no longer a repressive and retributive one, and juvenile offenders can "afford," as it were, to confide in them and to disclose many offenses, including offenses not even reported to the police. The large majority of juvenile offenders make correct statements to the police once they have been apprehended. One is confronted not so much with the tendency of juvenile offenders to lie, as with the qualifications of the interrogating policemen to interview juvenile offenders adequately.

Incidentally, it is this tendency to "tell all," together with a desire to make a clean breast of things, and also to make a sort of reparation, which prompt a considerable number of youngsters to tell about the offenses they have committed. This interesting aspect of the dynamics involved deserves more attention.

A considerable number of minor offenses which previously would not have been thought worthy of consideration come to the attention of the juvenile police unit. It may not be in the interest of the community or of the individual concerned that such minor offenses should be investigated and their perpetrators brought to court—particularly where children under twelve years and first offenders are involved.

Over the years, it has become the practice for the juvenile police unit and the juvenile probation service in consultation to decide, on the merits of each case, whether or not to take it to the juvenile court. On the average, close to 30 percent of the cases each year are not brought to court. Although in these instances no file is opened in the juvenile court, the police nevertheless keep a record of the offense and of the offender—a fact which may be of consequence only for those who later commit another offense. Further, because many files are closed by the police out of court, those which are actually prosecuted in the juvenile court ought to belong to a more serious category, although this is not always the impression on the bench.

The well-functioning police unit must constantly strive to improve standards, be alert to changing conditions, and foster appropriate relationships with other agencies that deal with delinquent and predelinquent behavior in juveniles.

The Police Ordinance of 1926 provided that the prison service should be part of the police force, a situation that was altered only in 1946, by the Prison Ordinance which made the prison service separate and independent. The turbulent political period which followed delayed the implementation of the ordinance, and only on 1 January 1949 did the prison service become independent. The minister of police, however, is also the minister of the prison service.

This ordinance and amendments introduced by the State of Israel in 1971 is in force today. The most conspicuous amendments are: the abolition of corporal punishment as a disciplinary measure in prison; the introduction of a wage scale for labor in prison; the operation of optional release by a release board; leave of absence from prison on compassionate grounds for a period of up to four days.

The prison service had to be built from scratch, because the prevailing methods were outdated in Israel, which was eager to introduce modern ideas and new methods into this field. This intention was greatly hampered, however, by the mere fact that there were no appropriate buildings available. Police stations were converted into prisons, and even today, more than twenty years after the establishment of Israel as an independent state, we have no prison building which was built for that purpose.

The prison service is headed by the commissioner of prisons, who is directly responsible to the minister of police and prisons, and is assisted by heads of sections and heads of such special divisions as classification, vocational training, general labor, education, social work, medical treatment, secure custody, early release, personnel management, finance, supply, etc. Confinement to a particular prison, and transfer from one prison to another is the responsibility of the commissioner of prisons.

The internal classification of the prisoners is made in relation to the length of sentence and in accordance with the behavior difficulties of the prisoner concerned. There are two maximum-security prisons, there are medium-security prisons, a prison for women, and one for young prisoners aged fourteen to twenty-one years. According to law, a person over fourteen years can be sent to prison proper—a provision also contained in the 1971 Youth Law. There are two minimum-security camps, located close to each other, where the atmosphere is designed to foster rapid rehabilitation. In these prisons the maximum term is two years, and the prisoners have considerable freedom and privileges. Prisoners who have served the greater part of their prison sentence in a maximum- or medium-security prison may be transferred to the minimum-security camps to finish out their sentences. The women's prison has accommodation for about 70 women prisoners, but the average has never reached more than 30–40 prisoners. This small number has created a serious problem: there is almost no possibility of segregating the major offenders from the petty cases, or the juvenile females from more adult ones.

The youth prison is part of the prison service, and is set up as such not by legal provision but by administrative arrangement. Section 58 (c) of the Prison Ordinance of 1946 stated only that prisoners under sixteen years should not be kept together with adults. Using this as a basis, the prison commissioner refers young prisoners up to the age of twenty-one years or so to the youth prison. He is not, however, under any legal obligation to do so.

The unit of the youth prison has space for about 250 prisoners at a time, allowing the possibility of an intensive and personal contact with each prisoner. On the other hand, 75 percent of prisoners in the youth prison are sentenced for a period of under six months, and approximately 8 percent up to one year. Those in charge of the prison maintain that genuine rehabilitation cannot be accomplished owing to the short sentences. There may be some truth in this, but it can by no means be overlooked that long prison sentences are no guarantee of successful rehabilitation.

The youth prison is a security prison. It is based on three gradings, interrelated but nevertheless separate. The first grade comprises all newcomers, who are kept under strict discipline for about one month. Those who make progress are transferred to the second grade, where they enjoy more privileges and where discipline is not so strict. In this group one finds the majority of prisoners. The third stage is reserved for prisoners who need no strict supervision; they are confined within the prison walls, but their rooms, as it were, are outside the prison proper, in the courtyard of the prison. These prisoners live in a "camp," in barracks or in tents, which they are allowed to furnish according to their liking. They enjoy privileges, and have a sort of self-government. A committee of prisoners is responsible for all arrangements pertaining to their program and discipline. To belong to this group carries with it considerable prestige, and each member of the group will try to maintain standards demanded. Public opinion in Israel most probably supports experiments of this kind, particularly if young prisoners are involved.

Since 1952, the youth prison has had a comparatively high number of social workers, men and women, to whom prisoners are assigned. There are prisoners who have regular hours with the social worker assigned to them; others have only sporadic contact, or whenever some need arises. The social worker is expected to foster or renew contact with the prisoner's family, and also to prepare him for release. Special emphasis is laid, however, on social case work with the prisoner himself, and a qualified case work supervisor is in charge of this department.

In our experience about 50 percent of inmates in the youth prison have had almost no regular school education, and a further 30 percent attended for some time, but never finished elementary education. For all of them the major problem is acquiring some formal education that may help them find a suitable job.

Elementary education classes are regularly held for younger age groups during morning hours, and for others, during evening hours. The school is under the direction of the ministry of education, which assigns qualified teachers from outside the prison. All those imprisoned for over three months are obliged to attend. One of the major difficulties for the prison authorities is to stimulate the interest of these young prisoners in attending classes. Sanctions are sometimes imposed for non-attendance—mostly by deprivation of leisure-time activities.

One activity has to be mentioned because of its uniqueness. The young people of a village near the youth prison "adopted" this prison, and for many years have come regularly once a week to spend an evening within the prison with the prisoners. They organize activities: games, playreading, drama circle, folkdancing, chess competitions, etc. These meetings with people of their own age from "outside" are of tremendous importance to the young prisoner. Furthermore, once a year all prisoners of the youth prison are invited to spend a whole day at the village with families and participate in whatever the family is doing. This fosters a feeling of belonging, which is of great importance and is much appreciated by young prisoners.

Those young prisoners who serve a term of more than one year may join one of the existing vocational training courses which are run at the prison by the ministry of labor. That ministry has gained great experience during the last few years with skilled labor training centers for new adult immigrants. These centers have been planned so as to enable newcomers from less developed countries, with no formal elementary education, to learn a trade during a comparatively short period, about a year. This very efficient system seemed to be appropriate also for the prison administration, and such training centers were established in prisons as well. Most Israeli prisons now have training workshops, where prisoners receive systematic training as carpenters, locksmiths, auto mechanics, tailors, shoemakers, weavers. The vocational training courses are complemented by lectures on the theoretical aspects of a particular trade, and visits to factories outside the prison.

Elementary education and vocational training are thus the responsibility of the ministry of education and the ministry of labor respectively. It is up to them to select suitable teachers, to prepare an appropriate curriculum and training program, and to supervise their implementation.

An examination board in the ministry of labor issues certificates to successful participants. These certificates do not mention where the training took place, and entitle a released prisoner to apply for membership in the appropriate trade union—an important step towards his rehabilitation.

The department of social work which is attached to the prison service itself is an additional asset. All its social workers are fully trained and qualified; they are all stationed in prisons proper, where they work with the prisoners, although their contact with the prisoner's family is mostly outside the prison; most social workers are women, who work in the men's prison on a basis with other staff members. Much of the social worker's time is taken up with the preparation of reports and recommendations arising out of the early release of prisoners, or applications for furlough. Decisions on these matters are based to a large degree on the social worker's report, which is based on thorough investigation.

Under the British mandate, a prisoner who was sentenced to more than one month of imprisonment was entitled to an automatic release after he had served two-thirds of his sentence. A new law passed by the Knesset in 1954 established these possible rules for early release:[2]

1. Where a person has been sentenced to imprisonment for a period exceeding three months but not exceeding six months and has served two-thirds of such period, the minister of police may release him if it appears to him that the prisoner may properly be released" [The minister of police is also minister of prisons].
2. Where a person has been sentenced to imprisonment for a period exceeding six months and has served two-thirds of such period, the minister of police shall release him if the release is recommended by the parole board.

[2] Section 17, Penal Law Revision (Modes of Punishment) Law, 5714–1954, in *Laws of the State of Israel*, Vol. 8, p. 208.

The release board for prisoners differs from that for juvenile offenders.[3] A juvenile offender, even one fourteen or fifteen years old, who is serving a prison sentence, can be dealt with only by the release board for prisoners.

Furlough for a period of up to four days (96 hours) can be granted by the minister on application of the prisoner or at the request of the commissioner of prisons. This is considered as part of the original prison term. The prisoner is under no direct supervision for this period, except in special cases.

The concept of furlough raises many questions to which no immediate answer can yet be given. One has to weigh carefully the security risk against the positive benefits for rehabilitation, although one has also to consider the possible negative repercussions following the return to prison life. Experience in Israel so far has shown that somewhat more than 50 percent of applications for furlough were granted by the minister, and of these only a very negligible number have failed to return to prison.

---

[3] Sections 38 and 39, Penal Law Revision (Modes of Punishment), 5714–1954, in *Laws of the State of Israel*, Vol. 8, p. 211.

V
Conclusion

13

Remarks
on Treatment
and Correction

There exists a widespread controversy over the treatment and correction of juvenile offenders. Opinions cover the whole range of prejudices and beliefs which are present in the field of crime and punishment, and are particularly evident when the issue is one of sentencing. Many believe that a punitive attitude is most likely to yield good results, whereas others are convinced that a permissive attitude is the best way to secure the desired effect. Attitudes are both rationally and irrationally motivated; they are deep-rooted, and therefore difficult to change. Time and again one can observe that a strong component of irrationality prevails in this field. One finds professionals and laymen, practitioners and academicians belonging to one or the other group, and adhering to beliefs and convictions which are irrational rather than rational. Even scientists, who in their own field of work are accustomed to examining and analyzing events on the basis of facts, may find themselves swept into propounding statements about the correction of juvenile offenders, without trying to find out what the real facts are.

When a judge of a juvenile court is confronted with the question of sentencing he is first of all faced with the practical issue that his decision may have far-reaching consequences, for good or for evil, for each juvenile offender concerned. For a judge the constant question is twofold: first, what to do with a particular offender, or what kind of sentence to impose on him; and, secondly, how to convey to the juvenile offender the meaning of that disposition.

The choice of a particular disposition is a most difficult decision, one which has to be very carefully considered. It is for this reason that the juvenile court is often assisted by probation officers and other experts, who provide the court with information on many aspects of the socio-educational background of the juvenile offender, aimed to enable the court to understand the upbringing and milieu of each juvenile offender and also to draw conclusions for the future, based on that background.

Often, the success or failure of a particular disposition may depend also on the approach which is used by the court at this particular stage of the trial. This applies equally well to instances in which a benign and permissive attitude is adopted, as well as to those instances in which a stern and punitive approach seems to be indicated.

The basic elements for a decision by a juvenile court can be summarized as follows:

1. A court's decision has to be based on legal grounds.
2. Actual needs of the juvenile offender have to be established.
3. Matters of general public interest and security have to be taken into account. There is general agreement concerning the first item, which has recently found its most dramatic expression in the decision of the Supreme Court of the United States in the Gault case.[1] On items (1) and (2) there are invariably differences of opinion about which has to be given preference. It boils down to the issue of the rehabilitation of the individual versus the safeguard of public interest and security. Decisions by the Israeli Supreme Court, the highest court in Israel, while sitting as a court of criminal appeal, have repeatedly affirmed that, all being equal, the rehabilitation of the individual deserves in special circumstances to be preferred. In two cases in particular an exceptionally lenient attitude was taken by the Supreme Court after information was received from a probation officer; the decision stated among other things that in the last resort the best safeguard for public security lies in a genuine process of rehabilitation.[2] In order to achieve such a goal, it was said, a calculated risk merits serious consideration.

Incidentally, the calculated risk is encountered in the field of psychiatry also. In many ways an analogy can be drawn between treatment methods in psychiatry and those applied towards offenders, and especially juvenile offenders. Treatment of the mentally ill is nowadays focused on their rehabilitation within the community. The risks involved in the new methods of treatment are justified because the alternative is eternal hospitalization. With the knowledge which is now available, this is an outdated attitude. Moreover, it can safely be assumed that, with the accumulation of experience, remedies to diminish these risks may be found.

[1] *Supreme Court Reporter*, June 1, 1967, Vol. 87, No. 15, p. 1428.
[2] C.A. No. 239/55 in *Supreme Court Judgments*, 1955, Vol. 9, p. 1796, and C.A. No. 69/63 in *Supreme Court Judgments*, 1963, Vol. 17 (II), p. 712 (Hebrew).

The conventional approach to the treatment of offenders would prefer, in many instances, a placement order, which may be equated to hospitalization of the mentally ill. Prima facie, different measures of disposal may seem more risky. In fact, this is not the case, as new methods of treatment such as probation, or new methods of correction, such as minimum security prison camps, home leave for prisoners, etc., make abundantly clear. In all instances a careful selection of cases is imperative.

It can be taken for granted that the juvenile court is constantly searching for new methods of disposal, because those that have been used hitherto have not necessarily yielded good results. A judge in the juvenile court should be aware of community resources and facilities for the rehabilitation of juvenile offenders. Whatever philosophy he accepts as the correct approach to juvenile delinquency, a judge of the juvenile court cannot operate in a vacuum. It is not suggested that he himself should become an expert on the manifold treatment and correctional aspects involved in rehabilitation—in their implication, implementations, and limitations—but he has to have firsthand knowledge of their existence and working principles. Otherwise it may happen that there are available adequate diagnostic treatment and correctional facilities of which the juvenile court fails to make use or which are not used appropriately. The responsibility of a court decision about juvenile offenders, i.e., young persons who are in a process of growing and maturing, make such knowledge indispensable. Equally indispensable is an understanding of the dynamics of human behavior and interpersonal relationships, and of the cause and effect of the social and emotional conditions under which children and young persons grow up. A special alertness and sensitivity towards the various needs of juvenile offenders has to be developed and fostered.

Adequate knowledge of available facilities confers upon the juvenile court a qualified authority to make a contribution towards the rehabilitation of juvenile offenders. The alertness of a judge to deficiencies in existing facilities may prompt him to draw the attention of the responsible authorities to them. Moreover, as a result of such alertness, he may become instrumental in activating authorities or citizens to make appropriate provisions to meet needs. Because of the prestige which a judge usually carries within a community, his recommendations may yield results. In many instances this is of particular importance because social services for juvenile offenders are often nonexistent or not properly provided with adequate facilities for rehabilitation. This is most probably due to the fact that those who are in need of them have practically no pressure groups to exert influence on legislators and on public opinion.

Although it is nowhere laid down in law that such activities constitute one of the functions of a judge in the juvenile court, it is in my view an indispensable and complementary function of adjudication in that court. Here we encounter one of the basic differences between the functions of the juvenile court and that of the adult.

It cannot be maintained that, since this is a court of law, based on procedure, no basic distinction should be made between juveniles and adults. Such an approach would prevent the juvenile court from operating on principles which belong to the field of child welfare. Clearly, contemporary complexities of technological society, of social and family relationships in a fast-changing society, make a specialized and professional approach in a juvenile court imperative. Obviously, the yardstick for treatment or corrective measures is quite different in the juvenile court from that which is used in a court for adults. For, although the legal definition of offenses committed by a juvenile offender is generally based on that for adult offenders, the disposition of juvenile offenders rests in most instances within the realm of an educational and social approach. Yet, legal and socioeducational aspects are not always reconcilable, because the measure which may be adopted by the juvenile court at the stage of disposition may be out of proportion to the offense committed, if compared to the standards used in a court for adults.

The standard for a "serious" offense is by no means the same for juveniles as for adults. A serious offense by an adult invariably implies severe punishment, whereas among juvenile offenders a serious offense does not necessarily and *should not* necessarily imply such punishment. Among juvenile offenders a serious offense, or for that matter a nonserious offense, may manifest very serious behavior problems, many of which are beyond the control of the juvenile concerned. A judge of a juvenile court cannot but take such conditions into account, without making use of a punitive approach. This does not exclude punishment in appropriate instances. We are here concerned, however, with the basic issue, one of outlook and approach, which is at this point decisive. In a juvenile court a philosophy of treatment and correction is of paramount importance. Such a philosophy may insure a rational and balanced attitude, which in turn may enhance the chances of rehabilitation.

The disposition taken by the court is undoubtedly one of the most crucial and difficult aspects in the adjudication of juvenile offenders, and may have direct bearing—for good or for evil—on their future development. It is at this stage that the individual approach of the juvenile court finds its most pronounced expression. It is manifested, for example, by different decisions which may be taken concerning an offense committed by several offenders together. For in most instances the disposition is based on the personality of the individual offender, and not necessarily on the fact that the offense was jointly committed. Naturally, there are instances of this sort in which the case merits a major emphasis on an equal sentence. Again a selective approach is important. Yet, the maxim that a juvenile court is "offender-minded," and not "offense-minded," is still valid.

I believe it is the professional duty of the judge himself to explain the decision of the court, because his is the responsibility towards the offender and towards society alike. This very important matter can by no means be delegated to assistants of the court, defending counsel, a probation officer or the prosecuting officer, a clerk of the court or a social worker. The announcement of a disposition is not a mere technical matter, but is part of a whole process of criminal adjudication.[3]

Obviously, there is no rigid rule as to which measure is the most appropriate one for a certain type of offense, and for a certain age group. In a society like ours, whose most characteristic feature is change, there are many causes for juvenile delinquency. Upheavals and changes following immigration and migration, the changing status of parents within the family setting, rapid economic development and industrialization, changes of attitude to religious values; the impact of mass media on the behavior patterns of young people; all create confusing situations which make a multidisciplinary aproach to treatment and correction imperative.

It would be, therefore, inappropriate were a juvenile court to decide that the very young should not be committed to an educational establishment, lest such an order might decrease the opportunity for an orderly upbringing. Although such an approach may be well-meaning, it does overlook the fact that children, particularly at a tender age, are often grossly neglected by their parents, and also emotionally and materially deprived. To let them continue to live under such conditions means in effect to abandon them to an almost predetermined course of events. Such sweeping generalizations as that even careless and neglectful parents are always preferable to favorable placement away from home, are in most instances incorrect, and implementation of such views may lead to disastrous results for the children concerned. It is as inappropriate to assume that the same policy should apply to all first-trial situations. On the assumption that a minor who is being tried in court

[3] Peter D. Scott, "Juvenile Courts: The Juvenile's Point of View," *British Journal of Delinquency*, Vol. IX, No. 3 (January, 1959).

for the first time should be given an opportunity to prove that the offense was a matter of accident only, some advocate not using certain measures. Such an approach would dismiss, beforehand, the fact that it is often a matter of chance that a juvenile offender is caught and brought to court. Sometimes he may have committed a large number of offenses, and he may be badly in need of care through an appropriate court order, but no such action could previously be taken because he was not brought to court. A social welfare agency may have tried to take care of a wayward boy as a precaution against delinquency, but since this care is based on the voluntary agreement of the person in question, all endeavors are often in vain.

Therefore, to adhere to the formality that this may be a first appearance in court, disregarding a previous history of delinquent behavior, is to adopt an ostrich policy. It is by no means suggested that a juvenile offender should be held legally responsible for his deeds, unless they are clarified by proper legal procedure in court, but waywardness and delinquent behavior are important features in personality.

It would be difficult to argue at the stage of disposal that a first appearance in court demonstrates lawabiding behavior previously. Such reasoning is usually met with contempt by juvenile offenders. On the other hand, it is to my mind legitimate to dismiss a charge without punishment or other measure of treatment. Such a dismissal is in itself one measure of treatment, and in many instances a very effective one. But the reasons for a dismissal should be given frankly, so that the juvenile offender should know that the court has not chosen to punish behavior that is in fact delinquent. The real needs of a juvenile offender, not whether it is his first appearance before the court or a repeated trial, are the decisive issue at stake.

One might assume that juvenile offenders would be particularly attentive at this stage, trying to concentrate on what is being said or done in court. Experience has shown, however, that many juvenile offenders are distracted from concentrating on what is happening. Some are tense and anxious, some are upset and rebellious, others are subdued because of conflicts with their parents; there are still others who are apathetic and indifferent, or pretend not to care, and in some instances there is a pattern of "day-dreaming." One can observe what might be called an "emotional blocking," which is characteristic of such a situation. Personality or the stresses imposed by being in court, may be the cause. Whatever the reaction may be, and whatever importance one can attach to it, such reactions are of sufficient significance to be observed and to be taken into account at the stage of disposition. These are situations of crisis and stress, where one is confronted with failures by children and parents alike.

It has been my experience that one has to use a very direct approach, and explain in simple language the decisions which the court has taken, without, however, falling into the pitfall of using slang or street language. By a very direct approach, there is a greater chance of bringing home to the juvenile offender the seriousness of his position and the reality of the court situation. Otherwise too many "misunderstandings" may occur; that is, situations in which the juvenile offender (or his parent) maintains that a different disposition than that which actually took place was taken. Again, one must develop great sensitivity to match the needs of a particular juvenile offender to the measure which the court finds it expedient and necessary to adopt.

It is a characteristic feature of the juvenile court that its attitude and decisions have meaning for parents as well. At the stage of disposition parents are often anxious and tense, in the face of impending punishment, or because of conflicts that may exist between parents and their child. We may witness a situation in which one basic problem is manifested in the lack of communication between parents and children. And as children grow, estrangement between them and their parents becomes more and more pronounced. Lack of communication between members of a family has direct bearing later on lack of communication with society in general. Because of this lack, children and parents are suspicious and even hostile towards society. Such hostility may be, indeed, sometimes the only basis of understanding or communication between children and parents. The court situation accentuates such circumstances.

From time to time the growth of juvenile delinquency or a certain offense committed by juveniles provides a hue and cry, and demands for retribution and reprisals against juvenile offenders are voiced. Critics complain that the juvenile court is "soft" in its handling of juvenile offenders, and maintain time and again that more severe punishment by juvenile courts would inevitably contribute in the prevention of juvenile delinquency. All this leads to public confusion and bewilderment. In reality, however, all those who are in practice dealing, in one way or another, with juvenile offenders are aware that a large percentage of offenses committed by juveniles are very minor matters. By no means all those eventually brought for trial are from among the more serious offenders, or have committed a serious offense.

A juvenile court should not yield to panic, but should rather keep abreast of reliable information instead. There is, for instance, no justification for imposing severe sanctions on a juvenile offender, if circumstances do not warrant it. Severe punishment as a deterrent has to be applied very carefully. It can safely be assumed that a severe punishment for a minor offense has no salutary effect, but may lead to further delinquency, as a protest.

The statistical data in Chapter 3 have abundantly shown that there has been no increase in numbers of juvenile offenders. One must not, however, minimize existing problems and deficiencies. Although we are not facing serious, large-scale delinquency, much is left to be done.

From the point of view of the juvenile court, the following picture presents itself:

1. There exists a relatively small group of juvenile offenders, the hard core, who commit the more serious types of offenses, and are also difficult to rehabilitate. They exert their influence on their peers, and their impact on the social climate surrounding delinquent behavior is out of proportion to their numbers, arousing public anger and disgust, and leading to generalizations embracing all juvenile offenders.
2. A careful analysis of figures indicates clearly that the numbers of recidivists are increasing over the years. These stand as living evidence to human shortcomings, but to an even larger degree, as evidence of society's failure to make appropriate provisions for their rehabilitation. Often, no serious attempt was made.
3. Inadequate social services are to blame for a great deal of misery, and as part of it, for much juvenile delinquency. It seems to be difficult to convince administrators of the importance of securing appropriate budgets for preventive services, and for existing treatment and correctional services.
4. There is a strong impression that a great deal of juvenile delinquency can be prevented by proper and adequate planning.

In our case, the approach has to be made simultaneously in four levels: the abolition of inadequate and poverty-stricken living conditions; the provision of educational and job opportunities, geared specifically to the needs of underprivileged; the establishment of helping services— governmental, public and private—which, by consistent and concerted efforts can change the present state of affairs. For there will be many people who will find it increasingly difficult to keep pace with the developments of an affluent and technological society. Finally, although it may be difficult to prove mathematically that a certain treatment or correctional method was responsible for a success or failure, one can definitely state that a wide range of appropriate preventive services, the establishment of varying treatment and correctional facilities on a large scale, and a selective attitude in matching the needs of a juvenile offender to available facilities, are essential prerequisites for controlling juvenile delinquency.

Above all, in the competitive society in which we live, in an era preoccupied with science and technology, and characterized by mechanization and machinery, there is special need for a personal and human approach in implementing treatment and correctional methods. The feature common to a majority of juvenile offenders is deprivation. Personal interest and even an emotional involvement in the treatment may become meaningful to them. Indeed, this should be a challenge and a vocation for all who are concerned with the improvement of conditions for human beings.

Bibliography

Bibliography

Alexander, F., and W. Healy. *Roots of Crime*. New York: Knopf, 1935.

———, and H. Staub. *The Criminal, the Judge, and the Public*. New York: Macmillan, 1931.

Bach, W. "Kindliche Zeuginnen in Sittlichkeitsprozessen," *Psychologische Praxis*, Heft 21 (1957).

Baker, H. E. *Legal System of Israel*. Jerusalem: Israel Universities Press, 1968.

Bauer, F. *Das Verbrechen und die Gesellschaft*. Munich: Ernst Reinhardt, 1957.

———, et al. *Sexualität und Verbrechen*. Frankfurt a. M.: Fischer Bücherei, 1963.

Bennett, I. *Delinquent and Neurotic Children, A Comparative Study*. New York: Basic Books, 1960.

Bettelheim, B. *The Children of the Dream*. New York: Macmillan, 1969.

———. *Love is Not Enough*. Glencoe, Ill.: The Free Press, 1955.

———. *Truants from Life*. Glencoe, Ill.: The Free Press, 1950.

Bowlby, J. M. *Forty-four Juvenile Thieves*. London: Bailliere, Tindall and Cox, 1947.

———. *Maternal Care and Mental Health*. Geneva: World Health Organization, 1951.

Cavenagh, W. E. *Juvenile Courts, the Child, and the Law*. London, Pelican Books, 1967.

Chouraqui, A. N. *Between East and West*. Philadelphia: Jewish Publication Society, 1968.

Cohen, J. *Juvenile Probation in Israel*. Jerusalem: Ministry of Social Welfare, 1963.

Eisenstadt, S. N. *The Absorption of Immigrants*. London: Routledge & Kegan Paul, 1954.

———. *Israeli Society*. Jerusalem: The Magnus Press, 1967.

Elkin, W. A. *English Juvenile Courts*. London: Kegan Paul, 1938.

Frankenstein, C., ed. *Between Past and Future*. Jerusalem: The Henrietta Szold Foundation, 1953.

Friedlander, K. *The Psychoanalytical Approach to Juvenile Delinquency*. London: Kegan Paul, Trench, Trubner, and Co., 1947.

Garrett, A. M. *Interviewing: Its Principles and Methods*. New York: Family Welfare Association of America, 1942.

Glickman, E. *Child Placement Through Clinically Oriented Casework*. New York: Columbia University Press, 1957.

Glueck, S., and E. Glueck. *Delinquents and Nondelinquents in Perspective*. Cambridge: Harvard University Press, 1968.

———. *Delinquents in the Making*. New York: Harper & Bros., 1952.

Goitein, S. D. *Jews and Arabs*. New York: Schocken Books, 1964.

Great Britain, Parliament. *Children and Young Persons Act, 1969,* Ch. 54. London: HMSO, 1970, (Repr.)

Grunhut, M. *Juvenile Offenders before the Courts*. Oxford: Clarendon Press, 1956.

Jarus, A., et al., eds. *Children and Families in Israel*. New York: Gordon and Breach, 1970.

Kahn, A. J. *A Court for Children*. New York: Columbia University Press, 1953.

———. *Planning Community Services for Children*. New York: Columbia University Press, 1963.

Karpman, B. *The Sexual Offender and His Offences*. New York: Julian Press, 1954.

Konopka, G. *The Adolescent Girl in Conflict*. Englewood Cliffs, N.J.: Prentice-Hall, 1966.

Landis, J. T. "Five Hundred Children with Adult Sexual Deviation," *Psychiatric Quarterly,* Suppl., Part 1 (1956).

Mannheim, H. *Comparative Criminology*. Vol. 2, pp. 499–670. London: Routledge & Kegan Paul, 1965.

Mohr, J. W., R. E. Turner, and M. B. Jerry. *Pedophilia and Exhibitionism, a Handbook*. Toronto: University of Toronto Press, 1964.

Morrison, S. A. *Middle East Survey*. London: SCM Press, 1954.

National Probation and Parole Association. *Standard Family Court Act*. New York, 1959.

Plaut, P. *Der Sexualverbrecher und seine Persönlichkeit*. Stuttgart: Ford Enke Verlag, 1960.

Polier, J. Wise. *Back to What Woodshed?* New York, Public Affairs Committee Pamphlet No. 232, 1956.

———. *The Rule of Law and the Role of Psychiatry*. Baltimore: The Johns Hopkins Press, 1968.

———. *A View from the Bench*. New York: National Council on Crime and Delinquency, 1964.

Radzinowicz, L., ed. *Sexual Offences*. London: Macmillan, 1957.

Redl, F., and D. Wineman. *Children Who Hate*. Glencoe, Ill.: The Free Press, 1951.

———. *Controls from Within*. Glencoe, Ill.: The Free Press, 1952.

Reifen, D. *The Juvenile Court in Israel*. Jerusalem: Ministry of Justice, 1964.

———. *The Magistrate and the Welfare Worker*. Milan: Centro Nazionale Difesa Soziale, 1962.

———. "New Ventures of Law Enforcement in Israel," *Journal of Criminal Law, Criminology and Police Science,* Vol. 58 (March, 1967).

———. "Observations on the Juvenile Court in Israel," *The Prevention of Crime and the Treatment of Offenders in Israel* (Jerusalem, 1965). Report to the Third U.N. Congress on the Prevention of Crime and the Treatment of Offenders.

————. *Patterns and Motivations of Juvenile Delinquency among Israeli Arabs.* Jerusalem: Ministry of Social Welfare, 1964.

————. "Sex Offences and the Protection of Children," *The Canadian Journal of Corrections,* Vol. 8 (April, 1966).

————. *Yeud Umatara (Vocation and Goal) in the Juvenile Court.* Tel Aviv: Mifaleh Tarbut Vehinuch, 1969. (In Hebrew.)

————. *Noar Bamishpat (Youth in Court).* Tel Aviv: Mifaleh Tarbut Vehinuch, 1961. (In Hebrew.)

Reiwald, P. *Die Gesellschaft und Ihre Verbrecher.* Zürich: Pan Verlag, 1948.

Rogers, C. R. *Client-Centered Therapy.* Boston: Houghton Mifflin, 1951.

Rose, G. *Schools for Young Offenders.* London: Tavistock Publications, 1967.

Rosenheim, M. K., ed. *Justice for the Child.* Glencoe, Ill.: The Free Press, 1962.

Sellin, T. *Culture Conflict and Crime.* New York: Social Science Research Council, 1938.

————, ed. "Juvenile Delinquency," *Annals of the American Academy of Political and Social Science,* Vol. 322 (1949).

Shaw, C. R. *Delinquency Areas.* Chicago: University of Chicago Press, 1929.

————, and H. D. McKay. *Juvenile Delinquency and Urban Areas.* Chicago: University of Chicago Press, 1942.

Simonsohn, B., ed. *Jugendkriminalität, Strafjustiz und Sozialpädagogik.* Frankfurt a. M.: Edition Suhrkamp, SV. 1969.

Smilanski, M., S. Weintraub, and Y. Hanegbi. *Child and Youth Welfare in Israel.* Jerusalem: The Henrietta Szold Institute for Child and Youth Welfare, 1960.

Special Police Departments for the Prevention of Juvenile Delinquency. Paris: Interpol, 1960.

Spiro, M. E. *Children of the Kibbutz.* Cambridge: Harvard University Press, 1958.

Stawsky, M. *Hkfar Haarawi.* Tel Aviv: Am Owed, 1946. (In Hebrew.)

Stott, D. H. *Delinquency and Human Nature.* Dumferline, Fife: Carnegie United Kingdom Trust, 1950.

Sweden, Ministry of Justice. Child Welfare Act. Stockholm, 1965.

Tappan, P. W. *Juvenile Delinquency.* New York: McGraw Hill, 1949. pp. 167–489.

Teeters, N. K., and J. O. Reinemann. *The Challenge of Delinquency.* New York: Prentice-Hall, 1950.

The Treatment of Offenders in Britain. London: HMSO, 1960.

U.S. Department of Health, Education and Welfare, Children's Bureau. *Standards for Specialized Courts Dealing with Children.* Washington, D.C., 1954.

Veillard-Cybulsky, H. *La Protection judicaire de la jeunesse dans le monde.* Brussels: Association Internationale des Magistrats, 1966.

Veillard-Cybulsky, M., and H. Veillard-Cybulsky. *Les jeunes delinquants dans le monde.* Neuchâtel: Delachaux et Niestle, 1963.

Watson, J. A. F. *The Child and the Magistrate.* Rev. ed. London: Jonathan
     Cape, 1965.
Wessel R., ed. *A Case Work Approach to Sex Delinquents.* Philadelphia: Uni-
     versity of Pennsylvania School of Social Work, 1947.
Williams, G. L. *Criminal Law.* London: Stevens & Sons, 1953. pp. 641–74.
Wilnai, S. *Hamiutim Beisrael (The Minorities in Israel).* Jerusalem: Reuwen
     Mass Publications, 1959. (In Hebrew.)
Wolfgang, M. E., and F. Ferracuti. *The Subcultures of Violence.* London:
     Tavistock Publications, 1967.
———, L. Savitz, and N. Johnston. *The Sociology of Crime and Delinquency.*
     2nd ed. New York: John Wiley, 1970.

Index

Index

Absorption, *see* Integration, social
Acculturation
  of Arabs, 51–2
  of Jews, 3, 5, 7, 31, 105
  see also Integration, social
Adjournment of hearing, 118–20
Adjudication of children, xiii, 23, 57, 85, 91, 101, 191–2, 194–5
  and detention, *see* Chap. 8; *see also* Custody
  and imprisonment, 89–90, 129, 139, 161–2, 173
  and indeterminate sentencing, 175–6
  of sexual offenders, 64–5
  and speed of sentencing, 118
  written record required, 99–100, 152
Afforestation, 54–5
Agriculture, *see* Economics
Amnesty of 1967, 36–7, 39–41, 58–9, 61, 137, 162, 174
Anxiety
  causes of, 8, 52–3, 109
  in court, 116–17, 124, 196
  in detention home, 134
  and drug abuse, 47
  and psychological examination, 133
Appeals, 69, 87, 96
Arabs, 50–1; *see also* Population, Family
Ashkenazim, *see* Jews, European
Assimilation, 14

Bail, 129, 131
Baker, H. E., *The Legal System of Israel*, cited, 181
Behavior dynamics, xiv–xv, 13–14, 25, 48, 67, 72–3, 91, 101, 115, 122, 128, 135, 157, 183, 193
Black Panthers, Israel, 26–8
Bordau, David, viii
Boredom, viii, xii
Borstal, 132

Child care, *see* Child welfare
Child guidance in kibbutzim, 45

Child labor, 149–51
  exploitation by parents, 26
Child marriage, 106, 148–9
Child offenders, *see* Delinquency, juvenile
Child welfare service, xiv, 73, 85, 91, 115, 151, 194; *see also* Protection of children
City life
  among Arabs, 51
  among Jews, 8, 20, 24, 54
  temptations of, 60
Civil rights, 93, 96, 99, 112
Closure of files, 36–7, 86–7, 183
Clubs, x
Competitive society, 8, 10, 24, 27, 199
Complaints
  against judges, 91
  against offenders, 45, 62
Communications, mass, 25, 195
Conformity, social, 10, 47–8
Correction, *see* Treatment and rehabilitation
Court, adult, vii, xiii, 39, 42, 89–90, 170, 182, 194
Court, juvenile
  competence of, 85, 88–91, 154
  and drug abuse, 46–7
  establishment of, xiv, 155
  intervention by, 66, 86–8, 93–4, 128, 136, 151–2, 166, 171
  juvenile appearance in, 55–7, 71, 73, 80, 86–7, 94–5, 99
  jurisdiction of, 33–4, 65, 88, 90
  and parents, 87, 93, 101–12, 197
  paternalism of, 169
  philosophy of, vii, xiii, xv, 85, 90, 114–15. 122, 131, 156, 175, 194–5
  procedure in, 94–100, 113, 194
  and the public, 87, 96, 192, 197
  and social services, 167, 193
  as treatment, 127–8, 156, 170, 196
  see also Adjudication
Crime, 32, 34–5, 37–9, 41–3, 48, 88, 115, 145
  against control regulations, 42, 60
  against morality, 42, 60, Chap. 5, 163

209

210